# Mechanics and Manufacturers
# in the Early Industrial Revolution

SUNY Series In American Social History
Elizabeth Pleck and Charles Stephenson, Editors

Paul G Faler

# Mechanics and Manufacturers
# in the Early Industrial Revolution
## Lynn Massachusetts 1780–1860

State University of New York Press
ALBANY

Published by
State University of New York Press, Albany

©1981 State University of New York

For information, address State University of New York
Press, State University Plaza, Albany, N.Y., 12246

*Libary of Congress Cataloging in Publication Data*
Faler, Paul Gustaf, 1940–
    Mechanics and manufacturers in the early industrial revolution

    Bibliography: p. 256
    Includes index.
        1.  Shoemakers—Massachusetts—Lynn—History.
    2.  Boots and shoes—Trade and manufacture—Massachusetts—
    Lynn—History.   3.   Lynn, Mass.—Social conditions.
    I.   Title.
    HD8039.B72U657  331.7'68531'0097445  80–21619
    ISBN 0–87395–504–8
    ISBN 0–87395–505–6 (pbk.)

9   8

# Contents

# Maps and Tables

# Preface

I began the study that has resulted in this book with two goals in mind: to understand more fully the nature and impact of the industrial revolution and to extend my knowledge of working people's experience of social change. In comparison to those of England, most studies of industrialization in the United States were, I thought, inadequate. Perhaps because they were concerned chiefly with economic change these studies lacked concrete evidence and the vivid human detail that I wanted to see in history. The accounts that discussed social change were particularly lacking. I wanted to include in a single study areas of experience that were often treated as separate and distinct entities. Economic, social, cultural, and political were categories that I believed should be merged in a manner that showed the relationship of one to the other, that showed more accurately how history happened and how it was experienced. Local history was, in my judgment, the best way to explore the many facets of human experience in rich concrete detail.

I had learned a great deal from my reading in labor history, and I also learned that there were notable aspects of the experience of social change on which I wanted to focus more attention. John R. Commons and his collaborators provided valuable information and provocative arguments in their multivolume *History of Labour in the United States* and *Documentary History of American Industrial Society*. Although they were clearly aware of the social context out of which the labor movement arose, they did little to explore that social context. There were excellent studies of workers, but the emphasis was on workers' function as wage earners, the formation of unions and workingmen's parties, and their relationship to the politics of the Jacksonian Era. John R. Commons's famous essay on the shoemakers revealed a great deal about changes in the production of shoes and the formation of unions by the journeymen, but the essay said nothing else about their lives. Norman Ware's *The Industrial Worker, 1830–60*, though still unsurpassed as an overview of wage earners in this period, lay squarely in the economic-political realm in emphasis. There were, moreover, important parts to Ware's study that were clearly in need of revision. Edward Pessen's *Most Uncommon Jacksonians: The Radical Leaders of the Early Labor Movement* was an excellent analysis of ideology that shaped my own thinking. But I wished to inquire into the ideology of actual workers and attempt to connect that ideology to their experience as workers and citizens. Many other studies of the period were written within the framework established by Commons and his associates. Commons's critics rejected his conclusions but basically approached labor history in the same way: they studied workers as wage earners and voters. Scarcely any other feature of their lives entered into histories of workers.

I wanted to expand the scope of labor history to include social relations beyond the workplace. I wanted to follow the mechanics and manufacturers to their homes and neighborhoods, fire companies and social clubs, societies, schools and churches to see in what ways social relations were affected by industrialization. How did people get to be mechanics and manufacturers? What changes besides those in the mode of production were taking place in the lives of working people and their employers during the industrial revolution? What were the links between temperance and trade unions, education and industry, religion and reform? I wanted to discover if the economic conflict often found between employer and worker by other scholars had its counterparts in social relations or if economic and social relations followed a different pattern. In the broadest sense I hoped to combine labor history with social history, a term that I would prefer because labor history too often meant industrial relations, an approach I would no longer follow. I was most interested in uncovering the non-economic aspects of the industrial revolution. I would not ignore the series of economic changes that were part of industrialization; they were fundamental. But the economic part of the historical process was the one area that had been examined with the most thoroughness. Without lapsing into antiquarianism I wanted to give more attention to the non-economic realms and show the connection between them and the economic process of change.

Another shortcoming in labor history that I wished to avoid was the emphasis upon incidents of conflict. Strikes and labor wars were common in these accounts, often becoming the only subjects discussed. The analysis of struggle between social groups can indeed reveal fact facets of social relations that usually remain hidden. Many testimonies by participants in industrial clashes show that strike can trigger revelation, altering in the most profound way people's view of themselves and others. But to seek out and dwell upon this single aspect of industrial relations to the exclusion of nearly all else did not accurately convey historical experience. What of the long interims of apparent stability or relations that did not manifest overt conflict? I did not intend by any means to ignore conflict, but I did wish to give more attention to social relations that did not display outright struggle. I was as much interested in continuity as well as conflict. I wanted to discover the bonds that united as well as the issues that divided people.

It was with these inclinations that I encountered Edward Thompson's *The Making of the English Working Class* which came closest to capturing the type of history I wanted to read and write. He probed realms of experience that had somehow eluded "labor historians" (actually labor economists), who apparently recognized no relationship between religion and economic change or between work and temperance. In Thompson's hands the concept of class was broadened to become a social term rather than an economic one, and the experience of industrialization was seen as more than a series of economic changes and more than economic change with only economic consequences. Together with Eric Hobsbawm, Thompson also showed the importance of understanding first what people were like before they underwent the experience of capitalist industrialization. What was the nature and origin of the values and ideas by which working people would judge the new? Their prescription for writing a new labor history would certainly be more demanding but the results promised to be far more revealing. Unprepared to undertake a study as broad in scope as Thompson's, I was confirmed in my resolve to attempt a similar study on a smaller scale.

Herbert Gutman had made a promising beginning in this direction in his dissertation and series of articles in the 1960s in which he examined the experience of working people in several towns and cities during the Gilded Age. He shifted attention away from a particular industry or union toward the community in which workers lived. The first results of this approach were impressive. Gutman then began to analyze the areas of experience explored in Thompson's and Hobsbawm's work. His essay on "Work, Culture, and Society in Industrializing America, 1815–1919," was provocative. I wished to employ Gutman's approach but with a few changes. First, his work tended to lack the dimension of time. It treated situations in an episodic fashion.

Instead of breaking into history at certain moments in time or studying the clash in cultures between various groups at different times in American history I wished to study a community of people over a longer period of time. Secondly, after recognizing the clash between industrial and "pre-industrial" values, I wanted to see the differing ways in which workers responded to the new values, ranging from acceptance to persistent, outright rejection and, finally, to something in between. And what was the relationship of these cultural values to political ideas and class consciousness? Might we find in this cultural conflict an explanation to a question that has always intrigued labor historians: why the weakness, the divisions, in the American working class? Whatever its limitations, Gutman's scholarship was refreshing and stimulating.

The publication of many new works in the field of labor-social history during the 1970s suggests that other historians were pursuing many of the same questions that drew me to the study of Lynn. There were the books and articles on Philadelphia by Bruce Laurie, David Montgomery and Michael Feldberg; Daniel Walkowitz on Troy-Cohoes, New York; Susan Hirsch on Newark; Thomas Dublin on Lowell; Howard Rock on New York; and Leon Fink on Richmond. A good selection of recent scholarship can be found in Milton Cantor's collection on *American Working Class Culture: Explorations in American Labor and Social History*. There are similar studies in European history as well: Donald Bell on Italian workers in Sesto San Giovanni; William Sewell on Marseilles; Joan Scott on Carmaux; Robert Bezucha on Lyons. And there is a sizeable body of scholarship, both published and unpublished, by younger scholars like Jill Siegal, Roy Rosenzweig, Jonathan Prude and Jama Lazerow. Perhaps no other field in American history has attracted so much attention during the past ten years. Labor-social history has tapped an extraordinary interest among people of impressive talents who are enlarging our knowledge of American social history. Yet there is little evidence of a synthesis emerging from these fine local studies. We seem further away from an American version of Thompson's work on England than we were a decade ago. The concepts of sex, race and ethnicity are regarded by many as more significant, or at least as significant, as social class. Arriving at a synthesis on the American worker has thus become more difficult to achieve in 1980 than it had seemed in 1970.

Among the works that appeared during the 1970s are two on Lynn, John Cumbler's *Working-Class Community in Industrial America: Work, Leisure, and Struggle in Two Industrial Cities, 1880–1930*, and Alan Dawley's

*Class and Community: Lynn in the Industrial Revolution.* Cumbler's is a fine comparative study of Lynn and Fall River that explores some areas of experience that I examined for an earlier period. The greater part of Dawley's superb study focuses on the three decades after the Civil War, especially the appearance and growth of factories and the sharpening conflict between employers and workers. The first third, however, deals with the same period and many of the same topics that I examine. Since we met in 1968 while doing our research in Lynn, Alan Dawley and I have frequently discussed the Lynn shoemakers. Our joint article on the relationship of culture to political behavior among the Lynn shoemakers is one product of our collaboration. But more important has been the opportunity to exchange information, to challenge each other's theories, sharpen our ideas, and test our hypotheses. Over the years, Alan Dawley has been an energetic and stimulating coworker, a challenging and insightful intellect, and an unrivaled creator of revealing metaphors.

Judging from the numerous requests for copies of my manuscript, there has been a continuing interest in the novel approach to labor history that I employed in examining the early industrial revolution in Lynn, Massachusetts. I hope that with the publication of this model study that American labor historians will again take up the Thompson and Hobsbawm challenge and strive for a new synthesis on the American worker.

# Introduction

This is a study of social change in a Massachusetts town within the first half of the nineteenth century. It seeks to show the breadth and nature of the early industrial revolution. Most important in this period was Lynn's growth as a center for the manufacture of shoes, with an economic system based upon the private ownership of the means by which people made their living. Equally important is the historical relationship between those who owned the means to life and those who did not. This study then is as much concerned with patterns of social relations.

I chose the town of Lynn for several reasons. First, it existed as a town before it became a manufacturing center. Unlike Lawrence, Lowell, and other places, Lynn did not exist initially as an idea in the minds of Boston capitalists seeking a site for factories. Nor was it built from the ground up, with all social institutions the handiwork of employers and planners. Secondly, Lynn was the home of artisans making shoes in a manner that had persisted for generations. Lynn is thus unlike towns that were transformed from agricultural villages to factory towns producing goods that had never before been made there. It is thus possible to find, in a single period of less than a century, in a single town, each stage in the evolution of capitalism in a single industry. One can also discern in this era many of the features of social organization and structure that are ordinarily attributed to the industrial mode of production, suggesting perhaps an earlier origin than historians have maintained. An industrial society clearly began to emerge before the appearance of factories. Lastly, Lynn was nearly a one-industry town, a town of shoemakers and not of a variety of artisans experiencing changes of a somewhat different nature and magnitude, depending on their trade or the time in which the changes alternately took place.

This study falls into roughly three parts. The first deals with eco-

nomic change and organization: the origins and growth of shoe manufacturing in Lynn, the manner in which shoes were made, and the
methods used to increase production. Included also is an examination
of the social and economic origins of the manufacturers who at various
points in time presided over the industry and directed the productive
process.

The second section of this study is an attempt to explain the social
transformation that accompanied the growth of manufacturing in
Lynn. It seeks to demonstrate how an economy based upon manufacturing gave Lynn a peculiar identity in its ideology, religion, politics
and code of morality: why, for example, the mechanic ideology took
root in Lynn; why Methodism was so successful in Lynn and so unsuccessful in other areas of New England; and why Republicanism exerted
a strong appeal to Lynn mechanics in the midst of an area that was
largely Federalist. Lynn's experience may provide a possible explanation for the religious upheaval of the Second Great Awakening and the
appearance in the early nineteenth century of a moral reform movement that instituted profound changes in a way of life inherited from
the eighteenth century. The various facets of the moral reform movement are examined in detail, whether in the area of sexual customs,
drinking habits, the treatment of the poor, child rearing, or education.

A third part of this study deals with the response of the journeymen
shoemakers to both the social and economic changes of the period. Included is an assessment of how they fared as wage earners over a fifty
year period—that is, the value of their wages, the length and nature of
their labor, how they were paid, and the working conditions they faced.
There is also a statistical profile of the Lynn cordwainers, which attempts, first, to ascertain their geographical and national origins,
length of stay in the town, their movement within the occupational
structure, and secondly, to evaluate a number of theories of behavior
based on data of this sort. Included also is an examination of the distribution of property within Lynn over a generation and the extent of
property holding among some of the shoemakers. The remainder of
this section deals with the formation of class and class consciousness,
that is, the process by which the Lynn shoemakers, as a result of a
common experience as wage earners and as members of a society that
was falling under the domination of their employers, came to have a
sense of common identity, with interests different than those of their
employers. Class consciousness took two forms, both of which emerged
simultaneously. First, journeymen cordwainers applied to their present
condition ideas, values, standards, and expectations inherited from the

past. In this process of applying standards derived from the past, they produced an ideology that was distinctively their own, a means both for interpreting what was happening to them and for conceiving an alternative social system. A second form of class consciousness was the creation of institutions that answered to their unique needs as journeymen. A third indication of the presence of class consciousness was the tendency for the emerging struggle of journeymen and manufacturer to carry over into areas beyond the cash nexus and to influence the response of each to the social and political issues of the time. Finally, there is an examination of the Great Shoemakers' Strike of 1860, which dramatically revealed Lynn's dissolution as a community.

# 1. Lynn—The First Century

From its founding in 1630 until approximately 1750, Lynn remained a struggling agricultural village. A shallow harbor and land that was swampy or rocky restricted Lynn's growth as either a trading center or as a prosperous farming village. Although situated on the North Shore of Massachusetts, ten miles from Boston and contiguous with Salem and Marblehead, nature's gift to Lynn was broad stretches of sandy beaches and marshland rather than a harbor suitable for vessels of the size employed in the carrying trade. Membership in a mercantile empire might have enabled Lynn to obtain its share of the wealth that flowed into the trading centers of Essex County. But where Salem, Newburyport, and Marblehead, all important ports, turned outward to the sea and sent forth ships to the West Indies, Africa and Europe, Lynn turned inward, away from the shallow shore, and sought to develop the few resources lying within the town. Yet even efforts in areas other than shipping either failed or produced slim rewards.[1]

Population grew slowly, if at all. Many of the original settlers departed. Immigrants avoided the town; most continued on inland or remained in the prosperous ports along the sea coast. The shipping centers flourished and grew; they became the most populous towns in Essex County. Lynn could not keep pace. One Lynn historian informs us that in the century 1640 to 1740, the town's population remained constant. In 1765, the census reported 1798 people; twenty-five years later there were 2093, a gain of 95. In 1781, Lynn ranked eleventh among the towns of Essex County, smaller in size than the inland towns of Haverhill and Andover.[2] The absence of a harbor meant economic stagnation.

Lynn was one of the first towns in Massachusetts to be settled by those Puritans who left England in the heavy migrations of the decade following 1629. In that year five men and their families from Salem

1

moved to Lynn. The next year another fifty persons from Salem joined them. The procedure was repeated in succeeding years as Puritans by the thousand abandoned England for the Bay Colony. A portion of them annually joined the small settlement at Lynn, which the General Court had incorporated in 1630.

Lynn's origin lay in the general spreading of the Puritan immigrants from the few landing points along the coast to the unoccupied lands in between. They first settled lands bordering the sea. Eager for land and anxious to sow the first crops upon which their survival would depend, the Puritans wasted little time in possessing the nearest tracts of tillable soil. Located midway between Salem and Boston, Lynn understandably attracted the covetous eyes of settlers who were among the first to land in America.

In 1640, Lynn was one of several outposts, roughly equal in size, that stretched in a broad arc around Massachusetts Bay. The taxes levied by the General Court on the settlements in Essex County suggest that Lynn was slightly larger in population than Salem. Thus, after the first decade, when the economics of survival prevailed, Lynn was indistinguishable in size from her neighbors along the Atlantic.

The growth of shipping transformed the economy of Massachusetts Bay Colony and sharply differentiated the towns of Essex County. The turning point came during the English Civil War. Cut off from the sources of population and financial support, the settlers in Massachusetts were compelled to find alternative means of income. They turned to shipping and shipbuilding. They bought, sold, bartered and transported commodities within the Atlantic trading market. Upon the foundation of the carrying trade Massachusetts became the home base for a large mercantile fleet.

Lynn did not share in the rewards of commerce. The absence of a harbor was a crucial deficiency. Small fishing vessels, coastal runners, and barges could be accommodated at the wharves of Lynn but not the ocean-going ships that crowded the ports of Essex County. Salem, Newburyport, and Marblehead became prosperous ports, whose citizens built and manned the vessels that earned their fortunes in the carrying trade. With ports of call in the West Indies, Europe and the Mediterranean, they reaped profits from transporting cargoes of tobacco, sugar, lumber, fish, slaves and anything else that was marketable. They also became distribution points for imported goods from England.

The lack of a harbor also meant Lynn was an inappropriate site for the associated industries that arose in towns with ships engaged in the carrying trade: shipbuilding, cordage, and duck manufactories; cooperage works, and distilleries. Extensive commercial activity created a broad range of opportunities for merchants and clerks, bookkeepers and attorneys; for seamen, carpenters, joiners, caulkers and riggers; for sail makers and coopers; for wharfingers, dockworkers, shopkeepers, and artisans of all types. Trade was the foundation upon which the economies of the coastal towns of Essex County grew, raising them from the humble origins still present in Lynn. As commerce flourished, it furnished the capital that set in motion a cycle of prosperity and growth. The gap between the ports and Lynn widened. By 1781, Lynn ranked eleventh among the towns of Essex County. Among those with larger populations were Salem, Marblehead, Gloucester, Newburyport, Ipswich, Newbury, Beverly, Andover, Danvers, and Haverhill.

In Lynn the resources for agricultural development were limited. An extensive marsh in the western portion of the town stretches across the Saugus River all the way to Chelsea. Periodically inundated by the ocean tides, the salt marsh, although it did provide fodder, was unsuited for raising edible crops. The flat plain that receded into the sea also extended eastward, reaching its lowest point at the center of the town. The low-lying land formed the Black Marsh with its soil of heavy untillable muck. Land at higher elevations was tillable but rocky, yielding light crops of corn, wheat and barley. To maintain the fertility of the land, Lynn farmers had to engage in the laborious task of combing the beaches for organic matter or stripping the rich humus from the topsoil of the marsh and carting the heavy loads to their distant fields. In return to a heavy investment of labor, the land provided sustenance for a small population but not enough to permit much growth.

Lacking a harbor or another resource that might have formed the foundation for sustained growth through a profitable investment for capital and employment of the people in the vicinity, Lynn did not attract many outsiders. Ownership of land was crucial for membership in an agricultural economy in which the soil was the sole source of livelihood for nearly everyone. The earliest settlers in Lynn quickly obtained the rights to the choicest farmland, leased the pastures, and left the marshes or the upland for the few who chose to follow. The small growth of population indicates that the town could neither retain all those who had already settled in Lynn nor attract immigrants.

Two centuries after Lynn was settled, twelve families, totalling 1660 persons, made up 27 percent of the population and an equal portion of the voters. And four of these families—Newhalls, Breeds, Alleys and Johnsons—made up more than half of that 27 percent.[3] The kinship

4

group, based on the blood tie, would undoubtedly be larger, perhaps twice as great, yet a cursory glance at common surnames gives a rough indication of the continuity of the population over nearly two centuries. The lack of a harbor or an equally valuable resource served to deter outsiders from Lynn and, in the process, preserved into the late eighteenth and early nineteenth centuries ethnographic patterns that originated 150 or 200 years before. Yet there is no evidence that would indicate a reluctance on the part of the original landed settlers to support or sponsor industries that might have generated the growth needed to attract outsiders. In fact, there is evidence to the contrary.

Townspeople tried their hands at anything that seemed promising. They built a few mills to grind the corn raised in the town, but Lynn did not become a milling center for farmers in the neighboring villages.[4] Situated on the coast and close to fishing grounds that are among the best in the world, the residents of Lynn pursued the codfish as a source of food and as an exportable commodity. Yet fishing did not attain the importance it held in the economies of Gloucester and Ipswich, probably because Lynn did not possess a port for the ships that carried the dried fish to customers in the Mediterranean. They did build a few vessels. From 1726 to 1741 they constructed three brigs and sixteen schooners, but a prosperous shipbuilding industry did not grow from this modest beginning.[5]

Among the consequences of stagnation was dependence. As a backward agricultural village in the midst of prosperous mercantile centers, Lynn became dependent on Salem and Boston for many goods and services.[6] A Lynn farmer could not purchase a suit of clothes in Lynn because the town had no tailor. There were no shopkeepers selling spices, sugar, tools, or fabrics; most citizens traveled to Salem for groceries and dry goods.[7] The same was true for professional services. Anyone needing legal advice sought an attorney in Salem or Boston. Not until the nineteenth century did the probate court extend its circuit to Lynn; before that time one walked to Salem to have a will probated. Lynn showed other features of an undeveloped economy that was restricted to agriculture and deficient in services that are ordinarily found in a society with greater specialization. For example, there was no post office until 1793 and no notary public until 1799. Before the nineteenth century Lynn had no banks, no fire insurance companies, no newspapers, and no school for children over twelve. Prior to that time, the few people in Lynn in need of these services went elsewhere. If Lynn had intentions, in the early years, of achieving greater self-sufficiency and of providing the same goods and services that were easily obtainable in Salem, the lack of vital resources disappointed those intentions.

For the young, the ambitious and the talented, Lynn offered few opportunities of the order one might find in Salem or Boston, both of which, one should remember, were within walking distance. A young man skilled in the craft of woodworking and anxious to test his ability on something other than ox yokes or fishing dories, could find a job as a carpenter in the shipyards of Salem. A job as joiner, rigger, cooper, or clerk would bring a higher wage than one could earn raising corn, barley or flax on a plot of rocky ground. Seafaring lured others. Many young men from Lynn shipped out as seamen on vessels outfitted in Salem. Some returned after a few long voyages; others did not.

For those of entrepreneurial ambitions Lynn must have appeared a wasteland. Take for example, Billy Gray, born in Lynn in 1750, the son of Abram Gray, one of three master cordwainers who at mid-century sold enough shoes to require the assistance of a few journeymen. The elder Gray sold his shoes to Richard Derby, a merchant in Salem, to whom Gray apprenticed his son as a clerk at the age of eleven. Gray gave faithful service to Derby and, upon reaching his majority, started on his own, putting to use all that he had learned while assisting the man who commanded one of the largest mercantile fleets in Massachusetts. By 1810 Gray had surpassed his mentor. He was the largest ship-owner in Massachusetts and reputedly the wealthiest man in New England. Appropriately, he was elected Lieutenant Governor of Massachusetts in 1810. Although a Lynn historian tells us that Gray retained many friends in Lynn, there is no indication that any of the wealth Gray amassed in commerce found its way back to his birthplace.[8] This the is understandable in light of the absence of promising enterprises in Lynn and of the continued preeminence of the carrying trade in the economy of Massachusetts, a preeminence that continued until the second quarter of the nineteenth century.

The pattern of settlement in seventeenth and eighteenth-century Lynn is another indication of the town's reliance upon agriculture, its dependence upon Boston and Salem, and its peculiarity among coastal communities of the North Shore. In Salem and Marblehead, a short distance down the coast from Lynn, people clustered on lands close to the port. There one would find the shops of traders and artisans, the offices of merchants as well as the coffee shops, taverns, and warehouses. A short distance away were the churches, public buildings, and residences. The harbor was the center of economic and social activity and the source from which the town derived its income. These towns looked to the sea, and the concentration of population reflected this outlook. The sea was a giant highway that connected them with the world beyond, bringing riches, prestige, and power, providing opportunities for their citizens. As the towns grew and population density in the old areas increased, people reluctantly moved inland.

Lynn showed a different pattern. A large area near the sea was a desolate salt marsh, much of it land unused until heavy filling operations in the nineteenth century made it a suitable site for buildings. The people of Lynn turned away from the sea and settled on higher ground a considerable distance from the shore. The loose clusters of population that did form were strung out along a few points on the roads connecting Boston to Salem. As a result, then, of dependence on the land and of the importance of the tie to Boston and Salem, Lynn was a decentralized town of small farms located in several distinct sections or neighborhoods, the centers of which were determined by the routes that were used for travel between Boston, Salem, and Marblehead.

Despite muted ambitions and modest beginnings that came to naught, people in Lynn persisted in their efforts to find an alternative to agriculture. They tried milling, tanning, silk raising, printing, and salt making. Some of these flourished briefly and then collapsed. Others struggled along in a small way, survived the initial difficulties of infant industries, and quietly died in a piecemeal fashion.[9] People in Lynn were particularly reluctant to declare an end to their lingering aspirations for a place in the maritime trade. Well into the first half of the nineteenth century shipping was a lucrative investment that offered attractions that Lynn capitalists found difficult to resist.

In the decade 1829 to 1839, Hezekiah Chase, Nehemiah Berry and others bought or built a few ships, dredged the Saugus River at a cost of $1000, constructed a wharf, warehouse, cooperage shop, sailmakers' loft, and ropewalk, and tried to capture a share of a business that had long eluded Lynn. Chase and Berry used their vessels for trade with Capetown, the West Indies, and towns on the Atlantic seaboard. The whaling business gave a boost to the enterprise. Aided by funds from other Lynn investors, the group formed the Lynn Whaling Company in 1834. With five whalers and three fishing schooners for codfishing on the Grand Banks, the firm prospered until the panic of 1837 put an end to Lynn's final attempt to become a port city.

Economic prospects, however, were not entirely bleak. The people of Lynn persistently sought ways to supplement their meager living. Some probably peddled vegetables, milk, and meat in the market towns nearby. Others of greater manual dexterity may have fashioned in their homes a few simple items that could be sold or bartered to people like themselves, who were hardpressed for the cash to buy imported goods. Perhaps in this manner, not suddenly but over a period of decades, the people of Lynn began to make and sell shoes; rough, crude specimens in the early years to be sure, but an article suitable for everyday wear among people of limited means. And through a combination of circumstances that coalesced in precisely the right way, the town emerged as a manufacturing town from a century and a half of stagnation, beginning an ascent that carried Lynn beyond all the mercantile towns of Essex County.

## 2. Rise of the Shoe Industry

The natural disadvantages that denied Lynn a place in the maritime trade of the seventeenth and eighteenth centuries did contribute to the town's growth as a manufacturing center. Had the town possessed a sheltered harbor and deep water, it might well have followed the pattern of development that one finds all along the North Shore. A reliance on fishing and the exporting of dried cod to the West Indies and the Mediterranean might have made Lynn another Ipswich or Gloucester. Had the town possessed more fertile soil and less hilly terrain, it might have, like the inland villages, had less reason to turn from the soil to other economic pursuits. But in each case the lack of the appropriate natural resources stood as a barrier that deflected the town's efforts toward an alternative that was altogether independent of indigenous material resources.

If Lynn's proximity to Salem and Boston bred dependence, it also enabled the people of Lynn to use the services of these centers that were vital to the development of manufacturing. Vessels from Massachusetts returned to Salem and Boston with the raw materials from which the Lynn cordwainers fashioned shoes: calamancoes, russets, satinets, morocco leather, and Russian sheeting, among others. Although in the early years of the shoe industry Lynn readily obtained sufficient supplies of tanned cowhides for sole leather from the surrounding farming towns, increased production demanded new sources. Again, proximity, to the sea ports assured Lynn of a continuous supply of hides from the West Indies, Philadelphia, Baltimore, and later, California and Latin America. The mercantile towns also lent financial assistance to the shoe industry, providing credit to the manufacturers by discounting the notes they received from shoe buyers.[1]

The absence of natural resources may have encouraged an early adoption of manufacturing in Lynn as a substitute for subsistence agriculture, yet one cannot be sure why the town made shoes rather than hats, wagons, or firearms. There may be some truth in the contention of Lynn historians who located the origins of the shoe industry in the first decade of the town's existence. In that period two cordwainers, Philip Kirtland and Samuel Bacheller, settled in Lynn. Kirtland was also a butcher, and may have used the hides from slaughtered animals to make footwear for his fellow townsmen. But Bacheller's stay in Lynn was brief; he was in the contingent that emigrated to Long Island in 1640. The possibility yet remains that Kirtland and Bacheller did introduce the draft to Lynners who wished to supplement their incomes. Equally likely is the possibility that farmers in Lynn, like farmers throughout Eastern Massachusetts, chose to make in their homes a staple consumer item for which they could readily obtain the necessary materials.

The importance of shoemaking in Lynn's economy prior to the nineteenth century is difficult to ascertain. Blanche Hazard, in her valuable study, *The Organization of the Boot and Shoe Industry in Massachusetts before 1875*, claims that the arrival of Kirtland and Bacheller from England in 1635 sparked an economic revolution in Lynn. In her words: "They either took apprentices and spread the fever or found others there in the farming community all ready to join them." Careful scrutiny of the town's early records showed no evidence to support her statement. She also believed, on the basis of the importance she attaches to the coming of Kirtland and Bacheller, that from 1645 onward Lynn was primarily a manufacturing town. Yet she admits that, except for the arrival of the two cordwainers in 1645, "no one seems to know any more about the shoe industry in Lynn or any of the surrounding towns" until 1750.[2] The absence of any mention of shoemaking as an important part of the town's economy in the Lynn records from 1640 to 1650 would cast doubt on her assertion. In addition, one unidentified Lynn historian informs us that in 1750 there were only three shoemakers in Lynn who sold enough shoes to require the assistance of journeymen. Had the town been a manufacturing center throughout the first century of its history, one would assume that this peculiarity would have evoked notice. On the other hand, the steady increase in shoe production after 1750, reaching 80,000 pairs in 1768,[3] would indicate the presence of a considerable body of residents who had received some training in the craft. Although in 1750 there were only three master cordwainers employing journeymen, there undoubtedly were many more independent producers who sold enough shoes to keep themselves employed full or part time, many taking leave of farming in bad weather to make shoes. As Alonzo Lewis, the earliest chronicler of

Lynn's past, put it: "For the first hundred years from the settlement of the town, this business was very limited. Few persons followed it constantly and the farmers only pursued it in the intervals of their common employment."[4] The majority of people continued to extract a living from the soil, raising their own food and selling or bartering their surplus for the items they were unable to produce.

The slow growth of the shoe industry and its prolonged position as an economic pursuit subordinate to agriculture was not due to any unwillingness of the people to give their full attention to shoemaking. The reason lies rather in the colonial status of America and, particularly in the contrast between the mature economy of the Mother Country and the primitive, extractive economy of the colonies.

Several factors inhibited the growth of shoemaking, all deriving from Lynn's membership in a mercantile empire that discouraged colonial manufacturing. The first and most important was English domination of the American market. The other reasons were corollaries of the first: English wares were generally superior in quality and cheaper in price. In the eyes of the men who directed the affairs of the mercantile empire, the American colonies were primarily sources of raw materials and markets for goods fabricated in England. In the seventeenth century and for most of the eighteenth, the colonies were ideally suited for little more than these limited economic functions. They were particularly successful in growing crops, especially the Southern colonies, and in taking advantage of their proximity to other colonies in need of goods and services available from North America. Most valuable, for example, were commodities like tobacco, rice, indigo, and furs, commodities that could not be raised or gathered in other parts of the empire or that were most easily obtainable from the American colonies. For producers of grains, livestock, and fish, the rapidly growing sugar islands of the West Indies were a rich market: they were dependent upon outsiders for the bulk of their foodstuffs. And for the port cities that were parts of a mercantile empire there were opportunities in shipbuilding and the carrying trade.

Yet what of those communities unendowed with the resources that were prerequisites for securing a comfortable niche in the empire? This was the question Lynn answered with manufacturing. But England prohibited colonial fabrication of products that English capitalists so profitably sold in the colonies. The exchange of manufactured goods for raw materials was the foundation of England's commercial supremacy. The duplication in one part of the empire of economic functions

performed by another was a violation of mercantilism and a competitive threat to the interest groups in England who helped formulate colonial policy. Parliament acknowledged the importance of maintaining
the domination of English capitalists in the colonial markets by restrict-
ive acts that prohibited the colonists from manufacturing items made in
England.

The supremacy of English manufacturing, however, was only partly
due to formal, codified restrictions. More important was the maturity
of the English economy. With few exceptions, English craftsmen could
make goods that were superior in quality and cheaper in price than
those made in the colonies. There were many items which Americans
continued to purchase from England long after independence and the
dissolution of formal economic restraints. Thus for a town like Lynn,
the empire was an obstruction that inhibited economic growth.

Despite the supremacy of the Mother Country, the shoe industry did
make modest gains. Lynn shoemakers probably peddled most of their
goods in the surrounding towns, turning to advantage their willingness
to barter and trade. A shortage of specie, a chronic problem throughout the colonial period, undoubtedly restricted the market for English
goods to customers who had the money to buy. The American who
preferred English shoes to those made in Lynn may well have been unable to put together enough cash to purchase her first choice. Instead,
she perhaps bartered the products of her labor or her husband's craft
for the shoes made in Lynn.

There is also the possibility that in the years before the Revolution,
the Lynn shoemakers began to penetrate the large market for cheap,
rough brogans. The handful of shoe bosses who in 1750 employed
journeymen and carried their shoes to Salem did not sell directly to the
consumer. They sold instead to merchants like Richard Derby. The
Salem merchants who traded heavily with the West Indies, dealing in
rum, foodstuffs and slaves, may also have sent barrels of cheap shoes.
In return, the merchants may have paid for the shoes bought from the
Lynn makers with West India goods, ox hides for sole leather, and
rum, a staple beverage in New England. Whatever the procedure, the
Lynn shoemakers were apparently finding holes in the English trade
network that covered the colonies.

Another achievement that may partly explain the steady growth of
the Lynn shoe industry during the pre-Revolutionary period was the
improvement in the quality of the product. Much of the credit must go
to John Adam Dagyr, a Welsh cordwainer who settled in Lynn in

1750,[5] either coincidentally or through the recruiting efforts of a Lynn merchant. In his shop on Boston Street, the main-traveled road between Boston and Salem, Dagyr and his friends tried to emulate the highest standards of the shoemaking craft. Using samples of the finest grades of imported shoes, Dagyr reportedly dissected the shoes and tried to discover the features that made them superior to the American product. Together Dagyr and his friends tried to recreate the foreign models. By means of study, imitation and duplication, Dagyr produced shoes that won for him the title "the celebrated cordwainer of Essex County." In 1764, an item in the Boston *Gazette* observed that the shoes made in Lynn exceeded in quality, if not in price, shoes made in England.

The turning point in the fortunes of the Lynn shoe industry came with the American Revolution. Animosity toward England brought a corresponding increase in American nationalism. Some Americans became conscious of the intervention of English authority in American affairs and of the arbitrary exercises of power at the expense of colonial interests. In the nonimportation movement and the colonial boycott of English goods, one can discern the beginnings of a concerted effort at self-reliance. Although few colonists believed the non-intercourse movement would become permanent, making the colonies completely autonomous of the Mother Country, some advocates of independence recognized the economic implications of the boycott. The people of Lynn were probably more advanced in their thinking on this point than people elsewhere. During the excitement generated by the destruction of English tea in Boston Harbor and Parliament's reprisals, the town voted support for the boycott of English goods. They also urged Americans "to promote our own manufactures amongst us," and rely on themselves for the goods they ordinarily purchased from England.[6] "Buy American!" was the tone of their collective opinion.

The outbreak of war against England effectively banned English goods from the American market. With the departure of their major competitor, the Lynn shoemakers, already the major supplier of shoes for a local market, extended their market into more distant regions. Shoe production increased from 80,000 pairs in 1768 to 400,000 in 1783. By 1783 there were about fifty shoemakers in Lynn who gave enough time to shoemaking to warrant the building of small shops in which to carry on the craft.[7]

Although the growth in shoe production was dramatic, the growth of population did not correspond. The number of people in Lynn increased only slightly in the years from 1765 to 1790, from 1990 to

2093. Even if one grants that a few outworkers living in surrounding towns were making shoes for Lynn merchants, the increase in production indicates a drastic reorientation of the town's economy. A large portion of the population was directing its efforts to shoemaking. The stimulus of a vastly extended market for shoes had generated profound changes in the economic life of the town.

The end of the war for independence resurrected the old threat of competition from manufacturing in England. Fears that they would attempt to regain their position in the American market were justified. No sooner had the war ended than English manufacturers inundated the American market with their goods. And the Americans, though independent, behaved in the old colonial manner, making heavy purchases of English goods, including shoes. The backlog of purchasing power that had accumulated during the war years was expressed in large sales of goods that Americans had traditionally bought. Political independence had not brought economic autonomy. The trade patterns between England and America, as well as the tastes and needs of the colonists, reappeared in much the same form that had existed prior to the war. Regardless of the Anglophobia that flowed from the struggle and the nationalistic demands for self-reliance and economic autonomy, Americans needed what England offered.

The activities of a large Lynn shoe merchant provide valuable information about the steps taken to retain markets won during the war, to obtain new markets, and to erect barriers to foreign competition in America. Ebenezer Breed was born in Lynn in 1766, the son of a wealthy Quaker family and a descendant of one of the earliest settlers in the town. The numerous members of the Breed family, many of them in the shoe business, were prominent in the affairs of Lynn and gave their family name to the western part of the town in which they congregated—Breed's End.[8] Ebenezer Breed was a slim, diminutive man with a larger than average share of ambition and vision. He dressed in the Quaker style of the period—drab coat and pants, buckle shoes, and broad-brimmed hat. Breed was a commission merchant and a partner of Amos Rhodes, his agent in Lynn. At the age of twenty, Breed left Lynn and journeyed to Philadelphia, the mecca for people of his faith. There he made contact with a group of wealthy Quaker merchants headed by Stephen Collins, a former Lynn resident and the commander of a fleet of merchantmen. Breed probably obtained more than a friendly greeting from his new associates: an introduction to merchants in Pennsylvania, financial support for his projects, or perhaps assurances of transportation for the shoes he intended to sell.

Through his agent in Lynn, Breed contracted with Lynn shoe manufacturers for shipments of shoes that he probably paid for with orders
drawn on Philadelphia and Baltimore Quakers who dealt in leather,
flour and grain, and West India goods. Breed's ties to the merchants
who imported the materials from which shoes were made and his links
with the shoe dealers who sold the shoes gave him effective control
over the shoe producers. The Lynn shoemakers went to Amos Rhodes
for raw materials, made the shoes themselves or had them made by
others, and returned the finished products to Rhodes, drawing remuneration in groceries and dry goods and pay their workers in kind. A
prerequisite for this arrangement was Breed's securing of markets.

Although Ebenezer Breed began his activities in Philadelphia his circuit extended to distant towns southward. He traveled up and down
the Atlantic seaboard, as far South as Savannah, Georgia. He also operated in Baltimore, Richmond, Petersburg, Charleston, and Augusta.[9]
Wherever he went, his broad-brimmed hat and drab Quaker suit was a
badge that gained him admission to the Quaker business communities
that occupied an important position in the mercantile life of the ports.
He sought out shoe dealers and arranged for them to peddle Lynn
shoes. His success was due partly to his willingness to take payment in
goods rather than specie, assured that shoemakers in Lynn would be
eager to accept groceries and dry goods.

Despite Breed's success in disposing of considerable quantities of
shoes, he and his Philadelphia associates, as well as the shoe manufacturers in Lynn, were apprehensive of the competitive threat from
abroad. Breed's journeys to towns far from Lynn had located new customers for American producers. The growth of the shoe industry, if
slowed by the return of English goods, continued into the 1780s.
Nonetheless there was a desire to establish protective barriers for the
infant American shoe business.

Breed played an important role as lobbyist for a tariff on shoes.
Through his Quaker friends in Philadelphia, the seat of the new Federal government created by ratification of the Constitution, Breed
made the acquaintance of men prominent in the new regime. With
equal amounts of tact, persistence, and guile, he pleaded his case for a
protective duty. His Quaker allies aided him in his efforts to gain the
support of the men whose votes he needed for passage of this legislation. These merchants made available their sumptuous mansions for
banquets and balls to honor members of the new government. The
generous hosts also thoughtfully invited charming ladies whose presence no doubt served to insure the attendance of those invited. On one

of these occasions Breed delivered an impassioned plea for a protective tariff:

> Will you stand tamely by and see this infant industry swalloed up by the raging lions of Britain and Gaul? Will you see the homes of these operatives destroyed or abandoned and not hold out your strong arms to shield them as they shielded you when war bent his horrid front over our fair land? No, I trust, and New England expects that by your suffrages we shall obtain the desired relief when the matter comes before your honorable body.[10]

The nationalists of the Federal government needed little prodding from lobbyists. In the first session of the new Congress, the government passed a tariff that placed a fifty-cent levy on boots and a 7.5 percent duty on imported shoes. An additional 10 percent tax was levied on goods brought to America in foreign ships. In succeeding years, the Congress renewed and raised the tax on imported footwear. Ironically, as domestic shoe production expanded and the American producers became better able to compete with foreign manufacturers, the tariff duties on shoes increased. The level of the protective duties clearly depended less on the needs of the industry than on the political power and influence of the manufacturers. If in 1789 the lobbyists did not obtain all that they had wished for, they did gain an advantage in the American market. There remained, however, the task of improving the quality of Lynn shoes. The tariff may have served to obstruct the flow of shoes to America from England and France, but Lynn still had to compete with producers in this country who were equally eager to capture a share of the new markets.

The effort to maintain and improve the quality of the shoes made in Lynn was an ongoing process. Quality depended on two things: workmanship and high grade materials. John Dagyr—through his skill, ingenuity, and willingness to instruct others—had helped establish the reputation of Lynn shoes. The mere presence of English goods in the American market undoubtedly forced American shoemakers to emulate the work of their competitors. The Revolution banished the English product and, with it, the standard of craftsmanship that the Americans strove to equal; in the rush to replace the English as supplier of shoes for the colonial market there probably was a deterioration in the quality of shoes. A considerable portion of the shoes made during and just after the Revolution came from marginal producers who had been drawn into the occupation by the extension of markets.[11] And if the war disrupted trade between English manufacturers and the colonies, it also interrupted the movement of raw materials from Europe to the domestic shoe industry. Shortages may have compelled shoemakers to use inferior materials. Hence, a decline in the standard of workmanship and shortages of high grade materials caused apprehension among Lynn shoemakers.

This suspicion is borne out by their petition to the Continental Congress. In 1783, the "respectable cordwainers" of Lynn requested that the Congress immediately negotiate trade agreements with countries that supplied the American shoe industry with raw materials such as calamancoes, russets, and morocco leather. Secondly, they resolved, on their part, to stamp all shoes that they exported, informing buyers that only those shoes bearing the imprint of the respectable cordwainers of Lynn had met the standard established by the craftsmen of the town. All others came from "botches," footloose apprentices, and farmers.[12] Their demands, no doubt, gained urgency from their belief that the reappearance of foreign shoes would cause a contraction in the market. It was against this background in 1786 that the young commission merchant, Ebenezer Breed, went in search of new markets to maintain shoe production at its wartime level.

Breed also emerges as an important figure in the movement to improve the quality of the shoes made in Lynn. He sought simultaneously to maintain and improve workmanship and to insure his suppliers in Lynn of sufficient quantities of high grade materials. In 1792, Breed journeyed to England and France. In England, he visited Leeds, Sheffield, Birmingham, Manchester, and Liverpool, arranging for manufacturers and merchants there to ship to Lynn materials he thought would enhance the quality of Lynn shoes. At one point, he informed Amos Rhodes, his agent in Lynn, "I have ordered a considerable quantity of bindings; was at the factory and saw them making them." And in September, 1792, just prior to his departure for the United States, he wrote, "I have several hundred pounds' worth of goods in this ship, all insured and paid for." Breed obtained more than fabrics and leather from England. He is also said to have smuggled out two skilled cordwainers, whom he persuaded to emigrate to America to instruct shoemakers in the finer arts of the craft. Another craftsman he recruited was William Rose, a morocco dresser, skilled in the complicated process of converting kid skins into the soft, pliable, and attractive leather used in making the upper part of ladies shoes.

Breed's achievements were limited. Back in America he resumed his activities as an itinerant commission merchant, sending to Rhodes dispatches that complained of the trash sent to him in the form of shoes. In a letter from Philadelphia, July 25, 1793, Breed told Rhodes,

I wrote thee yesterday, since which I have seen Daniel Ruff and Company, and they want six hundred pairs, or six barrels of excellent satinet rand shoes. I want thee to write me by return post whether thee can have them made, and at what price we can afford them. Those shoes thee last sent are mostly on hand, and I am perfectly sick of doing business in the shoe line here, unless we can have such as will sell. If I call for the money, they begin to show me the large number of small, unsaleable ones they have left, that they never can sell, and say I must not expect my pay, etc. And what can I say to them? It is so, and so it will be, while the shoemakers in Lynn are a set of confounded fools. Ask Samuel Collins what his cousin Zaccheus has written him, and he will tell thee it is a rascally business to be concerned in, while the makers of shoes there have no principle or policy.

More indictments of New England shoes came a few years later from the cordwainers of Philadelphia. John Commons locates the origin of American trade unions in the efforts of Philadelphia shoemakers to resist the competition of the shoe merchants from New England.

In the rise of the Lynn shoe industry, nothing is more important than the extension of markets. Commission merchants like Ebenezer Breed appear in profusion in the years from 1790 to 1860. They extended their contacts to shoe dealers in cities and towns throughout the country, stimulating further growth of the Lynn shoe business, increasing production, and bringing greater pressure on shoe merchants to find additional customers for Lynn shoes. Philadelphia and Baltimore retained their importance as distribution points for Lynn shoes. As port cities connected by sea to Salem and Boston, they were easily accessible to Lynn shoe manufacturers. They also had ties to a vast agricultural hinterland that supplied them with the foodstuffs and hides, which they exchanged for Lynn shoes. Prior to the 1830s, New York City was less important. For the large commission merchant who wished to sell several thousand pairs of shoes to wholesalers, New York was an undeveloped commercial center lacking the facilities to handle the sale of large lots of shoes. Jacob Ingalls, in a letter to a Lynn partner in 1818, admitted his mistake in going to New York to dispose of 6,000 pairs of shoes. Its auction system was poorly run and its wholesalers small and unpatronized by large buyers.[13] Ingalls arranged to take the first boat to Baltimore and Charleston.

If the extension of markets was the single most important factor in the growth of the Lynn shoe industry, the South was by far the largest purchaser of Lynn shoes. Alonzo Lewis, who salvaged many of the town's earliest records, credits the South with the rise of the industry: "The reputation of Lynn shoes soon found its way to the cities of the South," he observed, "and the manufacturers began to tend their business by taking apprentices and employing journeymen." Many a fortune was made in the Southern trade during the years before the Civil War. The largest purchasers were the slave holders who annually bought tens of thousands of cheap footwear for their slaves, thus giving employment to hundreds of New Englanders who made nothing but "Negro shoes." The staple item for this vast market was the brogan or, in the women's branch of the business, "slaps"—a rough, poorly fitting shoe consisting of a sole and a single piece of upper leather that only barely conformed to the shape of the human foot. With the expansion of the South and a continuous growth in population, the demand for shoes further stimulated expansion of the productive capacity of the Lynn shoe industry.

The exact proportion of Lynn's trade with the South is difficult to ascertain, but scattered references in the memoirs and reminiscences of Lynn residents, many of them manufacturers, give a rough indication.[14] Ebenezer Breed's correspondence shows that in the 1780s he journeyed as far south as Augusta, Georgia to secure customers. Benjamin Johnson, a shoe merchant and founder of the first Methodist church in Massachusetts, did a considerable business with dealers in the upper South, particularly in the vicinity of Virginia and North Carolina during the late 1780s and early 1790s. Daniel Silsbee and Micajah Burrill, Jr., operated on a large scale in the decade after 1800: owning their own coastal vessels, they traded extensively with towns along the southern seaboard. An indication of the size of their business is revealed in the financial loss they suffered in the war of 1812, thirty thousand dollars in notes they could not collect.[15] A group of Lynn shoe bosses evaluated the importance of the Southern trade to their business in 1804. In their petition to the General Court for incorporation of a bank to discount their notes from southern buyers, the manufacturers attributed their need for a bank to the expansion of their trade in the South. They stated that they were "extensively engaged in the manufacture of shoes, which were chiefly exported to the Southern States." This trade alone "amounted annually to $500,000," and "the time which necessarily elapses before remittances could be received subjected them to many inconveniences." Inconvenience did not deter merchants from entering and expanding trade with the South.

Members of the Atwill family were for two generations engaged in shoe manufacturing. Major John D. Atwill built a considerable trade with the Virginia towns of Richmond and Petersburg in the years from about 1790 to 1820. His son, John D. Atwill, extended the business further south and was among the first of the Lynn shoe merchants to establish trade ties with New Orleans.[16] He opened a wholesale shop there in the 1820s. A few decades later, David Taylor—merchant, manufacturer, and Whig politician—was a familiar figure among New Orleans traders, recognizable by an oversized, gold watch fob, which decorated his vest.[17] New Orleans was also the town Stephen Oliver chose after the panic of 1837 when, hard pressed by his creditors, he journeyed south to exchange shoes for cash at discounted prices. One Lynn writer recalls that Micajah Pratt, perhaps Lynn's largest shoe boss, employing hundreds of workers and selling thousands of shoes annually, made his name a household word in those parts of the South to which he sent his stamped shoes. There is also John Houghton, a former Lynn resident, who became a shoe dealer in Augusta, Georgia, acting as the agent for Lynn manufacturers. Houghton spent most of his life in Augusta, made a fortune selling shoes to slave holders, and, in due time, became a slave owner himself. Yet Houghton retained idiosyncracies that betrayed his origins. His mansion in Augusta resembled the Yankee structures erected on Chestnut Street by the Salem merchants. And at his death, Houghton manumitted his slaves and used the bulk of his estate to establish a school for indigent children.

The extension of markets, especially in the South, greatly increased the demand for shoes, which, in turn, led to a rapid expansion in the industry. Thus, shoemaking became the most important branch of manufacturing in the Massachusetts economy. Secondly, there were important changes in the organization of labor within the industry, most clearly manifested in a division of labor to speed production.

The absence of machinery and factories in the shoe industry has caused historians to underestimate the importance of shoemaking in the growth of manufacturing before the Civil War. The appearance of the textile factory absorbs the attention of the historian only slightly less than it did contemporaries. The many studies of the textile industry have conveyed the erroneous impression that the only significant manufacturing in Massachusetts was the making of cloth. But shoemaking employed many more people than cotton and woolen manufacturing. As late as 1860, shoemaking employed 69,000 persons; the manufacture of cloth, 47,000. Textile firms were larger, capitalization greater, and the use of machinery more extensive. But as a source of livelihood, shoe manufacturing was far more important than the textile industry.[18] It is the peculiar status of shoe manufacturing, a status halfway between the cottage economy of the subsistence farmer and the mechanized factory system, that has obscured its importance.

Although the increased demand for shoes stimulated a search for methods to speed production, it did not lead to substantial mechanization and the factory system until after the Civil War. The tools used in production remained the same throughout the first half of the nineteenth century. Not until 1854, with the introduction of the sewing machine, was there any substitute for manual labor. Ten years later came the Blake-McKay stitching machine, which created the need for factories to house the machines and their operatives. Prior to the use of the sewing and stitching machines, shoemaking remained a hand industry carried on in much the same way as it had centuries earlier. There was, nonetheless, a change in the way this hand labor was organized to meet the growing demand.

Blanche Hazard, in her study of the shoe industry, has outlined these changes. Under the handicraft system, which in Lynn lasted until about 1760, the shoemaker made the entire shoe and sold his product directly to the customer. He was both producer and distributor. If his business were large enough, he would employ a journeyman or two and perhaps an apprentice. In the sparsely settled town of Lynn, the handicraft stage was relatively unimportant. There were not enough consumers in the town to keep more than a few shoemakers employed. As early as 1750, a few cordwainers were making shoes for Salem and Boston merchants who distributed the product to shopkeepers in distant markets. The separation of the shoemaker from his customers, with no attendant change in the mode of production, signifies the appearance of the first phase of the domestic system, the system which lasted until the appearance of the factory. In the first phase, the shoemaker, making shoes for sale to customers with whom he had no direct contact, was the producer but not the distributor. The task of selling the product was assumed by the merchant capitalist who entered the trade in anticipation of the profits to be gained from buying and selling. Access to the market gave him considerable control over the shoemaker, who became dependent upon the merchant for securing customers for his shoes. In addition, the merchant frequently extended his control over the raw material from which the shoes were made. Ebenezer Breed, for example, supplied the leather, lastings, and other materials that the shoemaker needed but did not have the capital to purchase on his own. Through his agent in Lynn, Breed contracted with the shoemakers for so many pairs of shoes at an agreed upon price. Because Breed owned the materials, he also owned the shoes. The shoemaker had no choice

Waayeel Hortiisaa Caano Loogu Badhxaa!

but to return the shoes he and his journeymen made to the man who provided the materials. Under this arrangement, the manufacturer had direct access neither to the market nor to the sources of raw materials. He consequently was little more than a subcontractor for the merchant, taking his income from the difference between the remuneration he received from the merchant and the payment he made to his journeymen.

A change in the relationship between merchant and shoemaker began to take place in the 1790s. There appeared merchants who did not possess nor seek as great a degree of control over the trade as Ebenezer Breed had exercised. Instead they limited their operations to buying and selling shoes or, if the manufacturer preferred, to loaning capital that the shoemaker could repay in cash rather than in shoes. A letter from Breed to Amos Rhodes gives a brief description of the altered relationship between merchant and shoemaker that emerged in the late eighteenth century:

> Capt. Needham leaves us tomorrow, and by what I can learn he intends to be in the same shoe business—to lend the shoemakers money on the usual interest, with the privilege of taking his pay in shoes, they allowing him five per cent commission for selling what price he can.[19]

Captain Needham was prepared, then, to lend capital to masters and to take repayment in shoes, which he would sell on the open market. Unlike Breed, he would not provide the materials, only the capital. The shoemaker thus gained the freedom to purchase his materials in the cheapest market directly from the leather dealer and sell the shoes, if he chose, to a merchant other than the one who furnished him with the means to carry on his business. Under the old system Breed acted as a leather dealer, shoe merchant, and capitalist. Although the distinction between the two appears slight, a supply of capital meant greater opportunity for the manufacturer-merchant to gain control over raw materials and to establish a direct relationship with the market, bypassing the merchant altogether.

A second change, one that was more ominous for the future, was the entrance into the market of many small shoe merchants who would buy and sell shoes for whatever prices they could get. Breed also comments on this change:

> Why, it is my opinion, and always has been, that I can never do any thing here while shoes are brought [sic] and sold in such a manner

... I think if several of us would join and take such a quantity of shoes at Lynn as to make them more difficult for so many hawkers to get, it would be an advantage.

But Breed deemed it unlikely that he and the other large shoe merchants could gain control of a sufficient portion of Lynn shoes to control prices. It was so unlikely that Breed suggested "we might as well think of raising Egg Rock [a rocky island in Lynn Harbor] from its bed and bringing it to Philadelphia on our shoulders to exhibit for a show in the streets." Merchants like Breed were thus being pushed aside amid the scramble of smaller, more aggressive merchants for a share of the shoe trade. This competition evidently quickened the search for new markets.

The growing demand for shoes also led to changes in the organization of labor that signified the transition from the first to the second phase of the domestic system. In the first phase, from about 1760 to about the 1780s, the cordwainer made the entire shoe: he cut out the appropriate pieces, sewed them together, and attached the upper part of the shoe to the sole. Before 1780, most shoemakers worked in the home, others in small shops, commonly called ten-footers, in which a man, his sons, journeymen and apprentices worked together. In 1750 there were perhaps a half dozen shops. By 1783 there were sixty or more. The growing demand had caused an increase in the number of people who devoted their full time to shoemaking. A separate room in the house or a seat before the fire was no longer adequate for the man who gave as much or more of his time to shoemaking than to farming. Small structures were outfitted with benches or seats, a fireplace or stove, and the sets of tools that each cordwainer brought to his place of work. Although the ten-footer became the primary productive unit in the Lynn shoe industry and remained so until the coming of the factory, an important change occurred in the work that was performed in the shop.

To speed production a division of labor appeared in shoemaking, marking the beginning of the second phase of the domestic system.[20] In the first phase, the shoemaker, whether master or journeyman, made the entire shoe. But as the demand for shoes increased and the master procured larger orders, he hired additional journeymen. He then devoted a larger share of his time to cutting rather than to making. His task was to keep his journeymen supplied with cut leather, doing his utmost to obtain from each role of leather, which he bought, the maximum number of usable pieces with the least possible waste. At first he performed this specialized task within the same shop in which his journeymen made the shoes. As his business further increased, the master abandoned the ten-footer and built the "central shop," often a one or two-story wooden frame building, in which the boss cut up the leather, doled it out to his workers, collected and inspected the finished shoes, and packed them for shipment.[21] The larger bosses relinquished the role of cutter and hired one or more workmen skilled in that particular job. The central shop also became a store in which the boss stocked the goods he used in paying his employees.

Another step in job specialization came with the division of shoemaking into two distinct operations—binding and making. The first involved stitching together the pieces that formed the upper part of the shoe. This job was performed primarily by women, often the wives and daughters of the shoemakers, although in hard times cordwainers who had received a full apprenticeship in the craft bound their own shoes. Making referred to lasting and bottoming; that is, fitting the upper over the last and attaching the upper to the inner and outer soles. Women rarely performed this job. The binders worked in the home; the shoemakers in the ten-footer. Whereas in the first phase of the domestic system the master owned and worked in the ten-footer, in the second phase most bosses operated out of the central shop. The journeymen took over the ten-footers, sometimes renting them as a group or purchasing them outright from the masters. A few small shoe manufacturers continued to operate under the old system, working in the same shop with their journeymen or dividing up the central shop into rooms for cutting and rooms for making. But the prevailing system was one in which the boss and his cutters worked in the central shop, the binders at home, and the journeymen in the shop.

Not all binders and journeymen employed by the Lynn shoe manufacturers lived in Lynn. In fact, the increased demand for shoes and the growing need to fill shoe orders more rapidly caused shoe bosses to expand their labor market. In 1832, the *Lynn Mirror* reported that of 582 shoemakers in nearby Marblehead, 432 worked for Lynn bosses. By 1845, a Lynn shoemaker reported from Maine that while on a visit to a Penobscot Indian reservation he witnessed the arrival of a freight wagon loaded with cases of shoes marked with the initials of Lynn's three largest shoe manufacturers.[22] The expressmen usually worked for the Lynn manufacturers, but in some instances they operated as subcontractors, taking out the cases of stock for a flat rate and pocketing the difference between the amount they received from the boss and the payments they made to outworkers in the countryside. Thus, not only did the Lynn employers extend the labor market to encompass workers hundreds of miles from the town, but they also began to hire these workers in larger and larger numbers. By 1855, it was estimated that three-fifths of the shoes sold by Lynn manufacturers were made outside the town. This growing tendency to give employment to out-workers at the expense of Lynn citizens ultimately embroiled boss and cordwainer in a struggle that shook the town to its very foundation.

Increased production under the domestic system was due, then, to an extension of the labor market and to the dividing of shoemaking into three operations performed by three specialized groups of workers. And in the case of the binders, this meant the utilization of a group that had not previously, in any systematic way, participated in the productive process. The use of female labor was an outgrowth of the domestic system of manufacture in which the entire family of a cordwainer, working in the home, participated as a group in shoemak-ing, each member performing the task for which he or she was best suited. Skill in sewing garments could readily be applied by women and girls to the leather and various grades of fabric that composed the upper part of the shoe. The entrance of females into the shoe trade was also facilitated by the muted growth in Lynn of the handicraft stage in which the cordwainer in the shop made the entire shoe and sold his product directly to the consumer. A small local market never provided a demand large enough to create a considerable number of full-time artisans working in the shop rather than in the home. There were no powerful craft customs that enforced strict apprenticeship rules and denied any role in shoemaking to workers who had not been admitted by the members of the trade. In Philadelphia, a large market for custom-made shoes gave employment to trained artisans who worked at the craft in the master's shop. Direct contact with the consumer helped maintain the standards of the craft. Both master and journeyman re-sisted the efforts of the merchant to subvert the craft, cheapen the product, encourage the use of untrained workers, and convert the shoemakers into subcontractors competing with one another for the business of the merchant. The skilled craftsman's access to a market large enough to preserve the handicraft stage of shoemaking thus obstructed the introduction of practices that in Lynn characterized the domestic system.

Lynn's concentration on the making of ladies' shoes rather than men's is also closely tied to the use of female labor. The towns in Mas-sachusetts north of Boston, especially those along the North Shore in Essex County, traditionally made ladies' boots and shoes. In the communities along the South shore, workers concentrated on the men's branch of the industry. One economic historian, Malcolm Keir, suggests that the coastal topography of the state is the reason for the difference. Along the North Shore, sheltered harbors and deep water were prerequisites for the thriving port cities of Boston, Marblehead, Salem, Newburyport, and others. Poor soil made farming unprofitable, encouraging the people of the North Shore to direct their efforts to fishing and shipping. As a result, these two occupations attracted the major portion of the male population. Along the South Shore the situation was different. A shallow shore line and more fertile soil made farming more feasible than either shipping or fishing. But in both areas of the state neither farming nor seafaring occupations were sufficient to provide the means to satisfy the wants of the population, and, consequently, in both areas the people turned to household manufacture.

Ladies' shoes were made from finer grades of leather and various fabrics such as satinets, wool, and calamancoe. The stitching of the pieces that formed the upper part of the shoe required much the same skill that women used in making cloth and leather garments. The male residents of the towns along the North Shore, like men elsewhere who became the skilled makers of ladies' shoes, could have acquired the dexterity needed for fine workmanship in sewing. But the attraction of seafaring occupations and the trades of shipbuilding, caulking, sail, and rope making made those activities more profitable than shoemaking. A great many men, therefore, avoided manufacturing as long as a better living could be made in other jobs. Keir suggests that the appeal of the sea drained from the area a large number of the males, leaving the females to constitute a majority of the remaining employable population.[23] Poor land and the arduousness of farm labor made agriculture an unfeasible alternative. Most appropriate was an activity that could be pursued in the home and one that utilized skills the women already possessed or could easily acquire. According to Keir, the binding of ladies' shoes suited these conditions perfectly. The making of men's boots and shoes was less feasible. Constructed from coarse, heavy leather rather than fabric, men's boots and shoes required as much strength and dexterity at nearly every stage of their fabrication. Consequently, in the farming areas of the South Shore of Massachusetts where the appeal of the sea could not be answered, the male agricultural population turned increasingly to the making of men's boots and shoes, while along the North Shore where women made up half or more of the number of people employed in making shoes ladies' shoes were produced. Yet in both instances it should be noted that a growth in manufacturing was contingent upon an extension of markets and an increased demand for shoes.

This is borne out by the early census returns from Massachusetts. In 1790, Essex County, on the North Shore, showed the largest surplus of females—3,383. Each of the three large inland counties—Worcester, Berkshire and Hampshire—had more males than females. It seems that dangerous seafaring occupations resulted in a population composed of more women than men.[24]

This hypothesis is further verified by an examination of the returns from the twelve largest towns in Essex County over a thirty year period. Lynn is the only town that consistently had more men than women in 1790, 1800 and 1810. Coastal ports like Salem, Newburyport, Gloucester, Marblehead, and Beverly consistently showed more females than males. Thus, shoe manufacturing provided an alternative employment for the young men in Lynn, while, at the same time, enabling shoe manufacturers to utilize the female labor of neighboring towns to bind the uppers.

It is not precisely known when females were first employed by the shoe industry in the town of Lynn. Keir suggests that John Adam Dagyr, in addition to his improvement in the quality of Lynn shoes, also introduced the practice of using women to bind uppers. But Keir cites no evidence for his opinion, and in no history of Lynn does one find mention of a division of labor in shoemaking earlier than the 1780s. A principal reason for difficulty in ascertaining the date of this important change in the organization of labor is the ambiguous nature of entries in the shoe manufacturers' account books. One can never be sure if "making" refers to making the entire shoe or to making (lasting and bottoming) as distinguished from binding (assembling the upper). It is, nonetheless, clear that the practice evolved inevitably from the household economy of the domestic system, from a growing demand for increased production, and from the availability of female labor.

By 1830, the contours of organization in the shoe industry were fairly well defined. At the top of the structure stood the shoe merchants and the larger shoe manufacturers, each of whom had access to the market. The merchants, most of them in shops on Pearl Street in Boston, were engaged only in distributing the product; they no longer furnished raw materials to the manufacturer. Their purpose was to buy in the cheapest market and to sell in the dearest. The largest shoe bosses acted as both merchant and employer of labor. From a room in the central shop or through their agents in distant cities, they dealt directly with wholesalers and retailers. They purchased their raw materials directly from factories and employed males and females to make the shoes. Smaller employers, commonly called "bag bosses," cut up their own stock in a closet-sized room in their house or store and hired a dozen binders and half as many jours.[26] With the finished shoes packed in saddle bags, they peddled their product from horseback in surrounding towns or haggled with the merchants in Boston for the best price.

The workers actually engaged in production fell into three groups. The aristocrats of the trade were the cutters or clickers, persons skilled in the difficult art of judging the quality, grain, and thickness of leather as well as in cutting out the maximum number of components with a minimum of waste. The clicker worked in the central shop, often beside the boss, received a higher pay than the common shoemakers and frequently learned enough of the business either to start in a small way on his own or to establish his son in the business. Whereas the shoemakers received their pay by the piece, the cutters received a salary.

The cordwainers, shoemakers, or jours worked on materials furnished by the boss at the central shop. They owned their own tools, or kits, and applied their labor to the shoes (uppers) and stuffs (soles, thread), fashioning their shoes on lasts (wooden models shaped like feet) borrowed from the boss. Most jours in Lynn worked in small shops scattered throughout the town. The jours who worked for Lynn bosses but resided outside the town in sparsely settled rural areas worked in the house or in a room set up in a barn. If the Lynn jour owned his own shop, he rented out berths or seats to his neighbors. Occasionally a group of jours shared the cost of building or buying a ten-footer.[27]

The third group of shoeworkers were the binders, women who assembled the uppers and stitched in the lining. Their tools were needle and thread; their place of work the home. Although most binders in Lynn were the wives and daughters of cordwainers and often received components of the upper from the cordwainer who collected stock for the entire family at the central shop, some binders dealt directly with the boss. They periodically took out cases of shoes from the central shop, returned them when completed, and obtained a fresh supply.

This was the structure of organization that prevailed in the shoe industry until the appearance of machinery at about the time of the Civil War.

# 3. A Community of Mechanics

The categories of manufacturer, cutter, binder and journeymen are economic ones that explain the particular function people performed in the production and distribution of shoes under the putting out system. They also define the economic realtionship of one to another and to the means of production as well. But they are not social terms. It is, therefore, unacceptable to use these categories as tools for understanding the framework of social relations and institutions that constituted the society of which the domestic system of manufacture, and the economic relations within it, was a single aspect. Nor can one assume, on the other hand, that membership in one or another of these categories was of no importance in determining relations outside the market place. Both forms of deductive logic are unsound as historical methods for ascertaining what actually happened and why.

The second is based on a view of society in which economic, social, and political activity are separate and distinct realms of experience, each with a unique and autonomous set of relationships. Applied to history, this approach recognizes, at best, only the most tenuous and imprecise connection between changes in one sphere and corresponding, but often delayed, alterations in another. The first interpretation professes belief in an organic society in which nothing may occur that does not affect the other parts. Like the human body, a malady in a vital organ produces symptoms elsewhere. If the interpreter applies the hypothesis of economic determinism to history and sees in capitalism an exploitative relationship between boss and worker, he assumes the presence, in all areas of society, of the antagonisms of the two forces contesting for supremacy. But too often the practitioner of this approach resorts to a mechanistic determinism so strong that it violates the premise of organic social development: the reciprocal relationship between the spheres of experience that constitute society. Instead, eco-

28

nomic relations stand as the head upon the body, directing the activity of the limbs, otherwise autonomous of the other parts.

The shortcomings and errors apparent in the work of those who professed to be applying an organic view of history does not invalidate the approach. The experience of the Lynn cordwainers attests to the utility of such an approach. The contractual relationship between boss and journeyman became increasingly important as a factor in social behavior as the domestic system matured. For the journeyman cordwainer, his status as producer, wage earner, and hired hand came to determine the food he ate, the neighborhood he lived in, his rank in the militia unit or fire company, and even the cemetery in which he was buried. But the contractual relationship between the boss and worker was never the only social tie between them. Both were members of a society with institutions and relations that frequently mitigated and softened the harshness that arose from their dealings at the cash nexus. In the same way that the contractual relationship came to influence, if not determine relations outside the central shop, relations outside the shop affected the behavior of boss and worker. Their consciousness or awareness of worth and dignity, their standards of expectations and self respect, derived in good part from the social groups to which they belonged. In the years from 1830 to 1860 there was a gradual dissolution in the institutions and customs that had imparted to both boss and journeyman a belief in the mutuality of their interests. The new relationship between boss and worker increasingly came to affect the entire spectrum of social experience, often producing interests and attitudes, values and standards, that were different from and hostile to the other. But there was, at the same time, a continuation of relationships that had originated in an earlier way of life. The putting out system in domestic manufacture in many ways served to preserve social relations and institutions and, with them, the ideas and forms of behavior they fostered.

Before turning to an examination of Lynn on the eve of its rapid growth as a manufacturing center, one point should be made clear. The following portrayal is highly interpretive.

Although Lynn's population was geographically dispersed in several fairly distinct sections or neighborhoods, it is possible to speak of a sense of community identity, a feeling that, among the towns of the North Shore, Lynn was distinctive and somewhat peculiar. This was the ideology or set of ideas of the mechanic. It is revealed in the names the people of Lynn gave to their institutions: the *Lynn Mirror and Mechanics' Magazine*, Lynn's first newspaper, established in 1825; the Lynn

Mechanics Rifle Corps (1818); the mechanics' privateer Industry, launched in 1812; the Lynn Mechanics Bank, chartered in 1814; the Lynn Mechanics Institute, 1824; and the Lynn Mechanics Mutual Fire and Marine Insurance Company of 1832.[1] It was an ideology claimed by master and journeymen alike. Gradually, as the two groups moved apart and pursued interests that were mutually antagonistic, each became more discriminating, choosing only those ideas that served their new interests. But over a considerable period of time, journeymen and master were mechanics, with more in common with one another than with other groups in society. The mechanic ideology that appeared among the shoemakers of Lynn in the eighteenth century and lasted well into the next century became the local creed. It was not the idle talk of village orators. It arose rather from the way people of Lynn viewed themselves and their history and from the manner in which they tried to explain why the town had developed in a way different from other communities. These ideas, which came from experience, passed into the consciousness of the people of Lynn and became values by which they judged the morality and desirability of certain politics. The journeymen cordwainers, reared in the ethos like their fellow citizens of other occupations, carried these ideas with them to the experience of industrialization.

The main tenets in the mechanic ideology originated in the social experience of the men who professed them. The most important was the belief that labor is the source of all value and wealth. The application of human labor, talent, and ingenuity to the raw materials extracted from the earth and from plants and animals produced the articles upon which humanity depended for its survival. Without the food harvested by the farmer, humankind would perish from the earth. Without the clothing, shoes, tools, and shelter fashioned by the mechanic, human beings would exist at the level of the animal, foraging in the woods for sustenance and crawling into caves for shelter. For the progress of human civilization it was first necessary, in all cases, to satisfy the basic material needs. Once these needs were met, human beings were free to accumulate the amenities and luxuries that enhanced comfort and made life something to be enjoyed rather than endured. They were also then free to pursue the activities of craftsmanship and art, embellishing articles with qualities of beauty and perfection. So too were they free to think, to contemplate their existence and relationship with their God and fellow beings. But in all cases human beings never entirely escaped the fundamental imperative of procuring essential material goods; without these goods nothing more was possible.

If there was a definite and clear hierarchy in the ranking of human needs, with material necessity first and other needs in various descending orders, human society should, in the view of mechanics, reflect that hierarchy. Society was composed of groups that performed different functions; each supplied some human need. But the most important group were the producers—the farmers and mechanics. Least important were the nonproducers—the idlers, aristocrats, capitalists, lawyers, bureaucrats, and paupers. They contributed nothing that was required for the preservation of human existence. They were mostly social parasites who existed off the labor of the producers, taking for themselves the fruits of others' labor. Somehow eighteenth-century society had become twisted and distorted, deranged from the proper base of a just social order. At the top, were legions of nonproducers: corrupt monarchies that ruled by the accident of birth; aristocrats who performed no useful labor but occupied the seats of power; and a host of sycophants and hirelings of the aristocracy entrenched in innumerable sinecures. At the bottom of society, were the producers who had patiently endured, from fear or deference, the injustice of their social inferiority while all the time supplying the goods and services that constituted the bedrock upon which the entire structure rested. The mechanic ideology of Lynn presented a different alternative for restructuring society.

The social structure should reflect the hierarchy of human needs, giving first rank to the producers and relegating the parasitic nonproducers to the bottom of society. Power, position and prestige should go to those groups that were essential for the maintenance of human life. Highest rank would go to men of talent and ability who stood at the top of the trade in which they worked. Respectability and the full rights of citizenship—equality before the law, civil and political rights—were the just due of farmers, journeymen, and other workingmen, who for centuries had existed on the peripheries of aristocratic society, a degraded and servile race. The mechanics were flirting with proposals that suggested a social revolution in human affairs, a complete reorganization of the social hierarchy, including the replacement of social leaders with men who for centuries had composed the mudsill of society. As one historian has noted, "A contempt for manual labor permeates aesthetic, educational, scientific and religious assumptions until very modern times." No social revolution ever occurred in Lynn or elsewhere in the United States. There was, nonetheless, in the mechanic ideology a number of ideas that, in the context of the late eighteenth and early nineteenth centuries, prompted radical social thought. That these notions existed is not surprising. What is important is their widespread acceptance in Lynn.

First of all, Lynn was a manufacturing town. Of the 1320 males listed in the town directory of 1832, 840 gave their occupation as cordwainer. Another 66 were shoe manufacturers. There were also 106 artisans and 56 farmers. The vast majority of the adult male population was made up of mechanics and farmers. Occupational data for the late eighteenth century would undoubtedly reveal a larger portion of farmers and fewer shoemakers and artisans, but the important point is the predominance of men who fall under the rubric of producers. These figures may not be so striking in light of the undeveloped nature of the town's economy, but they assume greater significance if the economy and social composition of Lynn's population are compared with those of other towns along the North Shore. Salem, Marblehead, and Newburyport were primarily commercial and trading centers rather than manufacturing towns. Although a majority of their citizens were producers—artisans, seamen, dockworkers, and the like—these towns were the epitome of all the social evils that the Lynn mechanics associated with aristocracy. The merchant princes of the North Shore, with their fine mansions on Chestnut Street, their contingents of retainers and retinues of slaves and servants, a haughty propensity toward ostentatious display in their life style, and their contempt for the producers whom they employed, sat abreast the social structure of their communities. From the counting house to the vestry and the town hall, they occupied the seats of power and, by their commanding presence, set the tone and tastes of their societies. In many ways they resembled the dominant social elements of the Mother Country, whose oppression the colonies had recently overthrown; they were, on a less grand scale, the counterparts of the English merchants to whom they looked for guidance in fashion and taste. This was the external source, the foil against which the local ideology of Lynn developed and sharpened. Lacking a sheltered harbor and deep water and thus the mercantile fleets needed for the carrying trade, Lynn was fertile ground for the growth of ideas that never took root in other towns along the North Shore: no shipping meant no strong aristocracy; manufacturing meant mechanics and laboring men. Each produced its distinct ideology. The Lynn mechanics described their town in a petition to the General Court for a banking charter in the following manner: "It is a fact that there are but few Capitalists in Town. Fortune seems to have destined us to move in the sphere of Equality."

The labor theory of value was accepted by Lynn residents because it seems to explain the town's historical experience. Without the resources found in neighboring towns, the people of Lynn had to make up with labor what nature had denied them. Circumstances alone constituted an economic imperative that forced the people to apply their labor to modest resources. Consequently, in nearly every household that formula for achieving wealth, or at least a livelihood, was applied. Hundreds of cordwainers, binders, and cutters, using the simplest tools, applied their skill to the tough dried hides, the rolls of morocco leather, and the bundles of fabrics to produce the shoes that brought wealth to the entire community. The primacy of labor seemed self-evident. And most people in Lynn, because of the unavailability of any other alternative, followed its injunction. James R. Newhall, in describing the economic life of Lynn's residents as well as the difference between Lynn and her neighbors, observed, "The social equality was more distinctly marked here than in most of the seaboard communities of New England. Scarcely any were above the necessity of labor of some kind, and their employments were such that accumulation was by slow degrees."[2] The achievement wrought by the mechanics increased their sense of worth, heightened their awareness of self-importance, and hence helped them to overcome the disability of social inferiority, which the larger mercantile society fostered. It was their minority status and those ingrained notions of inferiority that lent an aggressive, radical, and sometimes shrill tone to their expressions. They were struggling to overcome in themselves, the accumulated residue of social, political, and intellectual inferiority ascribed to manual labor. They were also preparing themselves for an encounter with the upholders of tradition, who would, in self-defense, invoke the customary arguments attesting to their own superiority and right to power and position.

The mechanics in Lynn were a rising, self-conscious class, which was becoming increasingly assertive of new rights and eager to secure a social status commensurate with its growing economic power. At the bottom of their claim was a belief in the labor theory of value. Their most valuable weapon was the credit they claimed for producing the goods and providing the services necessary for the maintenance of human life. Their major opponent was that vague and ill-defined group called nonproducers, a group whom they sought to overthrow. If there was a note of vengeance in their demands for recognition and due reward, it was because they held the conviction they were struggling against the wrongs accumulated over centuries and perpetrated on them by a

34

domineering aristocracy. To illustrate their contention, the mechanics frequently pointed to the mechanics and workingmen of Europe, who still labored under the stigma affixed to them in aristocratic societies.

The mechanics' belief in the labor theory of value and their antipathy toward "nonproducers" revealed itself in their behavior toward members of the parasitic class. On May 8, 1786, the town meeting drafted instructions for John Carnes, its representative to the Massachusetts General Court. He was told to work for a change in the "mode of proceeding in our law matters and to put it out of [remove from] the power of the gentlemen of the law." Should he fail in that modest endeavor at reform, he was instructed then "to bring about an annihilation of the office."[3] The town's contempt for nonproducers reappeared a generation later in 1808 when Benjamin Merrill, the first lawyer to settle in Lynn, arrived and opened an office. A delegation of Lynn citizens called on him and politely asked him to leave; he was likely "to stir up strife, and do more harm than good." The young man promptly complied and moved on to Salem where he met a warm reception and good fortune. If in Salem and Boston the dandies looked askance at the mechanic in his leather apron who toiled at the bench, in Lynn places in the social hierarchy were reversed. A dandy in Boston might be a figure of emulation; in Lynn he met ridicule, or worse. One woman in Lynn, whose daughter had attracted the eye of an overdressed young man, angrily drove him off with a broomstick. The editor of the Lynn paper commended her for her public spirit and good sense and reminded all that Lynn was no place for idlers and social parasites.[5] Cordwainer apprentices sometimes took stronger action. In one case, a youth attired in a suit of fashionable cut and highcollared shirt fell into the hands of young mechanics, who pushed him into a ditch and smeared his clothing with mud.

In the narrower context of the shoe industry, the spread of the mechanic ideology occurred simultaneously with the efforts of the manufacturers and journeymen shoemakers to overcome the power and control exercised by the merchant and jobber, the middle men who stood between producer and consumer and extracted a share of wealth greatly disproportionate to the functions they performed. It was unjust that the producer had to support with his labor a man who did nothing more than speculate in the shoe market, buying where cheapest and selling where dearest, and, if failing, leaving boss and journeymen with worthless notes. One small shoe manufacturer, Benjamin F. Newhall, described the humiliation and anger he felt at his first dealings with a

Boston merchant. Treated curtly and rudely, kept waiting for hours, insulted by the taunts of poor workmanship, he had no choice but to endure the calumnies of the merchant. He clearly recalled that experience many years later when he penned a series of historical sketches, and he remained both an implacable foe of the shoe merchants and an advocate of the mechanic ideology.[6]

As the common store of ideas for master and journeyman, the mechanic ideology lasted only as long as relations between the two remained harmonious. It was particulary prevalent from about the time of the American Revolution until the 1830s. It inevitably became a casualty of industrialization—extension of the market, a division of labor, intense competition, and the exploitation of the journeymen by the bosses. Aspects of the ideology continued throughout the century and reappeared whenever conditions spawned the rebellion of producers against entrenched nonproducers. Other aspects underwent a transformation. They were revived, refashioned, and employed by workingmen against the bosses in much the same way both boss and journeymen had used them against the aristocrats.

Another source of community identity was republicanism and the political struggles in which the mechanics had participated. As a rising social class, and not just an economic interest group, the mechanics were drawn to ideas that corresponded in a political way to their growing sense of worth, self-respect, and economic importance. Their rise more than paralleled the movement for independence and the growth of American nationalism. The larger movement and their own experience are so closely entwined, each supporting as well as drawing upon the other, that they are inseparable. They themselves laid claim to republicanism as the political expression of the mechanic ideology and claimed much of the credit for its success in overcoming the combined foes of foreign domination and aristocratic predominance. But as a political ideology broad enough to include among its adherents slaveholders and merchants as well as mechanics and farmers, republicanism became what its supporters wished it to be. The mechanics chose to emphasize those aspects of republicanism that conformed to the tenet of the labor theory of value, using this basic principle as the starting point for their political assault on those who would profess republicanism while adhering to policies that tried to resurrect the old order under a new name. As long as the bonds of unity between jour and master remained intact, they tended toward unanimity in their interpretation and use of republicanism against a common foe. But a deterioriation in their economic and social relations inevitably produced different views of republicanism, with the one claiming liberty and the other equality.

The American Revolution was a fruitful source of ideas that were incorporated into the mechanic ideology, incorporated primarily because they seemed so compatible with what, to the mechanic, was self-evident in his own experience. It affirmed the notion, as one mechanic put it, that "ALL MEN are born equal, possessed of equal natural rights, and ensigned to enjoy equal civil and social privileges."[7] If the Declaration did not recognize the social superiority of mechanics, farmers, or any other group or condemn those with traditional claims to social preeminence, it did nonetheless proclaim equality. For the mechanics, impatient with an overbearing merchant elite that had derived its legitimacy from a source other than the people, this was a clear gain.[8] The Revolution, in extending the promise of citizenship to all men, gave them the sole right of determining, against the claims of any class, the prerogatives of government: the right to make laws, to impose taxes, to administer justice. No special privileges were reserved for any group because of birth, wealth, or occupation. Equal rights for all and special privileges to none became the watchword of the freeborn American. And citizenship meant active participation in some capacity, whether as voter or officeholder, in political affairs. In fact, the Revolutionary creed assumed that each citizen was the best defender of his rights; they could not, if they were to endure, be entrusted to a self-perpetuating ruling class. In its stress on full political citizenship as a defense against tyranny, the republican creed made it incumbent upon the mechanic to be more than a skilled worker and a producer of goods; he was entrusted with the highest responsibilities of government, and was obliged as a matter of duty, as the guardian of republicanism, to develop those talents and abilities that would enable him to carry out the tasks required of citizens.

The aristocrats, in defense of their position, frequently contended that the mechanics, farmers, and other workers were deficient in the qualities required of rulers and were thus incapable of governing themselves. Left to themselves and freed of the restraints imposed by the forces of order, anarchy would result. They would attack property, seek vengeance upon their betters for the imagined wrongs imposed upon them, and thus return society to the state of nature in which brute force and base instincts prevailed. In response to such a low estimation of the character and ability of those who lived by manual labor, the mechanics turned to history. Like any group seeking recognition and struggling against the stigma of inferiority stamped upon them by social superiors, the mechanics sought to establish links with a glorious past and overcome any lingering doubts of their own worth. They ransacked history for mechanic heroes, men larger than life-size, of superior virtue and ability, preferably men who had been American patriots. Roger Sherman of Connecticut, a signer of the Declaration of Independence and a former shoemaker, became a folk hero. Sometimes, in their zeal for progenitors, they resorted to extraordinary license. Any famous person who had at any time in his life performed manual labor was designated a mechanic. The mechanics were merely attempting to establish the truth that manual labor did not necessarily make one unfit for other duties. That Sherman could be a tradesman and a signer of the Declaration of Independence, that the German Hans Sack could be a shoemaker and poet, demonstrated the versatility, intelligence, and ability to those who worked with their hands. There was not, as many seemed to think, anything inherently degrading or brutalizing in physical labor that made one unable to perform the highest functions of citizenship, that is, unable to make laws, to administer justice, or to lead armies. Self-designated members of the ruling class might well attempt to foist upon the people the notion that the rich, the wellborn and the educated, were the rightful heirs to high office and the emoluments of public life, but for the mechanics, history proved them wrong. As one Lynn mechanic insisted, one did not need "a volume of Blackstone under his arm" to be a good representative in Boston.[9]

As additional proof of the importance of mechanics in the making of American history, they reexamined the participants in the struggle for independence. The men of words, the lawyers and political theorists, may have played an important role in the debate over colonial rights, yet the mechanics doubted if that role was as significant as their own. When verbal exchanges gave way to direct action and when debate produced stalemate, new forms of resistance to British aggressions became necessary. Without them the movement for independence would never have moved beyond idle talk. In the extralegal assaults on tax collectors, on bureaucrats, and on friends of the King, the mechanics provided the manpower. If they were not adept at discussing the finer points of the common law and assembling arguments for legal briefs, they were, nonetheless, able to express, in their own way, their opposition to British infringements on colonial rights. When the first detachments of redcoats landed on American soil and began the forcible suppression of American resistance, it was the yeomanry, tradesmen, seamen, and laborers who rose to counter their force and drive the British from the field. Independence was thus gained by armed resistance in which all Americans, whatever their social class, were called upon to risk their lives. The mechanics "poured out their hearts' best blood," as one mechanic recalled, for the defense of common rights; their sacrifice entitled them to an equal place alongside all other groups in the new American society. Because "all had united in the common struggle for liberty . . . all should share in the blessings of freedom."[10] It was as if their efforts during the Revolution had destroyed the ancient justification for social disabilities and proved, for them at least, who were the final defenders of territorial integrity and republican purity.

The mechanics' class consciousness was more a product of the early nineteenth century than of the eighteenth, and their view of the Revolution assumes for mechanics a distinctive group identity that probably did not exist as early as 1776.[11] On the eve of the Revolution, there is no indication of a cleavage between producers and nonproducers, between the mechanics and the town officers drawn from the clergy and small commercial class, nor is there evidence that the shoemakers at that time advanced a claim for greater political power. In Lynn, the Revolution was primarily a movement for independence and not a revolution that witnessed the confiscation of property, the ouster of incumbent officials, or a reorganization of society on a new basis. Yet there is little doubt that the Revolution set in motion forces that altered the town's economy and, in so doing, produced a population of mechanics who were receptive to the republican ideas arising from the struggle against England. In this sense, the mechanics were correct in stressing the Revolution as a significant event in their own history. A review of the town's political history after the Revolution indicates the emergence of the mechanics as a self-conscious group, a recognition of their differences with other elements in the town, and their efforts to gain political power commensurate with their strengthened economic position within Lynn.

On the eve of the Revolution, Lynn had a population of about 2,100 with 465 adult males, 200 of whom served military duty at one time or another during the war.[12] In response to the events in Boston, residents of the town periodically assembled in town meeting to express their support. Invariably their declarations carried without opposition. A local historian, in comparing the movement for independence in Lynn to the movement in other towns along the North Shore, observed that "not a single instance has been found recorded of a Tory in Lynn, and no case where an unpatriotic 'towny' was made to swear allegiance to his country."[13] The movement did not produce new popular leaders because community leaders embraced the cause of independence. With the creation of the committees of public safety that signified the political break with royal authority, the town chose established leaders for their representatives on the committee. Two Congregational ministers, Joseph Roby of the West Parish and John Treadwell of the Lynn Church, served on the committee. Treadwell dramatized his acceptance of his dual role by appearing in the pulpit with a sermon in his left hand and a musket in his right. The choice of Roby and Treadwell, the widespread popular support for independence, the absence of Tories in the town, and the lack of evidence of serious political differences suggests a high degree of community solidarity as well as political continuity with the prerevolutionary period. The first deep cleavage within the town came nearly twenty years later. If there is a connection between the alignment of Republican and Federalist after 1796 and a split within the town during the Revolution, that connection was submerged and incipient.

In 1781, Lynn's forty-four votes went to John Hancock, the first governor of Massachusetts under the new constitution. Three years later, only twenty-seven votes were cast for governor. These conditions led Lynn historian Alonzo Lewis to observe that "there were, indeed, many more voters in the town, but they were so well satisfied with the wisdom of their rulers, that they gave themselves no anxiety on the subject." Like most towns in eastern Massachusetts, Lynn showed no sympathy for Daniel Shays and his agarian debtors. The town furnished its quota of militia for the force that the governor dispatched to western Massachusetts to suppress the rebellion. But political harmony in Lynn began to disintegrate in the late 1790s. A politics that had been conducted "altogether without animosity" gave way to contentiousness and bitterness, signifiying a heightened political consciousness: people who arose to challenge the handful of local citizens who had previously transacted political business without interference from their constituents. In 1800, Caleb Strong, the Federalist candidate, won 113 votes, and Elbridge Gerry, the Republican, 68. Four years later, the Republicans increased their strength and defeated the Federalists: 145 votes went to Strong, and 272 to James Sullivan. As Lewis and Newhall observe, "the parties now began to regard each other with manifestations of decided hostility, and the political arena presented a field of civil warfare without bloodshed."[14] It was as if an alarm had sounded, warning the mechanics of the threat to their liberties and calling upon them to assert their rights against leaders who had transgressed the bounds of public trust. In the process, "the rage of party continued several years, and was sometimes so violent as to be in danger of degenerating into animosity and personal hatred." This was not the last time the threat of aristocracy and the need to protect popular rights became a cathartic force that gave political activity an erratic, cyclical quality, much like that of religious revivalism.

Although it is difficult to fix the role of the mechanics in the conflict between Republicans and Federalists, there are indications of the factors that determined the political affiliation of Lynn citizens. Religious, sectional, and occupational background were important. Among the leading Federalists were the Reverend Mr. Thomas Cushing Thacher, controversial minister of the First Congregational Church; Hosea Hildreth, preceptor of the Lynn Academy, a private school established by wealthy citizens; the local merchants and traders who dispensed West India goods and groceries, which they imported through merchants in Salem; and prominent members of Lynn's oldest religious denominations, the Congregational and Quaker churches.[15] The Federalists were strong in West Lynn, that part of the town situated on the Saugus River.[16] The river emptied into the sea and supported a modest amount of mercantile activity. The headquarters of the Federalists was in West Lynn at the Lynn Hotel, a popular watering place for people traveling on the new turnpike that ran along the Federalist axis from Boston to Salem.

The Republicans tended to draw their strength from Methodists and from Woodend, the eastern section of Lynn.[17] Although the shoe business was highly decentralized, with cordwainers in all neighborhoods, the heaviest concentration of mechanics was in Woodend.

A number of Republican leaders were Methodists. Enoch Mudge, Lynn's first Methodist preacher, furnished his party with patriotic partisan odes on festive occasions. His brother Joseph was captain of the privateer *Industry*, which the Republicans outfitted in 1812 to prey upon British shipping.[18] A third brother, Benjamin Mudge, was a lieutenant and later captain of the Republican artillery company formed in 1808. Their two cousins, Ezra and Samuel Mudge, were also militant supporters of Jefferson and Madison. Ezra divided his time between the militia and the Legislature, serving as an officer in the Lynn Artillery and representing Lynn for sixteen years, 1807 to 1823, in the General Court. Samuel commanded the Essex County militia unit that rushed to Salem in 1814 to defend the coast against an anticipated invasion.[19] Two other Methodist Republicans were Joseph Fuller, representative and Senator to the General Court and the first president of the Lynn Mechanics' Bank, and Thomas Bowler, energetic Methodist proselytizer and, later, town clerk for sixteen years. Although not all Republicans were Methodists nor all Methodists Republicans, the affinity between the two is unmistakable. The Republicans met at Paul and Ellis Newhall's building on Market Square at the end of the Lynn Common opposite the Lynn Hotel.[20]

One method used by both groups to win popular support was an appeal to the Revolution, with its constellation of emotive memories. Each group sought to establish itself as the rightful heir of that tradition. The first formal fourth of July celebration of the Revolution in Lynn came in 1804, during the heat of party strife. The Federalists held their commemorative meeting, appropriately, in the First Church. The Republicans met in the First Methodist Church.[21]

In 1804, the Republicans gained control of town affairs and despite serious challenges from the Federalists, retained power throughout the war. In the same year, the mechanics made their first petition to the legislature for incorporation of the Lynn Mechanics' Bank.[22] They explained the need for a bank in the following manner. They were manufacturers who dealt extensively with shoe buyers in the South, who paid for the goods with long-term notes. Their trade amounted to a half million dollars, but they were greatly inconvenienced by the long delay between the sale of the goods and actual payment. They wanted a bank to discount their notes and extend credit on the security of the paper from Southern buyers.[23] The Legislature denied their petition. Perhaps the Federalist-dominated body was influenced by colleagues affiliated with the institutions in Salem and Boston to which the Lynn manufacturers went for credit and note discounts. The Federalists undoubtedly were aware that among the petitioners for a bank were the town's leading Republicans. A decade later, the shoe manufacturers obtained a charter for the Lynn Mechanics' Bank.[24] Its first president was the Republican State Senator Joseph M. Fuller; the second president was Ezra Mudge, the town's Republican representative.[25]

In the spring of 1806, an established tradition in Lynn history became a casualty of party strife. For a hundred and seventy-three years, the franchised citizens of Lynn had assembled in the first parish meeting house for the transaction of municipal affairs. But in 1806 the meetings shifted to the Methodist meeting house, a more familiar and friendly site for the Republican majority.[26] The spring election of 1808 showed a growth in popular support for both parties. In the balloting for governor, James Sullivan, the Republican candidate, received 418 votes as opposed to 273 for Christopher Gore. A few months later, in

August, the Federalists submitted to the town meeting a resolution criticizing the Jefferson administration and demanding an end to the embargo. Despite the harsh effects of the trade ban on the town's economy, the meeting rejected the notion and, instead, passed several resolutions commending the President's policies.[27]

With the opening of hostilities toward England, party lines hardened. The war did not rekindle a patriotism strong enough to overcome political differences. The Republicans assumed the responsibility of preparing the town for war. They formed two militia units: the Lynn Artillery in 1808 and the Lynn Light Infantry in 1812.[28] The following year they launched the privateer *Industry*. The Republican headquarters at Market Square became Liberty Hall to Republicans and "The War Office" to their opponents.[29] The Federalists, in an effort to siphon manpower from the war effort without suffering the opprobrium of treason, founded a voluntary fire company. Under Massachusetts law, membership in a fire company exempted one from military service. Draft evaders could parade in the guise of public servants.[30]

Although historians have frequently noted the strength of Federalism in Massachusetts, particularly in the eastern port cities, the manufacturing economy of Lynn produced a different politics. The Federalists repeatedly suffered political defeat in Lynn, while the Republicans retained enough popular support to maintain control of the town's affairs. Their success is particularly unusual in light of the hardship that the embargo on trade, passed by Congress on December 22, 1807, imposed on Lynn's shoe industry. The population of the town had increased from 2,837 in 1800 to 4,087 in 1810, a gain of 44 percent. But from 1810 to 1820 the population increased to 4,515, a gain of only 10 percent. Lynn's prosperity, heavily dependent on exports of shoes to Southern ports on the Atlantic, suffered severely during the naval conflict. There undoubtedly was strong opposition to the embargo and the war from large shoe manufacturers and commission merchants whose fortunes lay in the trade with distant markets. A few manufacturers tried to circumvent the ban by shipping shoes overland to the South: during the war, Theophilus Clark, Benjamin Alley, and Jacob Newhall outfitted heavy wagons, loaded them with shoes, and sent them to customers as far south as Baltimore and Richmond.[31] Yet despite the hardship created by the embargo and the war, and despite the persuasive, persistent arguments of the Federalists a majority of people in Lynn refused either to denounce the ban or to abandon republicanism.[32]

The period from 1800 to 1820 was an important phase in the

emergence of mechanics as a distinct group with a set of political ideas and principles that reflected their heightened sense of self-importance. A half century of economic growth in the shoe industry had produced a large body of mechanics who were increasingly impatient with an existing social system and class hierarchy that did not reflect the importance of manufacturing. In the larger society beyond, particularly the ports of the North Shore, shipping and its associated industries remained the basic economic activities, preserving into the nineteenth century the social and political relationships that mercantile life created. Manufacturing never took root. Political conflict thus took the form of contests between merchants, who organized their factions with forces drawn from similar groups. The object was, therefore, a redistribution of power, prestige and, position among elements that already stood at or near the top of the social hierarchy. In Lynn, the masters and journeymen entered politics with loftier ambitions. They carried with them different ideas about the proper social order, the importance of manual labor, the place of merchants and lawyers, and the dangers of "aristocracy." If the mechanics in Lynn were more successful than mechanics in other towns of eastern Massachusetts in gaining political power, it was only partly because of their strength in number. Caulkers, joiners, riggers, and seamen were numerically a large portion of the population in port cities, but they were splintered by craft loyalties, bound by habits of deference, and beholden for employment to a merchant class more powerful and wealthy than any in Lynn. In addition, there was not a class of men in the maritime crafts comparable to the small manufacturer who often occupied the unusual position of worker-employer-merchant, individuals who were still closely tied to the journeymen but, in other respects, much like the propertied class they challenged. In some ways, the shoe manufacturers were similar to the manufacturers in Europe who did not hesitate to enlist the aid of artisans in their struggle against the landed aristocracy. The manufacturers in Lynn were aided by the weakness of the town's commercial class, the debility of the orthodox Church, and a degree of control over the means of production, which enhanced their stature as the men most responsible for the town's prosperity.

The period from 1800 to 1820 is also important as a link between the Revolution and the generation that preceded the Civil War. In the contest between Republican and Federalist, the mechanics reexamined the Revolution in light of their present struggle for political and social power and formulated an ideology that merged their own rise as a social class with the broader national effort to overthrow foreign domination. In Lynn as in the nation, manufacturing and mechanics, republicanism and the mechanic ideology, constituted the contours of an emerging America. In the eyes of the mechanics, the Revolution planted the Liberty Tree, and the collective efforts of republicans had defended it both against England and against those in America who, in defense of economic interests or a fear of Jacobinism, countenanced England's designs. As a political threat, aristocracy had been repulsed. But arising as it did from the moral defects of human nature—avarice, greed, and the desire for power over others—vigilance was yet the duty of the free born American. For the mechanics, aristocracy was defined as "the exhibition of feelings and views at war with the equal rights of men." It was "the worm that lies at the root of democracy." As a constant tendency among men, it could arise anywhere. For the discerning, aristocracy could be identified by "some assumed gravity—some inflation—some straining of the outer man to a semblance of dignity, and not infrequently by a supercilious smile, all speaking in words as audible as Shakespeare's fool 'I am Sir Oracle, And when I ope my lips let no dog bark.' "[33] Benjamin Mudge's vague description of aristocracy suggests something of the nature of the mechanic's challenge to the established order. Theirs was not an attack on private property or on the possession of wealth; they favored both, but implied that each should come from toil and enterprise rather than from inheritance or the manipulation of trade and government. They also denounced the social behavior of people who failed to acknowledge popular sovereignty and made no secret of their disdain for manual labor. These people were overbearing and haughty, emphasizing not their oneness with their fellow citizens but rather their superiority. If they ruled, it was by right—not by the will of the governed. To the mechanics of Lynn, master and jour, such behavior became objectionable, and in the struggle to assert their rights for a more egalitarian society and a greater voice in public affairs for the producers of wealth, they fashioned a political outlook that lasted well into the nineteenth century. The contest against the common foe of "aristocracy" also tended to minimize the differences between journeymen and manufacturer: both were mechanics.

Although the small manufacturers were the leaders of the mechanics' movement against the Federalist-mercantilist element, there is no evidence that the journeymen viewed this as hostile to their own interests. On the contrary, the political ties between master-manufacturer and journeymen were strengthened by religious and social bonds.

Lynn was the first town in Massachusetts, and perhaps in all New

England, to welcome Methodism and establish a Methodist church. The actual founder was Jesse Lee, an itinerant preacher whom Bishop Asbury dispatched to New England in 1790.[34] On his journey through southern New England, Lee tried to establish societies in Connecticut and Boston, but made only modest gains: after months of preaching in Boston, Lee gathered only fifteen members. Massachusetts still loomed as the stronghold of Congregationalism, and the one area of the country in which the Methodists were dismally unsuccessful. Methodist membership burgeoned in the South and in the newly opened territories in the West, and began to increase in the Middle Atlantic States. But the disciples of Wesley found New England almost impervious to their message. Although they made small gains in Vermont and in the areas of Connecticut adjacent to New York, Massachusetts remained the steadfast symbol of resistance of the old to the new. The earlier efforts of Methodist organizers, efforts made before Lee's trip in 1790, had failed to create a foothold in the home ground of Puritanism. The cold rebuff given the Methodists indicated that theological repudiation of Calvinism would gain entrance deviously, passing into Congregationalism from the lips of its professed adherents, taking the form of Unitarianism and, later, Universalism. Bishop Asbury acknowledged the strength of the opposition a Methodist would face in Massachusetts by sending Jesse Lee, perhaps the most able of his traveling organizers. Although Lee failed in Boston, he enjoyed immediate success in Lynn.

Jesse Lee, preacher, theologian, and church organizer, came to Lynn at the request of Benjamin Johnson. Johnson was a prosperous master-manufacturer who did an extensive business in the South, especially in the upper region around Virginia and North Carolina. Legend has it that Johnson, on one of his visits to shoe dealers in the South, received his first taste of Methodism and made the acquaintance of Lee. Johnson is supposed to have convinced Lee to come to Lynn. More likely, Johnson tendered his invitation to Lee while Lee was preaching in Boston in the fall of 1790.

The first meetings were held in Johnson's home on South Common Street in the fall of 1790, but as the crowds of the curious and the devout increased, services shifted to Johnson's barn. Five months later, in May 1791, 108 persons withdrew from the old parish and signed certificates of attendance for the Methodist meeting. In the single year following Lee's arrival in Lynn, Methodist Church membership reached 118. The division in the old parish, occasioned by the appearance of Methodism, was reminiscent of the feud stirred up by George

Whitefield's arrival in Lynn a half century earlier. The local minister barred Whitefield from the pulpit and tried to dissuade his congregation from attending his meetings, but the people persisted. They took a door from a barn, placed it on upright barrels, and from this improvised platform Whitefield delivered his sermons to hundreds of listeners. According to one historian, this incident poisoned relations between clergy and congregation and left a legacy that endured for decades.[35] Most of the 108 persons who signed attendance letters by birth members of the parish and not of the church, suggesting they had long since shown their dissatisfaction with Reverend Thacher by staying at home.[36]

Those who actually converted to Methodism spread the message: many were fervent, unlettered mechanics who vigorously gave their testimonies in the idiom of their listeners. Although the Congregational Church was already in decline, lacking the enthusiasm and dedication generated by newcomers, the Methodists cut even further into their membership; the old church was left with five male members, and even lost its silver communion set to the secessionists.

The appeal of Methodism lay in its ability to appropriate to itself and infuse with religious meaning many of the popular sentiments that were undermining the old order. Its thrust was both doctrinal and social. Lee's first sermon given in Lynn included a critique of the Calvinist tenet of "unconditional election," rejecting the notion that an inscrutable, arbitrary God extended salvation to a select elite for whom the gift became an inalienable possession. Too often the categories of elect and nonelect corresponded closely to a social structure that was becoming unacceptable. The Methodists, if they did not democratize the hierarchical structure of church authority, did democratize salvation by dividing the prerogative of election between God and humankind holding out the promise that anyone, should he or she seek salvation earnestly and devoutly, could gain God's ultimate gift through grace. As one listener of Lee was said to have exclaimed: "Why, then, I can be saved! I have been taught that only a part of the race could be saved, but if this man's singing be true, all may be saved."[37] But one's salvation lasted only as long as one's piety. This tenet would have far-reaching effects on the social life of the community and on the behavior of its adherents in the succeeding years. It seems, then, that Lynn from 1790 to 1791 was ripe for Methodism. Lee, upon his arrival there, is said to have remarked that he, at once, felt himself at home. And Parsons Cooke, an unfriendly critic who became the Calvinist minister of the First Congregational Church in 1836, observed that Methodism produced great results "because it took hold of the doctrines which lay in the minds of almost all men here, and wrought them with the steam, levers, and pulleys of a new engine."[38]

Equally important as the theological message of Methodism was the manner in which its followers preached to the people. Lee himself set the tone. He was a man of "keen wit, much native good sense, physical endurance and burning zeal."[39] His successors, if they lacked Lee's experience and intelligence, struck the same posture: "They sympathized deeply with the common people, and made themselves perfectly at home in every family which they visited and became acquainted with. Their open, free social intercourse with the people was one of the great secrets of their success."[40] The Methodists won the bulk of their converts from the ranks of the rising mechanics, and not from the socially prominent families of the town. Of the fifteen incorporators of the Lynn Academy, a private school founded in 1804 to educate the children of the elite, not one was among the 136 incorporators of the Methodist Church.[41]

The connection between Methodism and Republicanism extended beyond a mere similarity in the doctrines they preached.[42] As noted earlier, the first formal celebration of independence occurred on July 4, 1804. The Federalists from the Lynn Hotel in West Lynn met at the First Church; the Republicans marched to service in the new Methodist Church. Several of the most prominent Republicans in Lynn were also active missionaries for Methodism.[43] Among them were Enoch Mudge, Lynn's first Methodist preacher, and his brothers Joseph and Benjamin; their two cousins Ezra and Samuel; as well as Joseph Fuller and Thomas Bowler.[44] On the other hand, the men of West Lynn associated with the First Church, the Lynn Hotel, and the Lynn Academy constituted the leadership of the Federalist party. This was not a contest between rich and poor, capitalist and wage earner. The Republicans and Methodists included well-to-do shoe manufacturers and men with considerable landed wealth. The Republican militia unit, for instance, had a uniform of plumed Roman helmet, blue jacket, and gray pants trimmed with red cord, the entire outfit costing about eighty dollars, well beyond the means of a common shoemaker.[45] The Federalist, non-Methodist group was drawn primarily from the small commercial enclave in West Lynn and from the town's Quaker community, which was also involved in trade and had particularly close ties with merchants in Salem.[46] There appears, then, to be on one side, a connection between manufacturing, mechanics, Methodism, and Republicanism, and on the other, between trade and commerce, merchants, the older denominations of Congregationalist and Quaker, and Federalism.

Not all the mechanics who were dissatisfied with Orthodox religion travelled the route from Congregationalism to Methodism. Joseph Lye, respectable journeyman mechanic and devout Christian, kept a diary and account book from 1817 to 1832, which reveals his disgust for harsh, uncompromising Calvinism as well as for the emotionalism of Methodism. Most objectionable to Lye was Calvinism's low estimation of humanity and its almost morbid obsession with the sinful nature of mankind. His entry for December 28, 1817, reports that he heard a Mr. Hopkins preach "an uncharitable Hopkinsian Calvanistical Sermon such as one I never wish to hear again." Lye began intentionally boycotting church services whenever a Calvinist was scheduled to speak. A few months later, on February 22, 1818, he returned, only to observe what he had observed earlier of Orthodox preaching: "very uncharitable, not profitable to any, cruel as the grave." Lye, in his disgust, returned again to truancy from the First Church, recording in his diary that a Mr. Lyman, "an high Calvinist preached at the first parish. I, rather than hear him, staid at home." Lye evidently did not know where to turn for the theology he wanted. He visited the Methodist and Quaker meetings, and occasionally walked to Chelsea to hear the Unitarians Joseph Tuckerman and Horatio Alger. Although Lye periodically attended the Methodist evening services from 1818 to 1822, his final break with evangelicalism came in 1822 after he visited the encampment in Duxbury. His entries for August 14 and 15, 1822 explain the reasons for his withdrawal from them:

> There religious _____ [illegible] in its wildest form was exhibited in the different tents. Singing, shrieking, praying, exhorting, shouting, groaning, laughing, etc. Two tents were occupied by Blacks from Boston & c. In them were a few whites. Their devotion as they pleased to call it, continued until nearly midnight.

> I have not been informed how many have been converted this meeting but when the passions are excited and the understanding unenlightened, not much fruit can be expected, except from fanatics; and how decent men and good christians can encourage such proceedings is best known to themselves.

Disillusionment with Methodism and opposition to Calvinism led Lye to join with friends in the First Church to establish, first, an Episcopal

Church in 1819 and then the Unitarian Second Congregational Church in 1822. His motive in lending support to both efforts was to "inculcate the doctrines of Liberal Christianity; and thus do away in some measure the pernicious effects of Calvanism." He sought a community of worship that believed in "the Rights of Conscience and of private judgment in Religion, and the principles of Universal Charity."[47]

Although Lye's religious affiliations over the decade were unusual, and atypical for most journeymen cordwainers in Lynn, his social relationships with men in the community who were not journeymen was, perhaps, not uncommon. His status as wage earner did not deter him from joining with men of other occupations in working for the common end of creating a religious association that would satisfy their spiritual and social needs. Lye united with several prominent shoe manufacturers to found the Episcopal society in 1819 and, for a time, served as secretary of the new body. Yet he remained a journeyman cordwainer, working regularly at the bench in his small shop next to his home until his premature death in 1834. His occupation was that of shoemaker, but he was also a mechanic, a term which at that time recognized no significant distinction between journeyman and master.

The collapse of St. John's Episcopal Church in 1821 was perhaps the result of the mechanics' antipathy toward a religion that they associated both with the Mother Country and with those elements in America who were as much like the English aristocrats in their political and social views as in their religious propensities. Another attempt was made in 1836 to form an Episcopal Church; it struggled along until 1841. Three years later a group of Lynn citizens were successful in forming another such society, but it never won support from many people in the town. Even as late as 1865, in a city with a population of over 20,000, the Episcopal Church did not have more than a hundred communicants. Again the comparison with other towns along the North Shore is instructive. Trade and commerce seemed invariably to create the social conditions in which an Anglican church could survive, if not thrive, abetted by the presence of a considerable element in the population for whom the English influence retained its alluring appeal.

In the community as a whole, manufacturing had produced a class of people who impressed upon Lynn, in politics, religion and social outlook, a set of ideas and institutions that is here termed the mechanic ideology. Its basic tenet was the labor theory of value, and its social objective the supremacy of the producers over the nonproducers. The components of the mechanic ideology were not novel or peculiar for the time in which they appeared, but that they could win acceptance among enough people to become the prevailing creed of an entire community in eastern Massachusetts is, indeed, peculiar. There were, of course, differences among the mechanics, differences that would become sources of a new conflict in Lynn during the first half of the nineteenth century. But from about 1790 to 1830, the common enemy of master and journeyman alike were the ideas, values, and institutions of mercantile society, especially the place alloted to the mechanics. Their first task was to clear the ground of the debris left by a declining way of life, a way of life that perished earlier in Lynn than elswhere because there it had never been strong. This was the context for the cooperation between master and journeyman. In all endeavors, whether in founding churches, building republicanism, or opposing the shoe merchants, master and journeymen moved together in common cause.

This point deserves emphasis because of its importance in understanding the behavior of both boss and journeymen, particularly the jours in the following decades. Many of the standards, values, and social traditions by which the journeymen judged the changes that accompanied early industrialization originated in this golden age of the "mechanic." Master and jour rose together as partners against a common foe. In the process, the relationships, ideas, and institutions that they created preserved and perpetuated, in actual experience and in consciousness, many aspects of their original historical experience. At the same time, or soon after, the productive relationship between master and jour, which had been conducive to cooperation, began to show signs of strain, deterioration, and dissolution. Yet the relationships, ideas and institutions that they had together created did not suddenly dissolve; neither did they, in many cases, break down at a rate commensurate with the increase in exploitation of journeyman by master-manufacturers. For many journeymen, the mechanic ideology, a belief in craft solidarity, and the preservation of social harmony between boss and wage earner, remained a powerful force in determining behavior.

There was another dimension to the relationship between master and journeyman mechanic that extended beyond cooperation in founding and supporting religious institutions and political parties. In the neighborhood, in the larger family, and in the customs and traditional activities of the communities, there was a network of integrated social life which tended to inhibit the formation of relationships based on one's occupation. The neighborhood and family were important sources of social relationships in Lynn. One's membership in either or both frequently determined one's political and religious affiliation, the militia unit or volunteer fire company to which one belonged, or the people with whom one associated in the informal activities of clearing land, raising a house, drinking and gambling, or celebrating a birth or marriage. Sometimes, family membership and neighborhood overlapped: particular families tended to concentrate in certain sections of the town, making one's friends and neighbors one's blood relatives. This was especially true in the outlying sections of Lynn. It was generally true that the more distant and isolated the neighborhood, the greater the importance of the family and section in insuring group loyalty and in limiting affiliations with members of the community outside the neighborhood. The early putting out system of manufacture, based on shoemaking in the home or small shop rather than in a factory, tended to preserve this network of family and sectional loyalties. The Quaker shoemaker in Pudding Hill who worked for his brother-in-law or next door neighbor felt more in common with them, socially, religiously, and ideologically, than he did with the journeymen in West Lynn whom he saw once a year at town meeting.[48] But in each case, one's status as shoemaker, in the years from 1830 to 1860, came to determine one's social experience, first in the section, and then in the entire community. New relationships and new bonds of loyalty, identification, and affiliation were fashioned from a common experience that seemed to depend more on one's economic position than on the neighborhood in which one lived or the family to which one belonged.

The absence of a harbor, slow economic growth, and a concentration on agriculture and household manufacturing preserved early patterns of settlement and social organization. The population in Lynn was scattered across the fertile land and did not concentrate at a single point, either along the shore or at the harbor, as did the population in other towns along the North Shore. There was no central focal point of economic activity to draw people from the outlying farming sections or to detach them from the social organizations built around the neighborhood. Secondly, because access to land was crucial to anyone wishing to settle in the community, early landholders who transmitted their property to their descendants effectively deterred newcomers from the town. Consequently, a significant portion of the towns' population was composed of people descended from the families who had originally settled Lynn and occupied the best lands. As noted earlier, one fourth of the population in 1832 had twelve surnames, suggesting a high degree of continuity in population over nearly two centuries of time.[49]

Neighborhoods in Lynn frequently took their names from the families who settled there. Many of their descendants remained. The

Breed family tended to concentrate in Breeds End, Mansfield in Mansfield's End, Graves in Gravesend, the Lewises on Lewis Street and so on. Intermarriage, exchange of property, and movement within the town tended to disperse these families to other parts of the town, but continuity in the family and in the composition of the neighborhood was a marked feature of Lynn's population well into the nineteenth century. Accelerated economic growth increased the movement of population and brought to Lynn a large number of outsiders whose presence reduced the numerical importance of the indigenous population and weakened the neighborhood as the basis of social affiliation. But this was a gradual, ongoing process and not a change that suddenly transformed the entire community and dissolved old relationships. Throughout the first half of the nineteenth century, the section retained its importance as the factor which determined the scope of social relationships.

To a considerable extent, then, social life in Lynn centered about the neighborhood in which one lived. Examined from the level of the entire community, neighborhood loyalties were the primary sources of political and social conflicts within Lynn until changes in the town undermined sectional cohesion and created alignments based more on class considerations than on geography. Sectional rivalries almost assumed the appearance of rivalries between separate and distinct communities that had grown up in partial isolation, communities with their own institutions and with social relationships that fostered identification with one's neighborhood rather than with one's "class." But when neighborhood institutions and relationships are examined more closely, from the perspective of the section itself, it is evident that in the distribution of power and position, they reflected the class structure that was emerging from manufacturing. The changes in social relations that accompanied economic change meant essentially the gradual linking of shoe bosses in one section with their counterparts in another for the pursuit of their class interests, as well as a similar process on the part of the cordwainers, with each forming relationships, ideas, and institutions more reflective of their collective experience than of those found in the "classless" neighborhood. In other words, journeymen and masters did not confront each other from across a sectional divide in which each had developed separately and independently with their own institutions and social relations. They emerged rather from a common historical past.

Decentralization fostered sectional loyalty. The clearest example of an almost autonomous community within the town is Swampscott, a section of Lynn until it withdrew in 1851 and became a separate town. Legal separation was in many ways merely the recognition of the section's autonomy for many years prior to 1851. Lying on the coast at the extreme eastern end of Lynn, Swampscott was primarily a fishing village and not a shoemaking center.[51] The Phillips family was the largest kinship group. As Ward 1 under Lynn town government, Swampscott shows its independence and distinctiveness as a political, economic, and social entity. It had its own schools, fire company, stores, and church. An indication of its community solidarity was the political unanimity that the fishermen demonstrated in town meetings. David Johnson, in his *Sketches of Lynn*, observed that in the early 1840s the Swampscott fishermen were "democratic almost to a man." At each election, they came to the polls en masse, marching to the tune of fife and drum, and voted as a bloc. Political consensus was clearly the outgrowth of a high degree of group consciousness.[52]

Every section of Lynn showed similar features of neighborhood loyalty and solidarity, though not to the extent of Swampscott, which, furthest removed from the center of Lynn, was the most isolated. In the field of education, for instance, the neighborhood had considerable autonomy. Although funds for maintaining facilities and hiring teachers came from town revenue, each section had a Prudential Committee that adopted a curriculum and hired a teacher. At the end of each term, the Prudential Committee gathered in the school and heard the students recite the lessons they had learned during the year. If dissatisfied with their performance, the Prudential Committee fired the teacher and hired another. Autonomy in education is also revealed in the case of the Quakers of Pudding Hill, undoubtedly the most tightly knit community in Lynn next to the Swampscott fishermen. They maintained their own school for Quaker children, prescribed the material used in teaching, and financed the whole operation with funds allocated to them by the town government from public revenues. Other citizens resented the dispensation allowed to the Quakers, but the Friends had the political and financial power to make their will prevail.[52]

Neighborhood autonomy appears also in the distribution of other formal social institutions throughout Lynn.[53] Each section had its own volunteer fire company whose social importance was no less important than its role in fighting fires.[54] The fire company was the outgrowth of the fire club founded by well-to-do businessmen who joined together to take precautions against the loss of property. Membership was voluntary but limited. Each member equipped himself with two buckets for

carrying water and a large bag to salvage valuables from the en-
dangered house of a member whose membership was signified by a
shield affixed to the front of his building. As the population in each
neighborhood became more dense and as hand water pumps became
available, fire companies were formed. Businessmen usually furnished
the funds to purchase the hand engine, while residents of the
neighborhood provided the manpower to operate the pump.[55] Membership was voluntary, but although in later years the fire companies
became exclusive clubs, in the early years each householder was expected to offer his support. In 1837, the town of Lynn began providing
public funds for engines and fire houses while, at the same time, allowing each company to choose its own members.[56] Efficiency of one's
neighborhood engine became a source of intense rivalry between the
Lynn fire companies, resulting in musters that attracted hundreds of
partisans from each ward. The membership rolls of the fire companies,
usually listing about sixty members each, show, as one might expect, an
overwhelming majority of mechanics, masters, and journeymen alike.
The fire company, with its weekly meetings and training sessions,
drinking bouts and contests with other companies, thus tended to foster neighborhood pride.[57]

The same was true of the militia companies: after partisan conflict
between Federalist and Republican subsided, they tended to organize
around the neighborhood.[58] After the war of 1812 and the diminution
of any foreign threat to America, the militia system, with its compulsory
service, tended to give way to the fire company as the vehicle for sectional contests of collective discipline, proficiency in handling public responsibilities, and public recognition of the superiority of one's
neighborhood unit over all others.[59] Training day in Lynn was primarily a social gathering and not a series of protracted military maneuvers.
There was some marching and firing of muskets, but the atmosphere
was one of a public outing or picnic in which men from the surrounding area gathered for the revelry of drinking and cavorting with women. Membership in a neighborhood militia company became the
source of one's social identification and the affiliation that distinguished one from the members of other companies.

There were other institutions that suggest the importance of the
neighborhood in determining the scope of social relationships. Young
men, many of them already cordwainer apprentices, belonged to
neighborhood gangs that engaged in sporting rivalries with one
another or occasionally joined in the mock warfare of a snow ball fight.
David Johnson mentions encounters between the "Black Mashers," who

lived in the vicinity of Black Marsh along Union and lower Broad Street, and the boys from Lewis Street and Woodend.[60] These youthful affiliations perhaps extended, in their later years, to the neighborhood drinking spots. In Woodend, mechanics gathered at the "Diving Bell" in the basement of a fire company club house for rounds of spirited discussion and glasses of rum.[61] In West Lynn, mechanics would gather after work at Caleb Wiley's store, where large quantities of rum were dispensed at two cents a glass. The Swampscott fishermen had their own drinking places as did the people in Dye House Village and Gravesend. Each neighborhood also had its own stores, which sold an assortment of goods. These stores, usually situated at the intersections along the roads between Boston and Salem, became important focal points for informal socializing and the exchange of gossip. Each section also had its complement of merchants and artisans to serve the needs of its residents: wood dealers, carpenters, bakers, tailors, and so on, all of whom made it unnecessary for a resident of Woodend or West Lynn to venture out from his neighborhood and establish even the most casual relations with people in other parts of the town. Each section also had its own cemetery—Western burial grounds, the Eastern, and the Friends. All residents of the neighborhood, whatever their occupation, went into the same plot of ground. An indication of the self-contained nature of the various neighborhoods is the observation of David Johnson on the importance of the town meeting. He noted that the town meeting served both a political and social function, presenting an opportunity for people to gather and exchange news with a cousin, to discuss the prices paid by the bosses in the different neighborhoods, and to renew old friendships. He implicitly suggests that were it not for the town meeting, many people in Lynn would have seldom seen anyone other than their neighbors.

Probably more important than the formal relations that took place within neighborhood institutions were the informal activities that naturally arose from people's living together. Picnics, excursions to the coast on holidays, pig killings, funerals, house raisings, and fishing parties were group activities and shared experiences that gave to each participant a sense of social identity with his or her neighbors. Here were tasks which, in a more complex and specialized society, might be contracted out to a specialist, a butcher or carpenter, for example. But in Lynn, most people could neither perform the job alone nor afford to hire an artisan. Instead, they cooperated and lent their labor to a neighbor with a recognition that what was given would be returned. Some residents, for example, kept a vegetable garden and a hog to supplement the family larder. In the fall, several neighbors and usually a crowd of boys would gather on a Saturday morning to slaughter and butcher the pig for a family's winter supply of meat. No remuneration other than a few refreshing glasses of rum was expected of the owner, yet it was understood that he would repay the gesture with his own aid. The same was true whenever a man built a house. He usually constructed the roof in sections and when ready for installation called upon neighbors for their help in raising the roof upon the walls. In times of serious illness, one seldom hired a nurse. Neighbors would assume the responsibility of "watching," taking turns at the bedside until the ill person either recovered or passed away. For the pleasurable occasions of picnics and fishing parties, mechanics from a shop or two in the neighborhood would load a wagon with cooking utensils, fishing gear, and a keg of spirits and ride to Nahant for an outdoor feast of fish and rum. They might also pack themselves into a boat and go to the Point of Pines to gather giant sea clams or to George's Banks for fish.

An idyllic society of perfect harmony? Undoubtedly not. Instead, Lynn was a highly decentralized society composed of semi-autonomous sections, whose social life was characterized by a strong sense of community. The foundations of community in all sections were the shared experience of an immobile population with deep roots in the neighborhood and a high degree of cooperation on nearly every level of endeavor. What conflict there was before 1820—social, political, religious and economic—also appeared in the forms of sectional rivalry, with the small mercantile community of West Lynn and the Quaker traders in Pudding Hill contesting with Methodists and mechanics, mostly in Woodend, for preeminence in town affairs. Manufacturing, republicanism, and the labor theory of value together produced the class conscious mechanics who impressed their own ideology upon the town. Their ideas also reflected the social relationships that existed in most sections of the town. The cooperation of journeyman and master was not a formal arrangement of convenience between two distinct classes of men, but the outgrowth of a common outlook and way of life that is shown most clearly in their high degree of social integration. Neither group had detached itself from the integrated institutions and activities of the neighborhood to pursue its class interests in alliance with counterparts in other neighborhoods. Both worked within the framework of social relations inherited from the past, their behavior as economic beings constrained, on the one hand, by an undeveloped market economy in which competition was not yet intense, on the other, by a way of life that of necessity required cooperation. A boss or journeyman was not a free agent able to do as he pleased, without any regard for the sentiments or needs of others. A master could no more gouge his jours than refuse to answer the call of the fire bell and help extinguish a fire. The pattern of social relations in Lynn indicates that in the early years there was no recognition of a contradiction between one's personal interests and those of the larger group to which one belonged. Lacking were the means to gain power and to increase one's control over others, the means to give free rein to one's propensities for wealth and prestige. There had to be both the opportunity to advance one's interests and the conviction that such behavior was necessary, morally right, and ultimately beneficial to all.

# 4. Rise of the Shoe Manufacturers

The origins of the shoe manufacturers lay in their command of capital. The possession of capital enabled them to gain independence from the merchant and to secure control of the raw materials from which the shoes were made. Ownership of shoe stock thus made the manufacturer the owner of the finished product as well as an employer of labor. In the absence of machinery and factories, it would be technically correct, but misleading, to stress the incompleteness of the manufacturer's control over the means of production. True, the shoemaker retained his tools, but those tools were useless without access to the materials from which shoes could be made. It was the command of capital and ownership of materials that distinguished the manufacturers from the journeymen. Possession of raw materials, access to markets, and employment of wage labor are the features that gave a collective functional identity to the shoe bosses.

The distinction between master and journeyman was at first slight because the master had neither sufficient capital nor a large enough market to be a supplier of materials. Thus in 1750, there were only three masters in Lynn who employed journeymen, and masters were themselves obliged to work alongside the journeymen, either in the capacity of shoemaker or cutter. But as the demand for shoes increased and the master gained control over sufficient capital to employ larger and larger numbers of workers, including cutters working in his central shop, a distinction that had seemed slight became crucial. The shoe bosses gradually emerged as a full-fledged separate group that no longer participated in the actual production of shoes.

Equal in importance to understanding the role of the shoe manufacturers are examining their social origins and discovering the process by which they became manufacturers. An attempt will be made to identify the manufacturers in the social structure from which they emerged and

ufacturers were, therefore, a large group whose operations varied greatly in size, from the manufacturer in the central shop, who employed several cutters and hundreds of binders and makers, to the bag boss in his small shop, who cut his own stock and worked alongside his jours. Under the highly decentralized putting out system of domestic manufacturer, the bosses were only slightly less scattered throughout the town than were the journeymen they employed. They lived and worked in all sections of Lynn and did not congregate in any single neighborhood. But the same conditions that eased the movement of aspiring entrepreneurs to the rank of manufacturer also conspired to cause a high turnover rate among the bosses.

The small amount of capital needed for a modest start in business created intense competition among the Lynn manufacturers. The struggle for a foothold in the market impelled many toward recklessness in granting long credits to poor risks in return for orders. Out of the approximately eighty bosses who were doing business in 1836, all but half a dozen failed during the depression that commenced in the spring of 1837. Yet the threat of insolvency was no deterrent to those anxious to make a small start. In 1841, there were 110 shoe manufacturers, 86 of whom were new men who had entered the business between 1832 and 1841.[6] Thirty-two had previously failed in business. The same erratic pattern continued during the next two decades. In 1851, there were 145 shoe manufacturers, 103 of them new men who were not bosses in 1841. By 1860, there were 210 shoe manufacturers, 179 of them new entrants who becomes bosses at some point between 1851 and 1860. An indication of the lack of continuity in the group of shoe manufacturers can also be gained from another direction. Of the 145 men who were shoe manufacturers in 1851, 44 had been bosses a decade before in 1841; 21 had been in business in 1832; and 16 had begun as early as 1829.

Although the turnover rate among the manufacturers was extremely high, not all who disappeared from the ranks were bankrupts. Some merely left Lynn and established businesses elsewhere. Isaac Cobb, for example, a manufacturer noted for the high quality and excellent design of his shoes, moved to Haverhill and resumed business. But most of those who withdrew, whether because of insolvency or the desire to establish a business elsewhere, probably would not have left had they been more successful. Some former shoe manufacturers remained in Lynn and either returned to the occupations they had followed before entering business or used the capital they had accumulated to establish other enterprises. Of 48 men who were bosses in 1841 but not in 1851, the largest portion, numbering 20, do not appear in the directories of the 1850s and, therefore, probably emigrated from Lynn. Of the remaining twenty-eight, 8 returned to making shoes, 5 became clickers, 6 established grocery and provisions stores, 3 became commission merchants or wholesale shoe dealers, two specialized in supplying cut soles to manufacturers, and each of the remaining 4 went into other occupations. For those who remained in Lynn, the attempt at shoe manufacturing had not been an altogether unremunerative endeavor.

The large number of men who became shoe manufacturers in Lynn between 1830 and 1860 and the modest nature of their enterprise has promoted several assumptions of their social origins. It is undoubtedly true that at no time since the period before the Civil War had there been so many independent shoe manufacturers in Lynn, and that never had it been easier for a shoemaker of small means to move from the bench to the central shop. Perhaps one reason for the propagation and acceptance of this notion is the change that occurred in Lynn following the Civil War. The introduction of the factory system brought enormous disparities of wealth and power between capitalist and worker, causing many people in Lynn to look back nostalgically toward the early nineteenth century. Their design to sharpen the contrast between their own generation and that of their fathers led them to overlook differences of status, to minimize the tensions, and to find abundant evidence of an equality of condition that was deficient in their own society. The ease with which a man could set out in business on his own fostered the notion that the opportunity was available to all. The need for small amounts of capital is overlooked.

Those with some knowledge of Lynn's early history are impressed by the town's humble beginnings. One does not find evidence of the opulence that is so clear in the early history of Lynn's neighbors along the coast. The town's reputation in the eighteenth century was undistinguished alongside the glories and fame that accrued to Salem and Newburyport. The physical appearance of Lynn does not reveal any of the imposing residences and public buildings, centers of government and learning, that represent the wealth garnered by merchants from the carrying trade. Nor is there much similarity between the merchant and the shoe manufacturer in either wealth, life style, or social philosophy, all of which suggest the different social origin and entrepreneurial experience of each. Furthermore, Lynn's industrial leadership does not resemble those of the textile towns of Lawrence and Lowell, towns built out of nothing by the outside capital of the men whose names they bear. The Lynn shoe manufacturers were not outsiders; they sprang from native ground and, according to popular view, must, therefore, have been cleaved from the stock of the mechanics and farmers who resided there. The Lynn of 1830 appears as a town composed of an undifferentiated mass of toilers—poor but respectable and hard working.

What were the social and occupational backgrounds of the men who became shoe manufacturers? Of the 86 who appear as shoe manufactuers for the first time in 1841, 44 (51 percent) were born in Lynn, and 70 (81 percent) were born or married in the town. Their average age was roughly 32 years. Of the 86, 36 were listed in the directory of 1832, a poorly compiled register that assigned the occupation of "cordwainer" to any male over 221 for whom no other occupation was known. Shoe manufacturers and shoe cutters also received the same innocuous designation. Of the 36, 32 were former shoemakers. But a more accurate indication of their economic backgrounds is ascertainable from an examination of the occupations of their fathers. Of the 35 fathers listed in the 1832 directory, 11 were shoemakers or shoe cutters, 20 were shoe manufacturers or merchants, and 4 were in other occupations.

In the decade from 1841 to 1851, 103 men became shoe manufacturers and were in business at the time the directory for 1851 was compiled. Of the 103, 60 (58 percent) had been born in Lynn, while 82 (79 percent) had been born or married in the town. Their average age was 33. Thirty-seven of the new men and 44 of their fathers appeared in the 1841 directory. Of the 37, 16 were shoemakers, 14 were shoe cutters or clickers who had worked at the cutting table, and 7 were from other occupations. Of the 44 fathers of new shoe manufacturers, 23 were bosses, 6 were shoemakers, and 15 had other occupations: 4 were farmers, 3 merchants, 2 morocco dressers; the rest were engaged in other occupations.

An increase of the number of shoe manufacturers accompanied the growth of the shoe industry. In the last decade before the Civil War, the demand for shoes greatly stimulated production. In the same period, shoemaking under the putting out system reached its highest point of development, bringing an increase in the number of bosses as well as shoeworkers. In the nine years from 1851 to 1860, 179 men became shoe manufacturers. Seventy-eight (44 percent) were born in Lynn and 100 (56 percent) were born or married in the town.[7] Their average age was 34 years. Lynn's growth in population from approximately 12,000 to 19,000 is thus reflected in an increase of 14 percent in the portion of new men who were born outside of the town. Of the 179 new men, 121 are listed in city directories that give the occupations they followed before becoming bosses. Thirty-seven were former shoemakers, 57 were shoe cutters, and 27 came from other occupations, the largest being that of clerk or foreman in the central shop (9), the remaining occupations included shopkeeper, carpenter, fisherman, salesman, mariner, bookkeeper, farmer, and tailor. Most of the fathers of the new men were connected with the shoe industry. Of the 67 fathers listed, 24 were shoemakers, 32 were shoe manufacturers. The remaining 11 included 2 farmers, 2 laborers, a tailor, a fisherman, a "gentleman," a mason, a deputy sheriff, and an accountant.

The statistical data on the Lynn shoe manufacturers suggest a number of conclusions. In a highly decentralized, unmechanized industry, a small amount of capital and skill in the art of leather cutting could gain one admission to the status of manufacturer. But the overwhelming majority of new men failed within a few years and were forced either to emigrate or follow another occupation. If the occupation of one's father was not crucial for a modest beginning as a shoe boss, it did greatly enhance the likelihood one would remain in the shoe business. Daniel S. Pratt first appeared as a shoe manufacturer in 1851, yet there was only the remotest chance of his failing. His father, Micajah C. Pratt, was Lynn's largest shoe manufacturer, a man who had been in business since 1812, a director of the Mechanics' Bank and the owner of extensive real estate. The same would be true of the score of other manufacturers who in a generation had built prosperous businesses that assured their male progeny of a more than equal chance of continued success.

Most Lynn histories, reminiscences, and memoirs assert that nearly all Lynn manufacturers came from the bench. This is a half truth. It is true that a considerable portion of the Lynn natives who became bosses in the years from 1830 to 1860 were either shoemakers or the sons of shoemakers, but most were the sons of manufacturers and merchants. Moreover, if they had worked at the trade, more often then not they had labored as a clicker at the cutting board in the central shop rather than as a shoemaker at the bench. Experience as a clicker or service in some capacity at the central shop was evidently important in acquiring enough knowledge of the business to begin on one's own. Furthermore, the higher wages paid to the cutter, usually twice that of a shoemaker, permitted accumulation of capital for starting a modest operation. It became increasingly common for shoe manufacturers to train their own sons in this manner, acquainting them directly with all phases of the business: cutting stock, keeping account books, selling to shoe buyers, and inspecting the work brought to the central shop by the binders and jours. Employees who occupied the same position, even if unrelated to the owner, could also use their training to start their own firms, provided they had access to capital. One's chances of becoming a manufacturer, therefore, were greater if one had been a shoe cutter or clerk in the central shop rather than a shoemaker. If the central shop in which one worked belonged to one's father or uncle, success was virtually certain.

Becoming a shoe manufacturer was less difficult than remaining one. The high turnover in personnel from one decade to the next, or even in a three-year period, illustrates the chronic problem endemic in manufacturing under the putting-out system. The industry in Lynn alone consisted of scores of small entrepreneurs struggling for a foothold in a market that was increasingly competitive. Growth in shoe manufacturing did not simultaneously lead to consolidation and the creation of a few giant firms that were able to dominate the business. All the firms in Lynn were owned either by one man or two or three partners. None was incorporated. If there was an economy of scale, with an optimum size reached by firms with the most efficient business practices, the market for shoes was diverse enough to permit the producer of high grade footwear to exist alongside the large firms that turned out cheap common work. But if the mortality rate was extremely high in the business, there were, nonetheless, manufacturers with sufficient capital to withstand competitive pressures. Although these large employers never monopolized the shoe business in Lynn, they did exert an influence greatly disproportionate to their numbers, especially in setting wage rates and in controlling the credit policies of Lynn banks. The shoe manufacturers of Lynn thus present the appearance of a large, unstable group, beset by constant changes in personnel with a solid, unchanging nucleus of prosperous employers.

The facile conclusion that all shoe bosses were former cordwainers also gives the erroneous impression that it was in the natural order of things for all journeymen to become bosses or that the most important prerequisite for becoming a master was skill. A first-hand knowledge of the business was important, even necessary in the early years, if one were to remain a boss for any length of time. However, more important than either of these qualities was the possession of capital, not a great deal for a start but enough for a few rolls of sole leather and several bundles of stock and preferably sufficient surplus capital to compensate for delayed payments or bad notes. The more capital at the outset, the greater the chance of success.

Those who became shoe manufacturers came to the position by different means. There was the young unmarried shoemaker who had learned the trade from his father and had managed to put aside enough savings for some leather and stuffs, a horse to convey the shoes to Boston, and a high credit rating at a neighboring bank. Another may have earned the confidence of an uncle or neighbor who was willing to risk fifty dollars on an ambitious young man with good family background, respectable manners, and an admirable way of "horse trading." Others "couldn't sew a stitch" but did enjoy the advantage of being well-connected by birth or of having religious ties with men who had wealth and standing in the community and who were alert to a lucrative business investment.

The careers of several Lynn Quakers illustrates the importance of the access to capital gained by habits of mutuality and collective self-help. Throughout the first half of the nineteenth century, the largest shoe manufacturers in Lynn were Quakers or men of Quaker stock.[8] In 1850, for example, of the seven bosses who employed more than a hundred cordwainers, all but one were Quakers. They were, in order of the size of their operations, Micajah C. Pratt, David Taylor, Christopher Robinson, Isaiah Breed, Moses S. Breed, and Samuel Boyce. Robinson was the only non-Quaker. As a group, the Friends dominated nearly every aspect of the business life of the community. In banking and finance, manufacturing, commerce, and real estate they were with few exceptions the leading entrepreneurs in Lynn. Even in the field of patent medicine, a Lynn Quaker, Lydia Estes, won fame and fortune with Lydia Pinkham's Vegetable Compound, a concoction she mixed and sold to raise money after her husband's land speculations collapsed. Though they tended to congregate at Pudding Hill around the meeting house, the Quaker school, and the cemetery, a few Friends remained in other parts of the town. A common religious heritage, the shared experience of living and working together, intermarriage among Quaker families, and an acute awareness and pride in their distinction from the general population of Lynn all served to foster the growth of group solidarity.[9] Collective effort and cooperation extended from meeting house and school to business activity, whether in Lynn or beyond. The Quakers patronized, and thus aided, one another's businesses: they bought morocco leather from the factory of Winthrop Newhall and his two sons Francis S. and Henry; shoe stock and findings from Isaac Basset and his son; fire wood from Daniel Breed; lumber from James N. Buffum; and docking facilites at John Alley Jr.'s wharf. Quakers played an important role in the Lynn Mechanics' Bank, The Lynn Mill Dam, insurance companies, and whaling company; they revived the charter of the Lynn Academy to train their sons; they established a manual training school; and they led the movement for a railway line through Lynn. The Quakers held no monopoly on entrepreneurial talent or the ability to accumulate wealth; dozens of examples in Lynn would disprove that allegation. Yet they did excel in business affairs and in comparison with the members of any other single religious or sectional group in Lynn their preeminence is decidedly pronounced.

The Protestant ethic in itself, the heritage of Baptist, Methodist and Congregational as well as Quaker, is insufficient to account for the degree of business success that nearly the entire body of Friends in Lynn attained. Equally important was the strength of their loyalty to one another and because of their isolation their relative freedom from the informal social restraints that the general society imposed on acquisitiveness pursued at the expense of others.

In the extension of markets for Lynn shoes, the Quakers found their religious affiliation of inestimable value in securing customers. There was a Quaker colony in nearly all the trading centers along the Atlantic seaboard—from Salem, Boston, and Providence to Philadelphia, Baltimore and Charleston. When the young Ebenezer Breed first embarked on his venture as a commission merchant for Lynn manufacturers in 1786, he went first to Philadelphia and established close personal and business relationships with Quaker merchants. A common religious tie became the basis for mutual trust and a confidence in one's integrity and good sense.

In the seventeenth and eighteenth centuries, merchants with extensive dealings in distant ports frequently used members of their own larger families to fill positions that required loyalty as well as ability and good judgment.[10] The merchant in Salem would prefer an agent in Jamaica whom he could trust and over whom he had some control other than purely legal. A son-in-law, brother, or nephew would be preferable to an agent whose only obligation was a contractual one.

With the extension of markets and a corresponding increase in commercial activity, the need for some foundation of loyalty remained. The Society of Friends filled this need by assuming the role of a large "family," which had training to furnish the rudimentary skills for business activity and a religious education that inculcated the virtues of honesty, dependability, and loyalty to one's associates. As a closely knit group, the Quakers also encouraged the conviction that one's fortunes as an individual would depend in good part on the support one received from members of the group. Membership carried with it certain duties and responsibilities. One was not a free agent able to do as one pleased with no consideration or respect for the mores of the body that possessed the powers of reward and punishment. Ostracism and expulsion may seem in an individualistic, market society an extremely feeble means of control. But for someone who by education and experience had learned the value of collective effort and had witnessed in actual practice the fruits of mutuality expulsion was a harsh and effective instrument. The Quakers were thus able to enforce a rigid code of behavior, holding out to any potentially deviant member the threat of ostracism from a group possessing considerable power and influence, while extending to those who remained loyal an assurance of mutual support and cooperation. This does not mean that the cash return accruing to those who maintained their affiliation with Friends was a primary consideration in the behavior of its members. Nothing so vulgar is intended. What is meant is that it was natural for members of a small sect who had learned the need for collective self-help in many areas of social life to extend this principle of behavior to the sphere of business.

One can discern the working out of this principle in the relationship of shoe manufacturers in Lynn to commission merchants like Ebenezer Breed and his successors. Breed obtained orders from Quaker merchants in the cities of the Middle Atlantic and Southern States. He transmitted the orders to Amos Rhodes, his agent in Lynn, who in turn passed the orders on to shoe makers, many of whom were also Quakers. Others did the same. In one of Breed's letters to Rhodes, he reported that Samuel Collins, a Quaker and Lynn manufacturer, acted as the agent for his cousin Zaccheus who, like Breed, was a commission merchant in Philadelphia. A generation later, another Lynn Quaker, Joshua C. Oliver, became a shoe agent in Philadelphia for himself and his Quaker partners in Lynn, who administered the putting-out end of the business from their central shop. Quaker manufacturers and merchants did not limit their dealings to men of their own faith, nor did they insist that a wholesale purchaser be a Quaker. The extensive and ongoing business relationships between Friends in Lynn and Friends in cities along the Atlantic seaboard was merely the extension to business of ties that already existed. For the Quaker shoe bosses of Lynn, orders from reliable merchants in Philadelphia and Baltimore who had good bank credit, vessels for transportation, and access to materials that Lynn cordwainers would accept in barter exchange gave them an advantage over their competitors. In the rise of the shoe bosses, the Quakers appear in the forefront.

The most notable Quaker boss was Micajah C. Pratt.[11] He was born in Lynn in 1788, the son of John Pratt, a shoe manufacturer and wealthy landowner in Pudding Hill and one of the strongest advocates of the mechanics' bank. Micajah began his business in 1812. The following year he moved into his first central shop, a common two-story wooden building on Broad Street near the corner of Exchange; it served as his manufactory until 1850 when he and Samuel Boyce, another Quaker boss, constructed a brick building. In the words of a sympathetic biographer, Pratt built his business on the southern and western trade, sending out "a cheap, strong and durable shoe, not warranted, not tasty, like many bosses." At the height of his career, he employed 8 cutters, 400 to 500 jours and binders, and produced about a quarter of a million pairs annually. "A good part of these operatives resided out of town, and not a few out of the state." As early as 1830, Pratt began sending shoe stock loaded on heavy wagons to outworkers living in Maine. Anyone who dealt extensively with the South had to accept the inconvenience and risk of selling large quantities of shoes for long term notes that frequently went unpaid. This was originally the main reason for the movement among Lynn bosses to obtain a bank charter. John Pratt was a founder of the bank and his son Micajah was a director of the institution for more than thirty years.[12] Sufficient credit was often the difference between life and death for a shoe manufacturer. Pratt and a few Quaker associates captured control of the bank in 1828 and used their position to determine the lending policies of the bank. Backed by the credit of their bank, they expanded their operations until they were the largest employers in Lynn and the owners of extensive real estate in the central part of town. They also invested heavily in railroad stock. Pratt's major business allies were the Breed brothers, Nathan and Isaiah.

Isaiah and Nathan Breed were the sons of James Breed and were born in Lynn in 1786 and 1792. James Breed, called "Taller Jeems" because he was a chandler by trade, was also like his neighbor and fellow Quaker John Pratt a shoe manufacturer and large real estate owner, his lands covering the area from Broad Street, down Exchange and across to Silsbee in Pudding Hill. An indication of the elder Breed's business acumen is provided by the story of his encounter with a cordwainer who asked for his pay in candles rather than in soap.

Breed's reply, which left little opportunity for a rejoinder was: "What 'Ammi! Don't thy wife wash? Won't thee take soap? Candles are cash, 'Ammi."[13] Chandler Breed's son Isaiah began an apprenticeship at shoe making at the age of fourteen and in 1804 at the age of eighteen began his career as a manufacturer. He carried his shoes to Boston merchants in saddle bags, taking payment in groceries, dry goods, and shoe materials, which he stocked in his house in a room fitted out as a general store. He paid his workmen with the goods he received from the merchants. Isaiah's younger brother Nathan took over his father's business in about 1825. With the great demand for shoes that commenced in 1833, Nathan Breed moved from his father's old central shop to a new structure built for him by James N. Buffum, another Quaker, for a thousand dollars. At that time, the shop, measuring eighty by twenty-two feet was the largest in Lynn. His business steadily expanded into the South and the West. In the mid-1830s he helped found shoe stores in St. Louis, Nashville, and Natchez, in order to gain a larger share of the trade in those growing areas.[14] Nathan and Isaiah worked closely together, pooling their resources and investing jointly in ventures neither could undertake alone. They seemed to have a hand in nearly every enterprise that was tried in Lynn: the bank, the Lynn Mill Dam Company, the Lynn Whaling Company, the Lynn Mutual Fire Insurance Company, a manual training school, and the Lynn Gas and Light Company.[15] But their greatest undertaking was a railway line through Lynn.

In 1823, Isaiah became a director of the Mechanics' Bank and within a few years joined Quakers from Pudding Hill led by Micajah Pratt in wresting control of the institution from a group of businessmen centered in West Lynn.[16] The following year, Isaiah and Nathan purchased a large parcel of real estate, the Black Marsh fields, for $638.40. The low, swampy land was considered largely worthless. In 1829, Isaiah became president of the Lynn Bank and held that office for the next thirty years. Within two years, the movement began for construction of a railway line from Boston to Salem. Although there was considerable support for a westerly route that would follow the existing turnpike through West Lynn, the directors of the bank invested heavily in railroad stock and thus gained the right to chart the road's course through Lynn. The railway line from Boston ran along the Black Marsh field and the Quaker settlement in Pudding Hill. The property that Isaiah and Nathan had purchased in 1824 surrounded the railroad station at Central Square and became the center for flourishing business activity. The earth that the Irish laborers dug from the rail line cut went into the swampy lowland the Breeds had purchased a decade before.[17] By 1892 the lands that Nathan and Isaiah had bought for $638.40 were worth $5,000,000. Nathan took another measure to maximize the profits of his property. He ordered mulberry trees planted along the streets. The leaves from the trees were used to feed the worms that produced silk for a mill in West Lynn, another enterprise of this remarkable man.[18]

Sketches of the careers of other Lynn shoe manufacturers provide revealing glimpses of their social origins. The extension of markets and the increased demand for shoes constituted the external forces that evoked changes in the economic life of Lynn. But the response of people in the town to the opportunities created by growth varied according to patterns of relationships and according to the distribution of property that already existed. Christopher Robinson, another one of Lynn's most successful manufacturers, was born in Maine in 1799, the son of a British naval officer who had married a woman from Lynn. In 1808 after his father's death, Robinson and his mother moved to Lynn. He worked under Micajah Newhall, a shoe manufacturer and landowner, and learned the trade alongside Newhall's two sons Paul and Nathaniel, both of whom became manufacturers. At the expiration of his apprenticeship, Robinson and Nathaniel Newhall formed a partnership; Newhall furnishing the capital and Robinson, at the age of eighteen, performing the task of cutter. The partnership dissolved within two years, leaving Robinson to continue on his own. Despite the dull business prospects of 1819, he was able to buy small amounts of shoe stock and sell the finished product to commission merchants. He weathered this shaky start and expanded his business. In 1822, he employed twelve shoemakers and twelve binders and moved into a central shop, twenty-eight by sixteen feet, on South Common Street. Although he had doubled his workforce by 1824, the customers to whom he had sold shoes could not make payments on their notes, forcing Robinson to suspend business. At this point Robinson might have returned to the cutting board in the employ of a boss who had survived, but Nestor Houghton—a Boston shoe dealer, son of a Lynn manufacturer, and a man who recognized Robinson's good taste in shoe design—advanced him enough capital to pay his workers in full and his creditors at sixty cents on the dollar. With Houghton's support, Robinson resumed production and retained enough business to warrant construction of a new central shop in 1832, but he still was unable to gain immunity from the erratic cycle of prosperity and depression so prevalent in the industry. He failed in the depression that commenced in the spring of 1837, resumed business again in the early 1840s and expanded his operations until in 1850 the number of shoemakers and binders in his employ reached 375. In 1849, his firm produced 115,000 pairs of shoes worth $100,000.[19]

Robinson was unusual in that although he headed one of Lynn's largest firms, he made high quality shoes and paid good wages. An item in the *Lynn Bay State* noted another eccentric feature of his business career: "It is a matter worthy of remark, that Mr. Robinson has for twenty-nine years past, until within the last three months, and with the exception of about five thousand pairs, packed all the shoes made during that long period with his own hands—every pair thus passing under his own inspection."

William Diamond Thompson was another immigrant to Lynn who tried to make a start as a manufacturer in the expanding shoe business. He was born in 1787 in the neighboring port city of Marblehead, a town that had seen its best days in the eighteenth century and had suffered during the Revolution. Thompson moved to Lynn with his family at the age of ten and a few years later began a stint at the shoemaker's bench. Possessing some capital and having acquired the skill of shoe cutter, he began a small business as a bag boss. Within a few years, however, he withdrew from the business and went to work as a cutter for his brother-in-law, Joseph B. Breed. In 1827 or 1828, he left this job and joined Nathan Breed, a fellow Quaker and one of the fastest rising bosses in the town. For about forty years Thompson served as factory manager, salesman, and work inspector for Nathan Breed. With Thompson as with a great many others, the pattern of mobility within the shoe business was from bench to cutting board to central shop.[20]

Perhaps the most complete account of how one man became a shoe manufacturer is that of Benjamin Newhall. He was born in the West Parish of Lynn, later the town of Saugus, on April 29, 1802. As a young boy working in his father's shoe shop, he had developed a strong distaste for shoemaking. Though eager to help support his family, he was determined to find an alternative to shoemaking. First, at the age of fourteen he took a job in Amariah Childs' chocolate mill, working from sunset to sunrise four nights a week. The labor was hard and exacting, but he recalls, "I hated shoemaking, and was yet determined to earn something for my mother. If I could earn eighty-three cents a day by working night and day, it was to me a great sum." In 1818, he quit his job in the mill and hired on with a farmer. He lasted one week: "I could not hold a heavy plough, with two yoke of oxen . . . the work was beyond my strength." Newhall then went to work for a Mr. Smith who owned a chipping machine that cut wood into chips. "All went well enough for a while," but one day, through carelessness, the axe cut off his left thumb. He returned home, rested for two months and during the next seven years probably worked alongside his father at the detestable job of making shoes, fulfilling an obligation to his family yet not losing his desire to find some other way of making a living. In 1825, he and another fellow opened a trading establishment in Canada, which collapsed in a few years. "After various other trials, successes, and mishaps," which the editor of his autobiography does not explain, "he arrived at the age of twenty-eight." The year was 1830.

After numerous but fruitless attempts to establish a business in some line other than shoemaking, Newhall was finally drawn into manufacturing, fortuitously at a time when the industry was about to experience unparalleled growth. He first paid his small debts with money lent him by his uncle Makepeace and obtained an extension on his largest debts. He hired a small room in the house of a neighbor and "got trusted for one bundle of leather from Isaac Basset and a dozen of kid from John Lovejoy." For operating capital, he borrowed fifty dollars from John Emerton, "giving him a mortgage on . . . [his] horse and wagon for security." He labored on, and found that after three months of "close application" a "little had been made." Newhall recognized the danger of overreaching himself and allowing his indebtedness to reach amounts he could not pay on short notice. He, therefore, settled all his accounts every six months, paying in cash or with notes from his most reliable customers: "I got this machinery of business well established, and never deviated from it in all the time that I followed the business." Thomas Raddin, his friend and fellow manufacturer, introduced him to the president of the Commercial Bank in Salem who, as Newhall says, gave "a discount as often as I wanted one." In return, Newhall was "very punctual" in all his payments and thus improved his credit standing at the bank.[21]

As a result of such measures of strict cost accounting and financing, and his favored position at the Salem bank, which according to him was "everything to me," Newhall became "firmly established as one of the most successful, shrewd, and wealthy business men in the vicinity." But as one who was aware of the cyclical nature of the shoe business and had witnessed the liquidation of some of Lynn's largest shoe firms, Newhall was careful not to reinvest all his profits in his own business. A Lynn historian familiar with his career reported, although without explaining, "He by no means confined himself to one kind of business, but commonly, to use an expressive phrase, had several irons in the fire at the same time; yet he was so active and watchful that none appeared to suffer for want of attention."

After his retirement from the shoe business, Newhall penned a series of sketches on the origin of the shoe industry in the West Parish of Lynn at about the time of the war with England and during the next decade. Writing for an audience living in an economy based on a mature, highly sophisticated putting-out system with a clear division of labor between boss and worker and equally clear disparities of wealth and life style, Newhall stressed the changes that had occurred in a half century. His account is an excellent portrayal of the early bag bosses and the demands made upon them for versatility and hard manual labor. The shoe bosses who were his contemporaries—Thomas Raddin, Jr., George W. Raddin, Sewell Raddin, Jacob Newhall, Jr., Abel Newhall—came from families which, if not wealthy, owned enough property to make them better off than the neighbors they employed. His reminiscences are rich in the details of the process by which small entrepreneurs secured a place as manufacturers.

The early bag bosses "were satisfied with meager accommodations, and arduous, every-day labor was their pastime. They were both bosses, foremen, clickers, leather cutters, salesmen, clerks, and even teamsters." Their operations were small and their profits meager. Had they tried merely to provide capital and refrain from participating directly in the productive process, they would have failed. According to Newhall, "nothing short of the aforesaid course of business could, at that period, have insured their success." An example of the conditions in which the early shoe bosses worked is found in Newhall's description of Thomas Raddin, Jr.:

> His accommodations were here limited to two small rooms, half-buried, dimly lighted, and furnished with a rude bench or two, whereon to cut his stock. A small closet or two furnished him with shoe rooms and, when found not capacious enough, his shoes would be carried home. His clicking and leather cutting were all done by his own hands, and, when his shoes were to be marketed, he would take a horse and wagon and do his own selling, either in Boston or in the surrounding country.

The rigors of entrepreneurship under the early putting-out system—intensive competition, small profits, a high rate of failure, scarcity of credit—should not divert attention from the essential features of the economic and social origins of the men who became bosses.

They were, as Benjamin Newhall and other chroniclers of Lynn's early history stated, men of ability, skill, and resourcefulness. They labored hard and long at the cutting board, battled endlessly with the merchants in Boston for a fair price on their shoes, and traveled hundreds of miles peddling their product. They were not absentee capitalists or money lenders. Nor did they live in sumptuous mansions in an exclusive section of the town, waited on by servants, and convinced that manual labor was a dirty business beneath their dignity to perform. But to whom does this corrective rejoinder need be addressed? Lynn was not Salem, and the manufacturers were not the merchants of Chestnut Street.

Yet once that fact has been established, there is no justification for the assumption that all who became masters arose from an undifferentiated, leveled mass of poor farmers and shoemakers, their new economic position the result merely of a measure of skill and ambition greater than that of their fellows. Both were necessary, but equally important was the possession of capital or access to capital. Lynn's population was composed mainly of farmers and mechanics, but not all were equally endowed with property. In the early years few men in Lynn possessed enough wealth to gain an exemption from the need to participate in some capacity in productive labor. Yet skill and ambition were rarely sufficient to establish and maintain a small business. The Lynn manufacturers were men who often owned real property and used that property as security for the credit needed to purchase raw materials. Owning the raw materials, they owned the means to labor and were thus able to purchase the labor of those who owned no property. The men and women whom they employed sometimes did own real property but chose not to use it in the same manner as their neighbors. However, a great many, particularly those attracted to Lynn by the growth of the shoe industry and the chance to earn a better living or to learn a trade, owned nothing but their labor power and sold that for a wage. The profits that accrued to the manufacturers came from the difference between what they received from the buyer and what they paid out to the jours, the binders, and their suppliers of materials. And it was the attraction of profits that motivated some men to become bosses.

The small, hard working bag bosses like Benjamin Newhall and Thomas Raddin, Jr., were the forebears and predecessors of the shoe manufacturers. But in the years between 1830 and 1860, profound changes produced a class of men who scarcely resembled either the bag bosses or the well-to-do "Taller Jeems" and John Pratt. The central shop of the larger bosses was not a rented room or a crude, dimly lighted cellar but rather a spacious, three-story manufactory with carpeted counting rooms and shoe rooms with beautifully painted and grained counters and doors. Bosses like Raddin and Newhall no longer spent their waking hours cutting stock and packing shoes. The new manufacturers gave "a few hasty orders in the morning to their foremen, and then with a splendid turn-out" went off to Nahant, the Ocean House, Lynnfield Hotel, or some other place of fashionable resort. Their attire was not baggy trousers and patched shirt nor were their hands calloused from wielding the cutting knife. Instead they could be seen "strutting on Exchange in the finest broadcloth and seeking to keep the sun from their delicate hands by the use of fashionable kid gloves."[22] In short, the Lynn manufacturers had become in wealth and life style much like the aristocrats and capitalists of Salem, who had been the traditional foe of the mechanic. Consequently, it is not surprising that the ideological weapons that the mechanics had fashioned in their long struggle with an aristocratic, mercantile elite were seized by the journeymen and used against their employers.

In the realm of social relations within the community, there was still much to bind manufacturer and jour. The dissolution of their relationships did not occur suddenly or completely; the process extended over a generation or more. But in the growing opulence of the manufacturers and in their withdrawal from the productive process, one finds the key to the breakdown of ties between manufacturer and worker. The Lynn shoemakers came to believe that the accumulation of wealth that lifted the boss from his sunken, dimly lighted cutting room to his fashionable office in the central shop was achieved largely at their expense.

# 5. The Shoemakers: Wages and Other Standards

The Lynn shoemakers fared poorly from the changes in the shoe industry during the generation prior to the Civil War. Not that the economic condition of the cordwainers followed an undeviatingly downward course with losses suffered in every facet of their experience as wage earners. There were rather both gains and losses, with the losses often of a different sort than the gains, presenting thus the difficulty of comparing unlike things. Money wages, for example, improved slightly in the prosperous years of the 1830s, declined sharply in the depression that began in 1837, and then slowly increased from the late 1840s to 1857. Regular payments in cash rather than in commodities was another clear gain for the shoemakers. But these improvements were not great enough to offset other losses.

The single most striking feature of economic change in the Lynn shoe industry, and the primary determinant of the shoemaker's economic position, was intense competition stimulated by the demand for shoes. The extension of markets in the South and the West as well as improvements in transportation brought to the labor market an equally great influx of jobbers, bosses and workers. Jobbers and merchants sought to purchase stocks of shoes at the lowest possible price to secure a larger share of the market. The bosses, in turn, were pitted against one another in the competition for orders from merchants and wholesalers. Their survival depended on their ability to have shoes made at the lowest possible price and to pay for them with the commodities they could obtain most cheaply. One result was a general decline in shoe prices throughout most of the period from 1820 to 1860. Another was the extension of the labor market to an agricultural hinterland that was already badly depressed by competition from the West, its inhabitants eager to work for the prices paid by the manufacturer.

There was also a migration of young men and women from the countryside to the industrial cities, further intensifying the competition among cordwainers and binders for work. The apprenticeship system deteriorated as the bosses concentrated on selling for the southern and western trade a cheap, simple shoe that could be made by inexperienced young men. The hours of work lengthened, and night work by candlelight in the shops became common. Cordwainers labored longer and more intensely to compensate for the decline in the price per pair of shoes. In addition, the material upon which the shoemaker worked became more difficult to handle. Soft pliable leather from recently slaughtered animals was inadequate to meet the needs of the industry. A new source of hides was, therefore, opened in Califronia and in South America, bringing to Lynn tough, dried hides that made work more difficult for the cordwainer but brought no greater compensation for the extra effort expended.

The shoemakers were also badly hurt by sharp fluctuations in the business cycle. These fluctuations became more acute as the industry expanded. The length of time between peaks of prosperity became shorter until by the decade of the 1850s sharp depressions in the shoe business came every three years. The business also became more seasonal. There were short periods of frenetic activity in the busy seasons and sluggish periods of unemployment and hardship in the interims. And as the cycles in the shoe business became more acute and frequent, they seemed less a part of a national or regional pattern and more a peculiarity of the shoe industry. Consequently, a sudden drop in shoe orders and an increase in unemployment did not simultaneously bring reductions in the prices of food and other staples. The shoe business, despite its improved efficiency and production gains, was assuming the condition of a chronically sick industry. The shoe business enjoyed good health intermittently but remained mired in a constant condition of relapse.

A brief look at the pattern of growth in the industry during the half century from 1810 to 1860 will demonstrate the contrast of expansion and contraction. In the absence of any machinery before the introduction of the sewing machine in 1854, increased production came from increases in the number of "hands" to make and bind the shoes, from greater productivity through a division of labor, and from increases in the number of shoe bosses to organize the productive process.

In 1810, the Lynn shoe industry turned out 1,000,000 pairs of shoes valued at $800,000.[1] There was a sharp decline in business activity during the war and from the accounts of contemporaries almost complete stagnation in the depression that followed the war. Although during the 1820s the industry slowly and haltingly recovered, not until 1828 did production surpass the 1818 figure.[2] In 1828, Lynn produced 1,138,189 pairs valued at $692,126, the total value indicating the drop in prices.

From about 1832 to the spring of 1837, a great demand for shoes from the South and the West stimulated a rapid expansion in output. In those years, anything that looked like a shoe found a customer. Output reached 1,675,781 in 1832, climbed to 2,205,384 in 1835, and reached two and a half million pairs, valued at $1,678,333 in 1836.[3] There were also corresponding increases in the number of shoemakers and binders: 3400 cordwainers and binders in 1832, 5100 in 1836.[4]

The panic of 1837, which marked the start of a long depression in the shoe business, began with wholesale cancellation of orders in April 1837.[5] Two months later nearly all the shops in town were deserted: the click of the cordwainer's hammer on the lapstone was nowhere to be heard in Lynn. Nearly a thousand people who had been drawn to Lynn during the peak years of prosperity left town, most of them in search of work.[6]

Despite a series of false starts toward resumption of production, permanent recovery did not begin until 1844. By May of 1849, output reached slightly more than three million pairs of shoes; the number of binders and cordwainers, 10,058. In the four years from 1849 to 1853, the production of shoes increased by a million and a half, reaching 4,633,900 pairs. Yet the number of binders and makers rose only by 151, showing the growing reliance of Lynn shoe manufacturers on outworkers in the countryside, who were devoting a greater portion of their home to shoemaking. By the mid-1850s output reached nine million pairs of boots and shoes; the workforce, slightly more than 11,000. Total production was valued at $4,165,529.[7] Thus there was steady and impressive growth over the long run, without the aid of major technological change.

The means of production throughout the first half of the century remained the same. No machinery was introduced until 1854, and the full impact of the first device operated by males, the Blake stitcher, was not felt until at least ten years later. Between 1854 and 1855, the English Parliament sent a committee to the United States to survey mechanical devices used in various industries and to ascertain if mechanization was the cause of rapid increase and improvement of American manufactures. The commission visited Lynn in expectation of viewing shoemaking machines that might account for the town's preeminent position in the industry. Although they found sewing machines in use, they were disappointed to find no other devices of importance. Their report states that "Whilst at Lynn they went over some of the shoemaking establishments there, but did not find machinery so extensively used as they had been led to expect."[8]

The Lynn shoe manufacturers introduced sewing machines in shoe binding as fast as they could be produced, still output of the machines failed to keep pace with the demand. In July 1855, the *Lynn News* estimated there were between 1500 and 1800 sewing machines, most of them operated by girls employed by the shoe manufacturers.[9] Six months later the same paper reported that "the demand for them [machines] is immense and without a parallel."[10] The sewing machine was the first of several major innovations which in the next generation transformed the shoe business from a highly decentralized putting out system of hand labor to a factory system with labor divided into a multitude of operations performed by machine operatives.[11] Yet prior to the period that began in the late 1850s machines and factories had little consequence for the shoe industry.

Expanded production and growth, with increases in the number of binders and cordwainers, also brought corresponding increases in the number of shoe bosses. There were about 50 manufacturers in 1829, on the eve of the period of considerable expansion that began in the 1830s. By 1836, the number of bosses had more than doubled; and despite the continuation of hard times and restricted demand during the early forties, the number of bosses stood at 103 in 1841. A decade later there were 155 manufacturers; by 1858 their ranks swelled to nearly 200, the highest figure for the entire decade.[12]

Although the amount of capital required for a small start in the industry steadily increased throughout the first half of the nineteenth century, the putting out system based as it was on hard labor performed in the house or shop with tools furnished by the workers, attracted large numbers of small entrepreneurs. In 1832, Parker Mudge had a capital of $500 and a horse, employed four journeymen and an equal number of binders. Forty years later, John Mansfield employed a work force of the same size, but the capital investment required for his small operation had grown to $1200.[13]

In assessing the economic impact of these changes on the wages of Lynn shoemakers, one must first ascertain if the shoemakers were wage earners and if so how dependent they were upon wages for their livelihood. Stanley Lebergott notes that there may be no relationship between real wages and real income because of "a relatively simple numerical reason. In 1800, about 90 percent of the labor force, and as late as 1850 no less than 70 percent of the labor force, were *not* employees. They were self-employed persons (farmers, mechanics, small tradesmen) or slaves."[14] If by self-employed he means a man who owned the materials to which he applied his labor and thus the product he made and sold, the Lynn cordwainers were not self-employed. Although they did own the tools of the trade and invariably referred to the remuneration as a "price" and not a "wage," they owned neither the leather on which they worked nor the shoes that they made.

Only the shoe bosses, admittedly a large group, were self-employed. There were shoemakers of unusual skill, who occupied the dual role of wage earner and independent craftsman, but in Lynn they were rare and their custom work never amounted to a significant portion of their earnings. One such person was Joseph Lye, whose account books and diary cover the years from 1817 to 1832.[15] Lye periodically made and repaired shoes for people in Lynn with whom he dealt directly. On May 13, 1820, for example, he recorded that he made one pair of welted shoes for his friend Zachariah Atwell at one dollar seventy-five cents, more than double the price he received from his employer. Other shoemakers, if fortunate enough to receive their pay in cash or leather, might in their spare time or during slack periods make shoes for direct sale to customers. But the local market for custom work—unlike that of Boston, Philadelphia, or New York—was too small to provide a market for more than a handful of the most skilled cordwainers.

Well before 1800, the shoe business was divided into two clearly distinct groups of men, one that owned the raw materials and one that, in exchange for a "price," manufactured the shoes. For inclusion in Lebergott's category of self-employed, only the bosses would qualify. The great bulk of cordwainers were wage earners.

If the Lynn shoemakers were wage earners, how dependent were they upon their earnings? A number of writers have fostered the notion that under the putting-out or domestic system of manufacture, most workers were farmers and fishermen who in bad weather set up a stool before the fire and made shoes for a neighboring boss. In spring and summer, the yeoman would return to his fields and the fisherman to the sea. Lebergott, for instance, notes that "men who went codfishing for the usual four-month run would return to farm work, and to cobbling shoes through the winter months."[16] Wages from shoemaking would supplement the family income and provide for amenities the farmer would ordinarily go without. But for the sustenance of his family, the principal source of income would be earned from a pursuit other than shoemaking. An implication of this hypothesis is the impression that the domestic worker could move easily from one occupation to another, making shoes at his convenience yet always able in hard times to shift back to farming or fishing. As Norman Ware put it, "the domestic worker at Lynn had been part farmer, part artisan, part fisherman. If one of his three props failed him, he could fall back on another. He felt that he could work in the fields or in the shop as he chose, and when disinclined for either he could lock up his 'tenfooter' and go fishing." Ware thus gives the erroneous impression that full wage status does not come until the appearance of the factory.

His description might be applicable to Lynn in the late eighteenth and early nineteenth centuries and to many areas of Massachusetts, New Hampshire, Maine and Vermont as late as 1860, but it is an inaccurate description of Lynn after 1830—and perhaps earlier. It is impossible to fix a date to mark the occupational shift from agriculture to manufacturing or even to determine at what point shoemaking became the major source of income for a majority of Lynn residents. The shift extended over many decades and did not bring a sudden transformation in the town's economy. As early as the 1780s there were fifty or more small shoemaking shops in Lynn that were used exclusively for manufacturing. The appearance of the shops suggest that a considerable portion of the adult population was devoting enough time to manufacturing to require a specialized structure. A man like Joseph Lye might own a shop and continue to work a small farm, which he leased from his mother, but had shoemaking been only an occasional pastime, a seat at the hearth would have sufficed. His account books, on the contrary, suggest that farming was subordinate to manufacturing.

In her visit to Lynn in 1834, the English writer Harriet Martineau also reported that the cordwainers were part time shoemakers; most were farmers and fishermen. The editor of the *Lynn Record* felt compelled to correct her error. "It is not true," he stated, "that almost all who carry on the shoemaking business in this town, are *farmers* and *fishermen*, who work at shoemaking in the winter and at other business in the summer." Instead, he reported, "very few are fishermen, and fewer farmers." The sole exception would be the Swampscott fishermen. The vast majority, then, of Lynn cordwainers had no other occupation to which they could seasonally turn.[17]

The notion that dual employment was characteristic of shoemakers under the domestic system also carries with it the implication that the cordwainers were not wholly dependent upon the wages from shoemaking. A farmer who worked occasionally at shoemaking could rely on a garden plot and a few head of livestock to provide vegetables, fruit, and meat. David N. Johnson, a former shoemaker, maintains that such supplements to the family larder were by no means inconsequential. He states that nearly every family had a pig and that Lynn probably had more hogs than any other town of its size in the state.[18] A sharp drop in shoe sales, long layoffs, and an end to earnings derived from shoemaking would not necessarily mean starvation if the cordwainer could harvest produce from his garden and slaughter a hog or two for a year's supply of meat.

But the Lynn tax records do not support Johnson's description. Inventories of the personal estates of adult males and heads of households showed that only a minority of Lynn's residents owned cows or pigs. In 1832, for example, there were 414 swine owned by 310 individuals, that is, by about one-fifth (19.7 percent) of the entire population of tax payers. In 1842, this figure dropped sharply to 235 or about 8 percent. By 1849 there were 265 pigs owned by 193 individuals, again by roughly 7 percent of the adult population of rate payers. In other words, in 1832 eight out of ten families did not own a hog, and by 1849 scarcely one family in ten owned a pig. As one might expect, a sizeable portion of livestock owners were farmers and manufacturers owning real property. The typical owner of a hog was not a man who owned a pig and nothing else; he usually had a house, a parcel of land, and a number of livestock—pigs, cows, horses. The great bulk of the Lynn shoemakers did not own animals that would furnish them with a supply of meat. Most had either to go without or purchase meat from the local farmers or provisions dealers.[19]

More difficult to ascertain is the number of people who had access to land upon which they could grow vegetables. At no time in the period from 1830 to 1860 did a majority of adults own real property, either land or a structure. In 1832, 966 (61 percent) of 1571 persons entered on the tax rolls owned no real property. Five years later, after a period of considerable growth, this figure dropped to 56 percent. By 1842, however, it increased again to 61 percent. Revival in the shoe business provided a gradual reduction in the portion of people owning no real property until by 1849, 56 percent or slightly more than half the rate payers were propertyless. By 1850, 51 percent of those whose names appear on the tax rolls were without some real property. Most of the propertyless were shoemakers. Not all cordwainers were without a small house or piece of land.[20] As a group the shoemakers were renters and not owners of property. Whether in renting their houses they also gained access to plots upon which they could grow food is impossible to determine. Population density increased steadily throughout the period from 1830 to 1860, thus accounting perhaps for the decline in livestock ownership. But congestion of the sort one might find in the more highly urbanized areas was uncommon. A small garden plot at the rear of one's house was entirely feasible.

Estimations of dependency must also consider the accessibility of the sea, with rich stores of clams and fish, which could be gathered at minimum cost. David Johnson, recounting the hard times for the Lynn shoemaker of a depression in the 1830s, recalled that "when the spring opened, the horizon of his hope expanded. Less clothing and fuel were needed. The clam banks discounted more readily; haddock could be got at Swampscott so cheap that the price wasn't worth quoting."[21]

On a scale of absolute standards that mark the difference between life and death, the Lynn shoemakers rarely faced death by starvation. They could always subsist, as they sometimes did, on fish, clams, potatoes, and dandelions. But such was not the scale of values by which the journeymen shoemakers judged their experience. Fish, potatoes, and greens might satisfy the hunger of a beast of burden; it was not a fitting diet for a respectable mechanic.

The Lynn shoemakers were not self-employed, independent artisans who owned the raw materials and the shoes they made. Nor, with few exceptions, were they part-time cordwainers who combined shoemaking with farming, fishing or some other occupation, as did the thousands of outworkers in the New England countryside. The economic status of the outworkers, connected to Lynn by expressmen who conveyed shoes and materials to and from the central shops, was reminiscent of a stage in development that existed in Lynn a half century before. But by 1830, and perhaps much earlier, the shoemakers in the town were full time wage earners with no important means of support other than what they derived from making shoes. Although in slack times they might have turned to the sea for food or cultivated a plot of ground, this was their only recourse. Very few owned a hog, and the great majority rented the houses they lived in. Their livelihood would depend almost entirely on their income from shoemaking.

The economic condition of the Lynn cordwainers in the half century before the Civil War depended on several factors: the prices or wages paid for making various types of shoes; the form of the wage payment, that is, specie, paper, commodities or orders; the hours of labor expended in making a pair of shoes; the price of staple commodities; and the unemployment caused by seasonal fluctuations in the shoe industry or the business cycle in general. Each of these changed over a half century, but never simultaneously nor to the same extent, except perhaps in times of depression. No single factor, in itself, can explain how the Lynn cordwainer fared. An example, the one most commonly used by economic historians attempting to assess the fortunes of workingmen and thus their behavior, is wages. Because of the extremely sparse records left by workingmen, wage data is often the only information available to the historians. In some instances alterations in wage rates are so marked, and the trend in wages so closely parallel to patterns in behavior, that the method seems justified. An illustration is John R. Commons' study of the Philadelphia cordwainers.

In his superb essay on the "American Shoemakers, 1648–1895," Commons explains the structure and behavior of cordwainers' societies by the changes caused by extension of the market. The most visible feature in the experience of shoemakers prior to the Civil War was their decline from the status of craftsmen making custom work for direct sale to the consumer to that of wage earners making shoes for sale by the merchant in the market place. The decline is revealed in the prices that the skilled cordwainers of Philadelphia received in the period from the 1790s to 1835. In 1792, they received 4s.6d per pair for custom or bespoke work. Although the journeymen's society that they formed dissolved in 1792, the same year in which it was founded, wages gradually increased until by 1794 they were getting 6s or $1.02 per pair. From 1796 to 1806, their wages remained stable at about $1 for custom or bespoke work. Jours who made order work for sale in the market did not fare as well. From 1796 to 1806 order work brought "five elevenpenny bits" or roughly half the price paid to the shoemaker for custom shoes. Because Commons limited his account of changes in the industry to records provided by the cordwainers' society, he is able to provide little specific information on price changes in the years between 1806 and 1835, the year in which the shoemakers organized to defend themselves against wage cuts. They stated in their address to the public that prices for making boots had fallen from $2.75 to $1.125, their weekly earnings from between $9 and $10 to between $4 and $6. The decline was sudden, occurring, according to the cordwainers, "a few years ago." They blamed the merchant-capitalists, "the cunning men of the East," who made large quantities of inferior work which they threw on the market at prices below that of first rate work. The sharp decline in the price of boots from $2.75 to $1.125 was due to the intrusion of the jobber who used his access to the market to undercut the masters and journeymen, forcing them to labor at the prices he offered to give.[22] The same situation developed in nearly all the large cities of the Northeast. But the experience of the Lynn cordwainers was somewhat different from that of the artisans in Philadelphia and New York.

Custom or bespoke work was never an important source of income for most Lynn shoemakers. The local market was too small to furnish a demand for bespoke work large enough to maintain wages at the levels that prevailed in Philadelphia. Almost from the start, the Lynn cordwainers made order work for sale in the marketplace rather than for direct sale to the customer. As early as the 1780s shoe merchants like Ebenezer Breed, Samuel Collins, and others were contracting with shoemakers for large lots of shoes, which they peddled in distant markets. The shoe merchants had thus gained a gree of control over the business in Lynn that merchants in Philadelphia and New York did not achieve until a generation or more later. As a result, one does not discern in Lynn the drastic decline in prices and wages that. Commons found in the case of the Philadelphia cordwainers. Declines there were, but the starting point for the wage level of the Lynn shoemaker was not at the level enjoyed by the custom craftsmen in Philadelphia who, in their address of 1835, stated that even the slowest in their trade could earn between $8 and $10 a week before the business fell under the control of the merchants.

The account books of two Lynn shoemakers, Israel Buffum and Joseph Lye provide a continuous record of their earnings from the early nineteenth century to the mid 1830s.[23] Buffum was a native of Salem, a Quaker, and one of several Buffums who moved to Lynn around the turn of the century. His brother Jonathan was a shoe manufacturer in the 1830s, publisher of the *Lynn Record* from 1830 to 1841, and after quitting the shoe business owner of a paint and hardware store. Israel Buffum married Ruth Oliver, a Lynn Quaker, in 1808.[24] Her brother Stephen was a prominent manufacturer, former editor of Jonathan Buffum's newspaper, and a leading foe of abolitionism. Israel Buffum made shoes for both Stephen Oliver and Jonathan Buffum, and his kinship tie with them was probably important in securing work from them.

Joseph Lye was born in Lynn in 1789. His father was a native of Marblehead and a veteran of the revolutionary war, who had used his military pay to build a house, a shoemaking shop, and a small farm. The senior Lye left an estate of nearly $4000, $2000 of which went for debts, and the remainder, to seven heirs.[25] His son Joseph was a devout Christian, hard working and frugal. He lived with his widowed mother and leased the farm from her for $150 a year. Although bank records and tax rolls clearly show that Lye was economically better off than most cordwainers, his account books are still a valuable source of information for wages and prices as well as for the work routine of a shoemaker under the putting out system. The following table gives Buffum's yearly wage from 1806 to 1837 and Lye's earnings from shoemaking every third year, beginning in 1818 and ending in 1830.

| | Buffum | | Lye |
|---|---|---|---|
| 1806 | $ 61.71 | | |
| 1807 | 164.79 | | |
| 1808 | 288.77 | | |
| 1809 | 146.65 | | |
| 1810 | 86.60 | | |
| 1811 | 241.73 | | |
| 1812 | 144.08 | | |
| 1813 | 250.94 | | |
| 1814 | 229.45 | | |
| 1815 | 263.83 | | |
| 1816 | 228.00 | | |
| 1817 | 244.12 | | |
| 1818 | 247.81 | 1818 | $279.46 |
| 1819 | 230.50 | | |
| 1820 | 156.69 | | |
| 1821 | 210.94 | 1821 | 257.81 |
| 1822 | 183.46 | | |
| 1823 | 384.55 | | |
| 1824 | 251.88 | 1824 | 267.13 |
| 1825 | 259.26 | | |
| 1826 | 309.76 | | |
| 1827 | 164.00 | 1827 | 168.82 |
| 1828 | 333.11 | | |
| 1829 | 98.00 | | |
| 1830 | 271.77 | 1830 | 168.48 |
| 1831 | 341.38 | | |
| 1832 | 297.02 | | |
| 1833 | 180.70 | | |
| 1834 | 325.35 | | |
| 1835 | 342.88 | | |
| 1836 | 409.76 | | |
| 1837 | 184.43 | | |

Buffum shows an average yearly earning of $234.78 from 1806 to 1837; Lye's average is $228.34, giving each a weekly earning of about $4.40. The statistics also indicate fluctuations in a business already dependent upon the market demand for shoes. Buffum's earnings, for example, fell from $288.77 in 1808, the year Congress voted the trade embargo, to $146.65 in 1809 and to $86.60 in 1810. There is also a decline of almost $100 from 1811 to 1812, and a decline nearly as great during the depression of 1819 to 1820. Although wage data for 1820 was not taken from Lye's diary, his entries suggest the difficulty he encountered in obtaining work: Saturday, January 22, 1820: "shoemaking very dull." January 25, 1820: "waited half the day." February 21, 1820: "waited three hours for work." March 7, 1820: "1 pr. @ 35; waited rest of the day for shoes." And for March 31, 1820: "My wages has this day been reduced to 30 cents for military shoes—and have concluded not to make any for that price."

Neither Buffum nor Lye were earning the $8 or $10 per week that the custom craftsmen of Philadelphia referred to in their appeal. Although Buffum and Lye occasionally made or mended shoes for neighbors at prices more than double their usual income from wages, custom work was an insignificant part of their earnings. Both depended on stock they received from bosses. Their wages were also comparable with the figures collected by the town clerk Benjamin Mudge for Louis McLane's *Report on Manufactures* for 1832. Cordwainers received about $.70 a day, or slightly more than $4 a week if they were fortunate to obtain steady work.

The lack of records as precise and continuous as those provided by Buffum and Lye makes wage estimations less exact for the period after 1832. Yet from various sources, it is possible to piece together the wage pattern that existed in Lynn's shoe industry in the generation before the Civil War. Although the demand for shoes slackened in 1827, one Lynn resident observed, in January of that year, that "the most laborious part of our community supports their families comfortably on an average of two hundred and fifty dollars a year."[26] A year later, the business was "uncommonly brisk," and the Lynn paper contained several advertisements from shoe bosses for workers.[27] But the trade became sluggish between 1829 and 1830. Cut backs in production resulted in unemployment for many binders and cordwainers and in lower wages for those able to obtain work.

The period from 1830 to early 1837 was one of enormous growth in production and a heavy influx of newcomers seeking work in Lynn, pushing the town's population from 6136 in 1830 to nearly 10,000 at the height of the boom in 1836.[28] David Johnson recalled that "the impulse given to trade soon after 1830 changed the condition of Lynn during the next six years more than any previous period in her history."[29] There were as many new structures built in those years as were constructed in the previous two centuries and "the number of new streets opened between 1830 and 1840 was nearly equal to the whole number previously existing." The town's second bank, The Nahant Bank, opened its doors in 1833, land speculation became rampant, and shoe production in 1836 doubled the 1828 figure. Heavy demands for shoes from the South and the West extended the lure of large profits to manufacturers who sought to capture a larger share of the trade. There was consequently a pressure to throw on the market shoes of inferior quality. Firm, stout soles were joined to uppers that "were spoiled by the miserable expedient of using paper stiffenings" made of a "tender straw-paper that a drop of water would penetrate through and through." "Shoes were sewed in such a manner that they dropped to pieces long before they were half worn out." "And when the sewing was good the labor was wasted by the senseless practice of trimming the uppers close to the stitch—a practice that made it impossible to wear a pair of shoes a second time—thus causing a waste that could be reckoned by tens of thousands of dollars, if not by millions."[30]

Business prosperity was a mixed blessing for the cordwainers. The increased demand for shoes gave the shoemaker steady employment and, initially, higher wages. But the boom in the shoe trade also attracted a large number of marginal workers from the countryside whose deficiencies in skill were inconsequential in a market whose capacity to absorb goods of whatever quality seemed limitless. As the migration to Lynn increased in response to employment opportunities, intensified competition led to a downward pressure on wages. At the same time, commodity prices began to rise rapidly, outstripping the wage increases that the Lynn shoemakers had won before the migration was fully underway. Flour nearly doubled in price, rising from $6.00 a barrel in 1829 to $10.75 in September of 1836.[31] Pork was up from $6 to $12 a barrel, butter from $.15 to $.28 a pound, firewood from $5 to $8 a cord, Indian meal from $.80 to $1.30 a bushel; and beef from $4.50 to $7 a barrel. Despite an increase of nearly 100 percent in the cost of staple commodities, "workmen's wages" remained "status quo."[32] In November, 1836, the editor of the *Lynn Mirror* reported that "It is a fact very well known, that the price of labor has not risen in any proportion to the price of provisions."[33] The early advantages that the Lynn cordwainers had enjoyed by virtue of their location at the center of the ladies shoe business was rapidly undermined by price inflation and by the heavy influx of new workers.

The end to Lynn's boom started in the spring of 1837 with the collapse of the shoe houses "in all the great cities of the Union, and especially in the South." They went under "one after another in rapid succession," leaving Lynn manufacturers with unpaid wages. As David Johnson observed, "the recoil upon Lynn was tremendous and overwhelming." "All but six of eight of the leading manufacturers of the town failed."[34] A citizen who walked through the business district of Lynn from east to west found but one cutter at work in a single central shop. "Then came such times as the shoemakers never saw before." Hundreds of cordwainers turned in their last lots of shoes and were given the "sack." A few of the more fortunate were kept on by the boss and put to making cheap shoes, "cacks" at $.04 a pair or scuffs at $.30 a day. The impact of this blow on the skilled cordwainer was often devastating: "when an old shoemaker had got down to making 'scuffs' his career as an artist was about ended."

Those who had migrated to Lynn in search of work abandoned the town by the hundreds in a stream more swift and voluminous than that which brought them. One writer estimated that 800 to 1000 shoemakers left Lynn to seek jobs in farming and fishing, jobs that would give them at least a subsistence.[35] Those who remained foraged for necessities, extracting dandelions and greens from pastures, clams and eels and fish from the sea, firewood from the sparse forest. If a shoemaker were one of the handful who owned a pig, his family would not be wholly deprived of the taste of meat. Although the town had grown enormously in the years from 1830 to 1836, there was still space available for vegetable gardens. Tillable land that had lain unused at the height of prosperity was called upon by the cordwainers to sustain life. Johnson believed that "more potatoes, more beans, more corn, more squashes and other vegetables, were planted as well as more hogs raised, than for several years before."

Conditions improved somewhat during the spring and summer as fuel became unnecessary and fishing less hazardous, but hard times dragged on month after month. Slight improvements in business that stimulated hopes for recovery proved illusory; the revival in 1838 was short-lived, and the shoe trade sunk again into depression.

The economic stagnation that had meant unemployment and wage reductions did not immediately bring corresponding declines in the price of provisions nor did the possession of scarce specie insure to purchasers a high quality in the foodstuffs bought. Johnson was probably correct in attributing the deterioration of quality to the poor harvest of 1836, which "was probably the lightest—taking into account the area planted—gathered since 1816." The shoemaker nonetheless had to accept the foodstuffs that he bought from the shoekeeper or that he obtained from the manufacturer in payment for his labor. And Johnson recalls that "perhaps there never was a year when so much miserable trash called provisions was eaten in the town of Lynn as in the panic year of 1837."[36] His description reads like excerpts from *The Jungle*: barrels of pork mess mixed with bristles and other "foreign" matter that ought, he believed, to have been used for fertilizer; shriveled beans carried to the East Coast round the Horn through alternating climates of tropical heat and freezing cold; stinking butter at $.60 a pound and coarse flour that was sold as "superfine" at $15.00 a barrel. A discriminating buyer with specie might have been able to purchase more wholesome food, but the depression resurrected the system of payment in commodities.[37] The few cordwainers who were fortunate to find work took their wages in orders and probably suppressed any impulse to quibble over the quality of the goods paid them. There undoubtedly were many others eager to take their places.

The economic cloud that had settled over Lynn in 1837 did not disappear as rapidly as it had come. Recovery was slow, painfully gradual for both those without work and those on short time at low wages. Nathan D. Chase, a well-to-do boss who accumulated enough wealth to retire in 1850 at middle age, observed that the prices for making shoes remained low from 1837 to 1842:

> 4 cents for red-bottomed cacks
> 8 cents for women's turned slippers
> 10 cents for thick-heeled runrounds
> 12 cents for set heels
> 20 cents for welts.[38]

These prices are roughly half those that Joseph Lye was getting in 1830, though he rarely made cheap shoes like cacks and slippers. The wage for making a pair of spring pumps stood at $.17 in September 1843; a year later it increased to nearly $.20. By May of 1845, spring pumps made for Christopher Robinson, a boss who paid wages above average, brought between $.28 and $.30, the price Lye was receiving in 1830. Thus, in 1845, the Lynn shoe business had not yet recovered its pre-1830 price levels.[39]

The earnings of the Lynn cordwainers in 1844 averaged about $4 per week, with variations according to the regularity of employment and type of shoe.[40] One shoemaker, writing in *The Awl* in 1845, addressed himself to the question of wages:

> Some of them, I admit, will earn eight to ten dollars a week, at certain seasons; and perhaps there are some who will earn three or four hundred dollars a year; but take them as a class, it is not so. Let any manufacturer take his account book and examine it carefully, and make an average of the earnings of his workmen, and I fear not the truth of his investigation; he will find, that upon an average, as a class, they do not earn five, or even four dollars a week.[41]

There was a slight increase in wages during the fall of 1844: prices per pair were reported to have increased anywhere from $.08 to $.18, and weekly wages, went from between $3 and $5 to between $4 and $6.[42] The female binders, who stitched the uppers were not, one shoemaker observed, "in starving or freezing conditions," but they are working, many of them, from twelve to fourteen hours a day for from two to four cents an hour for their labor."[43] In July, 1845, *The Awl* reported that "the shoe business has seldom been better at this season of the year, than it is now."[44] With business finally on the upturn and an increase in shoe orders, the Lynn cordwainer anticipated an end to the depressed conditions that had lasted for nearly eight years.

But no sooner had prices begun to rise than the chronic problem of competition with outworkers in the countryside reappeared and became more ominous by its growing magnitude. In the fall of 1845, the Lynn shoe market was flooded with "cripples," poorly made shoes from outworkers in New Hampshire who were employed by Lynn bosses.[45] Manufacturers in Lynn who made a high quality welted shoe for discriminating customers might pay their workmen $.28 to $.33, but the larger bosses on Broad Street boasted they could get "as many welts made and bound for 20 cents per pair" in the country.[46] Improved transportation and better roads had enlarged the labor market, bringing the Lynn shoemaker into competition with domestic workers hundreds of miles away. A Lynn cordwainer on a journey to Maine expressed his surprise at seeing freight wagons loaded with shoe stock from Lynn bosses rolling into a Penobscot reservation.[47] Maine may have been only the outer limit of an extensive labor market drawn into the shoe business by enterprising manufacturers, but the sophisticated putting-out system laid a more finely meshed net across Essex County. Binders and makers from farms, small towns, and port cities along the coast all found employment with Lynn bosses. An estimated

900 of the 3,358 men and boys, and 1600 of the 4,935 binders who worked for Lynn manufacturers lived out of town by 1849. These outworkers made 350,000 of Lynn's total output of 3,540,000 pairs.[48] By 1855, the *Lynn News* estimated that three-fifths of Lynn's nine million pairs were made out of town.

It appears that the increase was due to two factors: first, Lynn bosses employed more domestic workers than they had ten years earlier; and secondly, outworkers were devoting a greater portion of their time to shoemaking. In the decade from 1845 to 1855, production increased 286 percent, value of the product 185 percent, while the workforce increased by only 87 percent.[49] In the year ending May 1, 1849, a total workforce of 10,058 made 3,540,000 pairs of shoes. By June 1855, 11,021 binders and cordwainers, 963 more than in 1849, turned out 6,000,700 shoes.[50] An article in *Hunt's Merchant Magazine* lauding Lynn for its preeminence in the ladies' shoe trade evoked a corrective rejoinder from the editor of the *Lynn News*. He observed,

> It should be noticed . . . that a large portion of the work is done out of this city. Shoes are sent from Lynn to Maine, New Hampshire, and Vermont to be made; and a large number of expresses, running in all directions, find a great amount of business in carrying the stock and shoes out and back between the manufacturers and the workmen. It is estimated that fully three-fifths of the shoes sold by Lynn manufacturers are bound and made out of the city.[51]

An example is the business of Isaac Newhall, a leading manufacturer who sold cheap shoes for the Southern trade. He employed 1200 shoemakers, 100 to 200 of them in the single town of Newburyport.[52]

In addition to increasing competition from outworkers, there was the resumption of a heavy migration of workmen, mostly from New England, to Lynn in search of jobs. If one allows for the secession of two sections of Lynn, Swampscott in 1851 and Nahant in 1852, the town's population nearly doubled in ten years, increasing from 9,367 in 1845 to 15,800 in 1855.[53] In addition, there was a seasonal movement of population. In 1849, 600 to 700 workingmen entered the town in late spring to work during the summer months and return home in the fall. The decline of New England agriculture and the waning of the carrying trade, shipbuilding, and associated industries in the port cities of the North Shore released thousands of Yankees for emigration. Many poured out of New England across the northern states into New York, Ohio, Illinois and the states of the Northwest to resume farming. Farm girls by the hundreds took jobs in the new cotton textile mills. The geographic and economic origins of the female operatives of Lowell have been frequently mentioned in numerous histories of the textile industry, but what of their brothers? An equally large and perhaps greater number of men abandoned the farms and rural villages of New England for the growing nontextile industrial towns like Lynn, Haverhill, and Worcester.[54] This steady influx of newcomers, combined with the extension of the putting out system to outworkers in the countryside, acted as a depressant on the wages of the Lynn shoemakers. Moreover, wages resonded sluggishly to the revival of business in the shoe industry during the second half of the 1840s. In 1849, shoemakers were earning about $.75 a day; the binders, between $.25 and $.50.[55] A year earlier, George S. Teel, a recently arrived shoemaker informed his wife in Lowell that he was earning $.83 a day.[56]

Although some shoe manufacturers continued to pay their workers in commodity orders, an enlarged supply of money had led most bosses to abandon their order system. The purchasing power of the cash wages paid to shoe workers was, therefore, greater than the same amount in orders, which had ordinarily been discounted at anywhere from 10 to 30 percent. Many shoemakers consequently bought their supplies from merchants outside Lynn. In 1849, the News reported that half of the family supplies of Lynn residents were purchased in Boston and Salem.[57]

The decade of the 1850s was one of sharp fluctuation in the shoe business, periodic depression, and erratic changes in wage levels. The Boston Mail, in April 1852 reported that

> The depression in this branch of business is greater than it has been for twenty years, particularly among the workmen. Many, very many, have gone to California, but still wages are very low. Hundreds, nay thousands of shoemakers in this state hardly earn fifty cents per diem, though they labor from twelve to fifteen hours a day. A journeyman shoemaker who earns a dollar a day is considered an expert, and as forming an exception to the general rule.[58]

But a year and a half later, the Lynn News could report, that "trade is brisk. Activity prevails among business men, and high prices are paid for labor." Quickened demand meant large orders and steady employment at higher wages: "Shoemaking was never better, and those who 'stick to the last' . . . have plenty of work, and never earned better wages than at present. Anything that looks like a shoe will sell."[59] Yet in less than a year the situation was reversed, and the bright, almost ecstatic joy of the *News* gave way to the grim warning of continued hardship from Lynn's new mayor, Andrews Breed. In his January 1855 inaugural address he acknowledged there had been "stagnation in business for the last six months," and "many or nearly all of our manufacturers have curtailed their business, and it will probably continue dull during the present winter."[60] The upturn did come, and by late summer, the *News* could report that shoemakers were earning $6 a week.[61] Although the shoemakers were earning $1 a day in times of steady employment, seasonal employment evidently reduced their annual wages considerably below that level. In surveying the condition of Lynn shoeworkers in the fall of 1855, the *News* reported that "there is not a manufacturer in Lynn whose account with his workmen shows an average through the year of $5 per week earned; or an account with his binders of an average of $4 per week."[62] Another sharp decline began in the spring of 1857.[63] Shoemakers who had been receiving $.15 to $.25 a pair saw their wages drop to $.06 or $.08 per pair.[64] Despite a modest revival in business in December 1857, the depression extended into 1858, and not until May was the *News* able to report, "the shoe business is improving."[65] Again hopes for a prolonged period of stable prosperity ended in the fall of 1859. By February 1860, the *Lynn Bay State* observed that during the past three months the shoemakers' wages had not averaged over $2.50 a week.[66] On the eve of the Civil War, the shoe industry of Massachusetts, by far the single most important source of income for people outside agriculture, was assuming the condition of a chronically sick industry.

The alternating conditions of prosperity and depression that one can discern in the first decade of the nineteenth century, if not earlier, became sharper as the century progressed. Israel Buffum's account book reveals the periodic declines in shoe sales. But a significant change occurred in the decade prior to the Civil War. Earlier fluctuations closely paralleled the business cycle of a national market economy and seemed attributable to external causes such as the embargo or the panics in 1819 to 1820 and in 1837 to 1842. A general decline in business activity would expectedly cause a fall off in demand, lower prices, and curtailment of shoe production, as it did in the period from 1837 to 1842.

Yet in the 1850s there seems to have been something inherently wrong in the shoe industry. The business was still subject to fluctuations in larger market economy, but sharp depressions of increasing regularity struck the shoe industry in the midst of moderate prosperity for the national economy. Periodic declines became more frequent and acute, and the interim periods of prosperity more brief. As the pattern emerged in the 1850s, a demand for shoes evoked a burst of activity, with scores of bosses filling their orders as rapidly as possible, expressmen racing between Lynn and the countryside, and shoemakers laboring hard and long at the bench to make enough money to survive the next depression. Invariably the spurt in production created a surplus of shoes. Demand then diminished, prices dropped, and unemployment increased. Those who earned their livelihood from shoemaking could only wait until large inventories were liquidated and the market reissued its call for shoes. The productive capacity of the shoe industry had increased so greatly after 1845 that it could in one year or less produce enough shoes to last two. Yet in the intervals of inactivity and unemployment peculiar to the shoe industry, the price level of goods purchased by the shoemaker remained stable. If during the flush times of the decade the shoemaker could earn $1 a day or slightly more, wages fell to half that when the cycle dipped downward. Over the entire period from 1850 to 1860, his average weekly wage was probably about $5, with payment in cash.

Another factor that contributed to a worsening of conditions in shoemaking was the change in the quality of raw materials. The enormous increase in shoe production during the three decades prior to the Civil War evoked a demand for new sources of labor. Suppliers in New England could not satisfy the demand for hides, nor in later years could hide producers in other agricultural regions in the United States. Leather dealers consequently turned to South American and California, sending out vessels like the ones on which Richard Henry Dana served, providing the experiences that he recounted in *Two Years Before the Mast*. Collecting dried hides from stations along the California coast provided the young Dana with numerous adventures that fascinated thousands of readers, but the cargoes he helped gather meant something else to the cordwainer. Dry hide was, in Johnson's words, "the special abomination of the shoemaker." Unlike the soft, pliable "slaughter leather," which was tanned soon after being taken from the animal, the hides collected thousands of miles away had to be dried before shipment to tanneries in the East. The Lynn shoemaker had to spend considerable time softening the leather in a tub of water to make it workable. Shoemaking thus became more laborious and exacting for the cordwainer, and without any additional remuneration for his efforts.

The shoemaker's position was further weakened by changes that facilitated the entrance of new men into the craft. The apprenticeship system, never strong under the domestic system, broke down almost completely in the generation before 1860. Small shoe bosses struggling for a start in a highly competitive business, fitted out rooms in their shops for young men eager to work for low wages and a chance to learn a "trade." Instead they frequently learned only to make a cheap shoe. In other instances, competitive pressures encouraged both boss and journeyman to exploit apprentices by limiting their instruction for the first five years to sewing seams—a tedious, boring task—while allaying their dissatisfaction with a promise to complete their training in the final year of their apprenticeship.[67] But the deterioration in the quality of shoes sold on the open market deprived the craftsman of this hold over the novice and gave the apprentice an opportunity to enter the labor market. It no longer mattered if a man could make a melted shoe. The demand for "cacks," set heels, "scuffs" and "nigger shoes" was large enough for the young man to earn wages which, if low, were more than he received as an apprentice.

Lynn shoe bosses also devised a method for enlarging the workforce. In 1834, a group of Quaker bosses headed by Isaiah Breed and Jonathan Buffum purchased a farm in the Cherry Hill section of Beverly and established a manual training school. The purpose of the school was to build character by combining education in academic subjects with manual labor. Although most of the students were the sons of manufacturers being prepared to succeed their fathers, the founders felt it appropriate to provide materials for the manual labor they thought so edifying. They hired skilled shoemakers to instruct the students, supplied the leather and stock, and paid the young scholar-workmen a flat daily wage of $.50.[68]

At about the same time, a group of Lynn manufacturers instigated a "reform" in the town's system of poor relief. Residents of the poor farms on Tower Hill had traditionally limited their labor to raising enough food to sustain themselves. The proponents of change decided that the rising cost of in-the-house relief could best be reduced if the labor of the inmates, many of them aged cordwainers, were applied to more productive tasks. In looking about for some form of useful employment whose pecuniary return would offset relief expenditures, the shoe manufacturers chose shoemaking, with Isaiah Breed providing the stock and paying the overseers of the poor with orders drawn on his Union Store. This practice continued throughout the first half of the century. On the eve of the Civil War, one opponent of the practice reported that the poor were making shoes for a shilling a day (seventeen cents).

If the shoemaker's real wages were slightly higher in the 1850s than in 1830, there is evidence that he was working a good deal harder. Wholesale prices declined in the half century before the Civil War. One reason for the decline was the tendency of Lynn manufacturers to produce a larger portion of common work in place of the higher grades of welted walking shoes. This meant that a cordwainer would have to make three pairs of common shoes to earn a wage equal to what he received for a single pair of welted shoes. A welted shoe required more time and greater degree of skill, but these were competitive advantages for the Lynn cordwainer, who competed with the less skilled outworkers. Consequently, the additional effort expended was more than offset by the higher wages paid for finer grades of work. Joseph Lye, for example, occasionally earned nearly a dollar a day making two or three pairs of welted shoes. In recording his earnings, Lye divided his working day into two parts, forenoon and afternoon. He does not seem to have worked into the night. Thomas Bowler, shoemaker and shoe manufacturer, also served as town clerk for nearly two decades. If called upon by a fellow citizen to draft a legal document, Bowler charged a fee equal to the rate he made as a shoemaker, ten cents per hour.[69] By the 1840s, some shoemakers were working a fourteen-hour day for a wage only slightly higher than the amount Lye and Bowler received. David Johnson, in recalling the work routine in the small shop, mentioned the crew's practice of sharing a meal of clam chowder at nine or ten in the evening before leaving for home. And Nathan D. Chase provided an anecdote of reminiscence that should evoke caution in assessing the change that occurred in the economic condition of Lynn shoemakers. Two shops' crews engaged in a contest to produce as many shoes as possible. Each group of about five or six men began at 4:30 A.M. and worked without recess until 9:30 in the evening. Of the dozen or so shoemakers involved, one man earned $3.12 for seventeen hours of uninterrupted, competitive labor. Chase does not inform us how the others fared.[70] It was, therefore, possible for a shoemaker who was willing to labor long and hard to make a decent daily wage. But it was precisely this implacable imperative that aroused in the cordwainers a determination to resist their exploitation and search for alternatives to so harsh a system.

As a wage earner, the Lynn shoemaker lost ground in the years from 1830 to 1860. Wages advanced slightly during the boom of the midthirties, but were quickly eroded by inflation and the order system of commodity wages that cut heavily into the shoemaker's earnings. A man earning $1 a day in orders took a discount at the combination store that left him with $.70 worth of inferior goods. The depression of

1837 to 1842 cut wages to a bare subsistence level for those able to find work and forced others either to abandon the town or forage the land and sea for their food. With partial recovery in 1843 to 1844, the shoemaker was receiving an average of $4 a week in orders, giving him an income about equal to what he was making a dozen years before. Although wage levels rose slowly during the next decade to about $5 a week in cash, other forces intervened to diminish these gains. Commodity prices increased during the fifties, competition with outworkers in the countryside intensified, migration to Lynn doubled the town's population, new forms of leather made shoemaking more exacting, the weak apprenticeship system nearly disappeared, and sharp fluctuations in the shoe business made the economic position of the shoemaker in the 1850s more insecure than at any time before. The few economic gains he made were shortlived and purchased at the cost of longer and more intensive labor. By the eve of the Civil War, the shoemaker's conditions of employment had deteriorated in almost every respect.

# 6. The Origins of Industrial Morality

The first quarter of the nineteenth century witnesses the birth of a moral reform movement that wrought profound changes in the social life of the American people. There were attacks on intemperance, infidelity, profanity, lax sexual customs, promiscuous fashions, gambling, and a host of other practices that fall roughly under the rubric of "sin." The moral reformers also cast a critical eye on the status of women in American society, the treatment of the insane, the education of the young, and the condition of the poor. There was scarcely a social institution or aspect of personal behavior that escaped the scrutiny of the moral reformers.

Most historians trace the origins of moral reform to the religious upheavals of the late eighteenth and early nineteenth centuries. Usually manifested in the form of revivalism, the rebirth of Christianity was of such immense proportions that it has been accurately termed "The Second Great Awakening." Dixon Ryan Fox viewed the upsurge as the Protestant Counter Reformation, while Merle Curti, noting related changes in many aspects of American thought, described it as The Conservative Reaction. The revivals originated in the South in the late eighteenth century and swept across most of the new nation, enlisting in the cause hundreds of passionate preachers who brought their message to tens of thousands of people. The Methodists were leaders in the movement and reaped the greatest harvest of souls. The Baptists and Presbyterians also made striking gains. The Second Great Awakening, if most successful in the South and the West, also made rapid headway in the older areas of the Northeast. What caused this profound change in the religious and moral life of the United States, this transformation from indifference or hostility to religion to passionate sectarianism?

A recent interpretation of the Second Great Awakening offers the provocative hypothesis that the movement "was an organizing process that helped to give meaning and direction to people suffering in various degrees from the social strains of a nation on the move into new political, economic and geographical areas." The post-Revolutionary era was one of social disorientation produced by forces of national liberation: geographical mobility, the breakdown of authority and deference, and the absence of any accepted sense of national purpose or direction to fill the void. The revivals themselves are less important than the thousands of churches that sprouted like seedlings in a hothouse and grew to become perhaps the most important social institutions in American society. To the convert, the churches gave a sense of community, a common world of experience, a code of morality, and a sense of meaning and purpose in life.[1] Although this interpretation helps explain the appearance and growth of Protestantism, it does not explain why the churches prescribed for their members a particular code of morality.

One of the clearest and most persuasive statements of the connection between religion and reform is Joseph Gusfield's interpretation of the temperance movement. He suggests that temperance originated with the declining Federalists, especially in New England, who adopted temperance reform in an attempt to regain the social prestige which they had once enjoyed by virtue of their political power. Although the Federalists initiated the reform, they were unable to implement it. More important for the success of temperance was the rising middle class evangelicals, who adopted temperance as a sign of piety and social respectability. It was a sumptuary insignia that distinguished the saved from the damned.[2] Although Gusfield clearly discerned the relationship between temperance reform and evangelical religion, there still remains the larger question of why evangelicals chose a particular brand of morality.

It is significant that American evangelicals did not borrow their peculiar version of piety from a St. Francis of Assisi or a Simeon Stylites. Their pietism would not have won much support in a society convinced of the importance of productive labor and the accumulation of wealth. Much of the success of American evangelical religion lies in its compatibility with the prevailing values of the dominant economic system.[3] It is, indeed, possible to find in the United States during this period a number of religious groups that adopted, in varying degrees, codes of celibacy, asceticism, common ownership of property, and social withdrawal that approximated medieval monasticism. But the main strand of evangelical religion runs in the opposite direction. Evangelicals preached frugality and self-denial but tended to drop the injunction against acquisitiveness, usury, and accumulation. Coveting another's property was both acceptable and a sign of superior virtue. Slavery may have been the grossest evil under God's heaven, but the morality of appropriating wealth from a man in one's hire was unquestioned. There were some evangelicals whose reading of Scripture led them to condemn the accumulation of property and the exploitation of labor, but again they remain exceptions.

The manufacturing town of Lynn may help explain the relationship amongst a number of important social changes that were occurring simultaneously: the quickening of economic activity, the revival of religion, and the emergence of a code of morality that is often called Victorianism. But if Lynn's experience is at all instructive, it suggests that historians have given insufficient attention to the economic awakening in the first half of the nineteenth century as the principal source of a particular form of piety that became the hallmark of evangelical Protestantism.

In Lynn it was the growth of manufacturing that provoked profound changes in social customs, institutions, and standards of moral conduct. There was a concerted effort to destroy or alter any practice that was deemed incompatible with the emerging capitalist order. Customs that had existed for a century or more came under attack and either disappeared or were driven underground to be carried on clandestinely. The movement extended its influence to all areas of life: the school room and the poor house, the militia training field and the fire company, the marriage bed as well as the grog shop. There was a general tightening up of the moral code and a growing emphasis on self-discipline, industry, sobriety, self-denial, and respect for authority. There was an equally strong condemnation of idleness and leisure, lewd and lascivious behavior, self-indulgence and prolonged celebrations. In pursuing these ends, participants in the movement either infused their values into existing institutions and used them as instruments for change or created new institutions. The Methodist and Baptist Churches assumed a prominent role in the movement, but one no greater nor more influential than that of the older denominations, the Congregational and Quaker. Voluntary associations were formed to unite people of different faiths in the struggle for specific reforms. A logical outgrowth of the movement was the attempt to capture political power and to use legal coercion to attain the success which moral suasion had failed to win.

Before turning to the achievements of the moral reform movement in Lynn, it may be helpful to trace the development of the religious and secular forces which together produced the reform movement. First, the revival of religion in the Second Great Awakening was not limited to the evangelical denominations. The Methodists did achieve the most spectacular gains in membership from about 1790 to 1850, but other groups also showed considerable growth. A Baptist church was founded in Lynn in 1816, forming with the Methodists the bulk of evangelicals in the town. The orthodox First Congregational Church, despite wholesale losses to the Methodists, showed a remarkable recovery in the late 1820s and 30s under the direction of two Calvinist pastors of the old school—Otis Rockwood, who served from 1822 to 1832, and his successor, the cantankerous and garrulous Parsons Cooke. A Unitarian Church was established in Lynn in 1826, drawing most of its members from people of the First Congregational Church who withdrew rather than accept the Calvinist tirades of Rockwood. A religious controversy also shattered the staid, placid Quaker Meeting in Lynn. A group of Hicksite "New Lights" attempted to return the Society of Friends to the original principles of George Fox and to cleanse the Meeting of worldly corruption. Expelled from the Society for disrupting services, carrying weapons, and assaulting prominent members who held 'the high seats,' they joined disgruntled members of the First Church, who had founded the Unitarian Congregation. Another group of Lynn citizens united to establish a small Episcopal chapel in 1841, while a second group founded a Universalist parish soon after. Thus, the revival of religion in Lynn encompassed all major Protestant denominations. The Second Great Awakening was not merely an evangelical phenomenon.

Each of these groups supplied its share of supporters to the movement for tightening the moral code and purging society of the corruptions it inherited from the eighteenth century. Whether the issue was drinking or gambling, rowdiness in the streets, nude bathing, or idleness, one could identify Methodists, Baptists, Quakers, and Unitarians in the grand coalition for moral reform. Although a strict morality is frequently attributed to the piety of the evangelical groups, Lynn's experience suggests that people from a variety of religious faiths agreed in their opposition to a libertine morality. This, in turn, suggests that the representative of the different denominations derived their values from a common source: the milieu of a society in the initial stages of industrial capitalism.

A second reason for stressing the importance of manufacturing in spawning the moral reform movement of the early nineteenth century is the marked contrast between Lynn and her adjacent neighbor,

Salem, in response to specific moral issues. A cosmopolitan, mercantile community, Salem maintained an implacably cool attitude toward the temperance movement. Reformers in Lynn who carried their cases against local liquor dealers to the county court in Salem found an unsympathetic if not hostile reception. Defendants often gained acquittals, while the plaintiffs sometimes suffered the humiliation of being insulted by the presiding judge, who shared none of their idiosyncratic notions on tippling.[4] Perhaps the clearest illustration of the contrast between the industrial town of Lynn and the mercantile community of Salem is the case of Samuel Cheever.[5] Cheever was a young clergyman imbued with an intense desire to halt the use of distilled spirits and put an end to the indifference with which the practice was viewed by respectable opinion. He was particularly outraged by the discovery that the church not only tolerated the imbibing of spirits but even showed its indifference by giving the owner of a distillery the position of deacon in the parish. In 1835, Cheever penned what must have been one of the first pieces of polemical fiction against the liquor traffic. His villain was Deacon Giles. But instead of gaining public acclaim for performing a valuable service, Cheever was sued and convicted of slanderous libel.[6] He also suffered the additional rebuke of being assaulted in the street by the foreman of Giles' distillery. His assailant went unpunished. If in Salem the intrepid Cheever was a cowardly slanderer and disturber of the peace, in Lynn he was a hero. During his term in the Salem jail, women from Lynn called on him daily with gifts of baked goods and clean linen. During the next twenty years, the temperance movement invariably found Salem an extremely wily and elusive foe; at the same time, it gained increasing strength in Lynn.

A third consideration that merits attention in exploring the link between early industrial capitalism and the new moral code is the growth of Methodism in Lynn. The Methodist church was the largest denomination in the town, holding first rank in membership from its beginnings in the eighteenth century through the nineteenth century. In 1850, there were 8 Methodist churches, 8 pastors, 6 lay preachers, and 2000 members. Lynn was the center of New England Methodism and a stronghold of the denomination in the heartland of Congregationalism. As noted earlier, Methodism began in Lynn with the arrival of Jesse Lee, one of the church's most able itinerant preachers. Lee made his way from New York to Boston, stopping in several Connecticut towns only long enough to sense the hostility of his presence. His reception in Boston was simply more of the same. Although determined to lay a modest cornerstone in the ancestral home of Puritanism and thus create a symbol of his church's momentous achievement, Lee failed dismally. After eleven weeks of fervent preaching, he gained scarcely a dozen converts.

But on arriving in Lynn in December 1790, Lee seemed to have gained Providential favor. Speaking from a crude platform in the barn of Benjamin Johnson, a prominent manufacturer, Lee attracted hundreds of listeners. In a few months, 118 citizens withdrew from the first parish and signed letters declaring their adherence to Methodism. Five months later, 200 members formed a Methodist church.

Lee's singular success in Lynn can be attributed to the peculiarity of the town among other towns of eastern Massachusetts. It was a manufacturing town, a town of mechanics who were disillusioned with the old formalism and elitist doctrine of the established church. Most had simply drifted away, thus demonstrating their rejection of a theology that preached salvation for the few and damnation for the many, categories which paralleled in a manner discernible to the mechanics a class structure that was becoming increasingly intolerable. Parsons Cooke, an unfriendly critic of Methodism, stated that the people of Lynn were Methodists before they heard Lee preach. A way of life based on manufacturing rather than on agriculture or shipping had loosened the ties of tradition, raising up a class of people who found in Methodism a religion that in theology and in the manner of its clergy gave religious expression to values they derived from their experiences as producers. The egalitarian evangelical churches formed during the Second Great Awakening thus may have existed in the minds of the converts before they joined.

It should also be noted that the assault on the objectionable customs and practices of the eighteenth century did not commence with the formation of the Methodist church in Lynn. Although one writer, for example, recalled that 'cold water societies' had existed in Lynn before 1820, the temperance movement and its allied causes did not get underway in Lynn until the mid-1820s. Likewise, a study of the policy of the Methodist Church on the temperance issue indicates that the denomination was somewhat indifferent toward tippling before the second quarter of the nineteenth century. The evangelical churches as well as their more conservative counterparts were evidently swept into a movement whose origins were secular and social rather than religious. But once the movement began, the churches played an extremely important role in marshalling support for changes in standards of moral conduct and of social respectability. As the religion of the rising middle class, it expectedly reflected the social ethics of its founders.

Another force that advanced and stimulated the process of social disciplines was the peculiar definition of republicanism that emerged in Lynn. As with religion, republicanism grew simultaneously with early industrialization and was thus infused with values that mirrored the ideology of people who were on the rise as an ambitious, confident, and able economic group. Spokesmen for the mechanics, in carrying the fight against the objectionable features of the eighteenth century cultural legacy, tended to associate those practices with the corrupt, class ridden, mercantile society of Lynn's North Shore neighbors. They desired a break with the past, a new departure, a new nation cleansed of vices that flourished in both England and among her proteges in America. The editor of the *Lynn Record*, for example, in describing the high moral standards of the community, observed that "the inhabitants of Lynn are truly republican in their principles, habits and manners; and equality prevails to an unusual degree." If rich mercahnts elsewhere elicited praise and emulation, in Lynn aristocracy was frowned upon. Moreover, "an idler or a drunkard . . . [was] scarcely known and would not be tolerated." Any visitor who doubted the accuracy of the editor's description could see for himself by "passing the length of this extensive village, and glancing at the dwellings, nearly all . . . neat, simple, and convenient in their appearance and construction—no lordly palaces—no beggarly tenements, with old hats, garments and other badges of rum-drinking, substituted for glass, to shut out the light of heaven." In short, Lynn was "a miniature likeness of a well regulated republic."[7] And the factors that made Lynn a miniature, well regulated republic were manufacturing, and a population composed mainly of mechanics.

An underlying, unifying feature in the tightening up of morals was a new conception of time. John C. Warren, a Boston physician whose life spanned the period from 1778 to 1856, noted this change in his recollection of the customs prevalent in Massachusetts around 1800. There was "the general and pernicious habit of a morning draught of flip or other stimulant." Men of all classes whiled away the morning drinking hot punch, porter, brandy and water and eating bread and cheese while arguing and chatting about topics of the day. "It may readily be imagined," Warren recalled, "that a conversation under such circumstances was not likely to be brief, and that no small part of the morning was wasted in this relaxation." But the reason for the extent of this social custom was that "time was not very important to most men at that period." The pervasive torpor that permitted "much time to be occupied in eating, drinking and cardplaying" was the result of business lassitude. Warren noted that "from the peace of '83 until near the beginning of the present century, very little business was done in Boston. About half a dozen merchants were sufficient to carry on the greater part of the foreign trade; and the rest were condemned to small business, which did not fill up their vacant hours."[8] And if this were true of the merchants and shopkeepers, if was probably true also of the mechanics and workingmen whom they employed. But with the revival in economic activity, time took on new importance. Hours spent in a public house drinking flip or playing props were hours wasted, hours that could have been devoted to productive labor. There was much time wasted during prolonged holidays like 'lection day that dragged on from Wednesday to the following Monday. And this would be especially true in a town like Lynn whose survival and prosperity depended not on the utilization of natural resources such as fertile soil or a sheltered harbor but on the constant and close application of labor to raw materials. What seems to have developed in Massachusetts after 1800 was the appearance of opportunity. The desire for material improvement and personal gain was probably present before that time, but the opening of new avenues of entrepreneurial activity brought the realization that the desire could actually be satisfied. Self-denial and self-discipline would be rewarded as they never had been before.

There is another feature of the process of social discipline that should be mentioned. There seems to be a popular notion that the rigid code of morality that achieved cultural hegemony in the nineteenth century and lingered on well into the middle of the twentieth originated with Puritan settlers of Massachusetts in the seventeenth century. Although there are similarities, this view either expunges the eighteenth century from history or misrepresents the period. It was as if John Winthrop lived for two centuries or sired progeny who, in their social ethics and standards of morality, were identical to their Puritan forebears. The late eighteenth century suggests rather that Winthrop and Bradford were forgotten, while Joseph Morgan and his merry bunch of revelers, gathered about their maypole with jugs of strong drink and Indian women on their arms, were the dominant figures of the age. There is no unbroken line of descent from the Puritans to the nineteenth century Victorians. What people today call "Puritanism" is a product of the nineteenth century and not of the seventeenth.

One group that has confronted this unpalatable fact with embarrassment are genealogists who are partisans of strict morality. When encountering, for example, an otherwise respectable ancestor who participated in and supported the practice of bundling, which permitted premarital sexual intimacy among courting couples, the genealogists either expunge the practice from the record or fabricate something called a "bundling board" and insert it between their ancestors to prevent any indiscretion. Or to explain away a vast collection of handsomely carved drinking bowls, many with amusing lyrics singing the praise of Bacchus, they state emphatically that they had contained only unfermented beverages. One may be entertained by these heavy-handed attempts to "clean up" a generation of ancestors, but this distortion contains a germ of historical significance. It suggests the extent and magnitude of the revolution in manners and morality that occurred in the half century before the Civil War. The assault on the libertine morality of the eighteenth century brings to light an older way of life that loved a good draught of strong rum, a game of props, or craps, lengthy political discussions at the public house, prolonged festivals, and, in general, gave the human need for enjoyment its fair due.

# 7. Lynn and the New Industrial Morality: "A Well-Regulated Republic in Miniature"

The movement in Lynn to alter the manners and morals of the community formally began in 1826 with the founding of the Society in Lynn for the Promotion of Industry, Frugality and Temperance. Officers of the society were prominent Lynn citizens, mostly shoe manufacturers, occasionally a shopkeeper or professional.[1] They were drawn from each of the town's religious groups, with Micajah Collins, teacher of the Friends' school, heading the Quaker contingent and Otis Rockwood leading the representation of members from the orthodox First Church. The Society frequently held its meetings at the newly constructed First Methodist Church. Except for the minority of shopkeepers and professionals, the bulk of Society members belonged to the rising class of manufacturers. There was Thomas Bowler, cordwainer, shoe manufacturer, Methodist lay preacher, and Republican town clerk; Micajah Pratt, prominent Quaker and Lynn's largest shoe boss; Jonathan Bacheller, owner of a prosperous dry goods store and postmaster of Lynn from 1808 to 1829; Jonathan Buffum, a Hicksite Quaker and then Unitarian, shoe manufacturer, hardware and paint dealer, and owner of the *Lynn Record*; and two other prominent Quaker shoe manufacturers—Isaiah Breed and Ebenezer Brown.

As the name of the Society stated, it sought to promote values that would better enable Lynn to prosper as a manufacturing town. Industrious habits required self-discipline, a concentration on productive labor, and a repudiation of idle, wasteful habits that rendered no material improvement in one's life.[2] Frugality also required self-denial and resistance to the temptation to squander the fruits of industry on such harmful pleasures as draughts of rum at the neighborhood grog shop. Industry, frugality, and temperance if conscientiously followed, would necessarily result in savings that would bring a material reward to the practitioner of these habits.[3] It is, therefore, no coincidence that several officers of the Society were also founders and directors of the Lynn Institution for Savings, which was likewise chartered in 1826, the same year in which the society was formed. Isaac Story—a native of Marblehead and brother of Joseph Story, justice of the United States Supreme Court—was cashier of the bank. Other directors included Josiah Newhall, shoe manufacturer; Isaac Bassett, leather dealer and shoe boss; and Robert Trevett, lawyer.[4]

A sign boding ill for the future was the slim representation of respectable citizens from West Lynn.[5] The Quakers from Broad Street were present in force, and there was a sizable delegation of manufacturers from Woodend, but only a handful of men from the western portion of town. Most prominent by their absence from the list of officers in the Society were Hezekiah Chase, Samuel Huse, Nehemiah Berry, and Henry A. Breed, all of whom were engaged in mercantile and trading activities rather than in manufacturing. West Lynn was the one portion of Lynn that had developed a modest shipping business, gaining access to the Atlantic by way of the Saugus River. It was the one section of Lynn that most resembled the mercantile centers of the North Shore. Although the carrying trade, which had brought wealth to eastern Massachusetts, was on the decline, Hezekiah Chase and his associates had not been deterred from investing heavily in shipping. They had purchased several small vessels, constructed a rope walk and sail loft, and were preparing to extend capital to the whaling industry. It was not evident to them in the 1820s that Lynn's economic future lay solely with manufacturing or that shipping and industry were mutually exclusive. A struggle for control of Lynn was emerging between West Lynn, on the one hand, and Broad Street-Woodend, on the other. It would involve economic issues such as transportation, banking, and the location of a railway line through Lynn as well as cultural differences. West Lynn defended the libertine morality of the eighteenth century; the rising manufacturers upheld the emerging values of industrial morality associated with the Society for Industry, Frugality and Temperance.

One of the first institutions in Lynn to fall under the scrutiny of the reform movement was the poor house and the town's policy toward poor relief.[6] The poor were of two kinds. First, there were indigent persons—orphans, widows, the aged, and the crippled—who were unable to care for themselves and were thus dependent upon the town for food, shelter, and clothing. The town therefore constructed a poor house at Tower Hill in 1819 and placed it under the care of a resident superintendent and his family. A second and larger group were the poor who had some means of support but could not get by without aid from the town. A widow who had inherited a small house from her husband might remain at home but obtain food and other necessities from the town. A man unable to find sufficient work might be able to provide staple foods for his family but turn to the Overseers of the Poor for the remainder of his necessities. Aid to the first group of indigent poor was called "in-the-house relief," while support for the second was termed "out-of-the-house relief."

In 1827, there were eighty-one persons living in the Alms House, most of them children or elderly, but some were employable males whom economic depression had reduced to dependency. The cost of maintaining them was $603.10.[7] A larger number of people outside the house obtained some relief from the town, primarily because of "the great depression experienced of late in the staple manufacture of the town."[8] The value of supplies furnished out-of-the-house totaled $752.34. The Alms House must have also served as a detention center for persons convicted of misdemeanors.[9] One occasionally finds in the Lynn papers a notice of an escape.[10] Discipline at the Alms House was lax. Ebenezer Breed, the former merchant who had been instrumental in opening new markets for Lynn shoes, was a resident of the Alms House for about twelve years before his death in 1832. Although opium had reduced Breed to absolute dependency, Breed was a familiar figure on the streets of Lynn. He chatted with old associates who could recall the brighter days of his career, poached their tobacco, and sometimes joined them at the dinner table. The fluctuation in the number of residents of the Alms House also suggests that some persons entered the house for brief periods during the year, especially in the cold winter months, and left in the spring to find work. It was the presence of employable males in the Poor House and the increase in the cost of poor relief in the depression of 1827 that evoked the attention of the "reformers."

The direction of the town's new policy for poor relief was outlined in several letters to the Lynn paper by a citizen writing under the name of "Civis." He was angered by the abuse of the poor relief system. There were, he began, two classes of poor: the infirm aged, and crippled; the intemperate and lazy. The first should be cared for; the second were parasites and should be treated as such. He was particularly appalled to see men "in the prime of life and able to earn a good living, inmates of a poor house, and these live better than many industrious men, who support their families and pay their taxes." He warned that "men from twenty one to forty five years of age, and even older, will labor hard to break off their evil habits and learn to do well rather than submit to such rules and regulations as I shall recommend." His motive was to discourage idleness, "banish it from the world," by making confinement "a punishment" and "a terror to the intemperate and idle." He proposed that shoemakers in the Poor House be leased to a contractor who would supervise their work and see to it that they performed their daily tasks. All inmates would be locked up and not allowed to converse with anyone but the keeper. Their diet would be limited to bread and water; misconduct punished by solitary confinement. The treatment of the poor, he hoped, would produce "a strong sense of fear accompanied by absolute humility and contrition." As an additional humiliation to those requesting poor relief, Civis urged that their names be posted in public places.[11] Although the town did not adopt Civis's plan in all its details, the town meeting did adopt a series of important changes that altered the poor relief system.

The town first changed the procedure used in dispensing aid to applicants living outside the house. It had been the custom for the Overseers of the Poor to give needy citizens orders drawn on local grocery stores, allowing the recipient free choice in the selection of items she or he needed most.[12] But the auditing committee appointed to investigate this procedure reported that the poor did not always buy the items that the committee felt they should have bought. One might buy meat instead of fish, or flour instead of indian meal, or coffee rather than material for clothing. To remedy what they considered an abuse the committee proposed that the order system be abolished and that the poor no longer be permitted to purchase supplies like their fellow citizens in the town. Instead, provisions would be stocked at Alms House by the Overseers, who would choose those commodities they felt were best for the poor. The Keeper of the house would dispense the goods sent by the Overseers, giving each the amount deemed sufficient by the Overseers.[13] Under no condition would any ardent spirits be allowed the poor. In 1827, $120 was spent on liquor for inmates in the poor house. At the town meeting in the spring of 1828, this practice was abolished.

The town also resolved to redirect the labor of the poor toward more productive tasks. Residents of the Poor House who were shoemakers would be required to devote all their working time to shoemaking in the house rather than to laboring on the poor farm. In 1828, indigent cordwainers earned $461 to defray the expense of relief.[14] Although the town did not adopt the suggestion of "Civis," urging that cordwainers be let to a contractor, who would supervise their labor, the Overseers did obtain work for the cordwainers from Isaiah Breed, taking their pay in orders drawn on the Union Store, which Breed owned in partnership with several other manufacturers.[15] Of the three Overseers who devised this arrangement all were Quakers and two, Isaac Bassett and Isaiah Breed, were also officers in the Society for the Promotion of Industry, Frugality and Temperance. Their control over the Poor House gave them a splendid opportunity to implement their reform of the relief system.

The lax discipline that had allowed residents of the Poor House like Ebenezer Breed to wander the streets of Lynn also came to an end in 1828. Regular visiting hours were established for each Saturday morning. For the remainder of the week, the poor would be confined to the premises of the Alms House and would not be permitted to converse with outsiders. To enforce this order, the town voted $100 to construct a ten-foot fence topped with iron spikes. The *Lynn Mirror* observed that the barrier was "the beginning of our economy in the Poor House Establishment."

The immediate effects of these reforms were gratifying to the architects of the new relief policy. Relief to out-of-the-house paupers declined from $1000 in March, 1828 to $277 in 1829 and $27.25 in the spring of 1831.[16] A similar improvement was evident in the decline in the number of inmates of the poor house. There were 81 inmates in the Alms House in 1827. Two years later, the number dropped to 60, and by 1831 there was an average of 50 persons living in the house.[17] Although there was a slight increase to an average of between 50 and 70 in 1832,[18] the number again declined in 1833; in July of 1833 there were only 27 persons living in the Alms House. There were corresponding economies in the amount of money spent for each pauper. The achievement was explained by the editor of the *Lynn Record*, leading organ for reform opinion in Lynn:

> For instance, we are told by a former Overseer of the Poor in this town, that five years ago the average number of paupers for several years amounted to between seventy and eighty. Now the whole number supported on the farm is twenty-seven only, and the whole expense year before last for the support of inmates over the income of the establishment, was but $606.10, although the inhabitants [of Lynn] have greatly increased since that time, numbering at the present time, it is believed, over 7000. Average expense per head per week, twenty-three cents and three mills. . . . The average number of paupers in the poor house last year was fifty.[19]

The editor attributed the reduction in expenses to good management;

that is, stringent rules and the application of sound business principles. He estimated that if the current policy were conscientously followed, there was no reason why the Poor House should not become a profit-making enterprise: "Should the number of paupers continue to decrease in the same proportion a little longer, the inhabitants of the town will have the profits of the farm to themselves.

Yet he felt compelled to encourage his fellow citizens to take a greater interest in poor relief. The town may not have relished the responsibility of caring for the poor, but it was best that Lynn care for its own and note permit paupers to migrate to other towns. There was the danger that poor folk from Lynn would settle in neighboring communities whose poor law administrators were not as efficient as the Overseers in Lynn. Under Massachusetts law, Lynn would be obligated to send remittances to other towns for the maintenance of paupers born in Lynn. If relief procedures elsewhere were inefficient and discipline lax, the economies implemented in the administration of the poor law in Lynn would be negated.[21]

There were other measures designed to enlarge the stigma of poverty and make dependency more odious and humiliating than it had been in the eighteenth century. In 1828, an item in the *Lynn Mirror* reported that most physicians in Lynn had agreed not to attend a family whose head was poor and a drunkard. The doctors were apparently convinced that the threat of withdrawing their services from the intemperate would cause them to renounce strong drink and at a stroke remove the major cause of poverty.

In 1831, the Commonwealth of Massachusetts repealed a law of 1815 that had been designed "to protect the sepulchres of the dead." Under the old law the use of cadavers for medical purposes was prohibited. Many people thought it horrifying and disgusting to have one's body or that of a loved one desecrated by dissection. The new law conceded that such fears were founded on superstition and ignorance. Old inhibitions that impeded medical research were, therefore, removed by the new statute signed into law on February 28, 1831.[22] The act granted no medical schools the right to practice anatomy on the bodies of deceased paupers if they were not claimed by a relative within twenty-four hours of death. The new law, thus, not only met the research needs of the medical profession but also, in light of widespread opposition to such uses of the human body, calmed the fears of all respectable citizens. Only the corpses of paupers would be turned over to the medical schools, creating an additional incentive for avoiding the Alms House.

The long range achievement of a more stern policy toward the poor was ambiguous. The reformers were most successful in reducing the number of paupers admitted to the Poor House, making their labor more productive, and keeping down the expenses of in-the-house relief. If one considers Lynn's continual growth in population during the years from 1830 to 1860, the new policy was effective in deterring admissions to the Alms House. In 1833, the number of inmates averaged about 50. In 1840, 80 persons received in-the-house relief. A dozen years later, after an increase in population of nearly 4,000, there were 80 who received in-the-house relief. The ratio of paupers to the general population dropped from 1/117 in 1840 to 1/317 in 1850. Although there was a sharp decline in the number of inmates of the Poor House after 1854, the change was due primarily to the transfer of non-Lynn paupers to regional poor houses, which the Commonwealth established and maintained. In January of 1855, for example, there were only 33 persons in the Alms House, while the town's population climbed beyond 17,000. But the new poor law policy was less successful in reducing out-of-the-house relief, though here again the increases were not proportionate to the growth in population. The number of persons receiving aid outside the house increased from 202 in 1842 to 260 in 1852.[23] In 1855, this figure dropped slightly, to 250, but increased again in 1856 to 275.[24]

Although there is a close correlation between increases and declines in the number of relief recipients and fluctuations in the shoe business, defenders of the poor law system invariably drew a distinction between the working poor and paupers. Despite the hardship of unemployment and severe wage cuts, the great majority of shoemakers were able, through their own collective efforts, to survive hard times without aid from the Overseers of the Poor. Yet this situation began to change during the late 1850s as the most frugal and industrious workers were thrust toward pauperism, evoking among citizens a new view toward poor relief. Throughout most of the period from1830 to 1860, however, the assumptions and policies of the administrations of the poor law remained undisputed.[25]

Another step in the tightening of the poor law came in 1854 with the opening of a state poor house in Tewksbury, Massachusetts and the transfer of inmates from Lynn to the state institution. Lynn would care only for her own; the others would become wards of the state. The response of the paupers to their removal suggests that many feared detention in the new institution. Proximity to friends and relatives, familiarity with their surroundings, and a long standing association with the keeper would no longer serve to mitigate their treatment. The *Lynn*

*News* reported that "many of them were dragged out screaming." To explain their behavior, the *News* warned: "They must either labor or be kept on hospital diet—an alternative which is rather unpleasant to many of the inmates, who had taken refuge in the 'house with six chimneys' for the purpose of getting rid of work. Several of these escaped before the appointed day of their removal."[26]

The impact of this policy toward the poor on workingmen was profound. The originators of the policy succeeded admirably in inculcating a profound dread of poverty and a compulsive drive to do all humanly possible to avoid pauperism, which was precisely tbe object of those like Civis and members of the Society for the Promotion of Industry, Frugality and Temperance. A feeling of dread is expressed in communication to the *Lynn Pioneer* in 1848: "No person can contemplate the idea of becoming a pauper, without a feeling of horror. It seems like becoming a criminal. Many would as soon go to prison, as to a Poor-house, and others would sooner go to their graves than to either."[27] The accuracy of this assessment is shown in the suicide note of an aging shoe cutter, Joseph Dwyer:

> As I grow old, and my health fails, and I find myself less able to provide for myself and live as I want to, and not be dependent on others, who have as much as they can do to provide for themselves (no doubt they would do what they could for me in an emergency, but I prefer to help myself, one way or another), I take the method you will find when it happens. I have enjoyed life as well as the most of men, but cannot bear the idea of being a helpless, dependent old man. I have paid my way so far, and owe nothing. Goodbye to all.[28]

Although the dependency of the poor made them especially vulnerable prey to the effort to enforce industry and frugality, the regulation of public behavior extended to all members of the community. In 1828, the town adopted a series of bylaws to prohibit objectionable forms of social conduct. Placed under the ban was the use of profane, obscene, or insulting language; shooting dice in any street, lane, or alley; making tumultuous noises and being rude in either speech or behavior toward females.[29] Passage of these ordinances may indicate an increase in the practices that the laws made illegal. There were on several occasions complaints from citizens against the crowds of unruly boys who gathered in public places and spoke to women as they passed.[30] In addition, the growth in population during the 1820s, bringing to Lynn a great many newcomers, may have loosened the informal social restraints that had inhibited such behavior among residents of the town. It is more likely though that there had been little or no increase in gambling, coarse language, or noise in the streets but that these practices had become objectionable by their incompatibility with the values of good order, industry, self-discipline, and a high standard of morality. There was thus a need to codify and formalize the values of good order, industry, and self-discipline that were emerging, incorporate them into law, and make obedience mandatory. Upon the recalcitrant, the indifferent, or the rebellious would fall the odium of arrest and financial penalty as well as the censure of respectable opinion.

A similar effort to propagate these values and enforce compliance extended to the educational system.[31] Beginning about 1830, there was agrowing interest in schools as institutions for training and educating future citizens, equipping them with sound moral and spiritual values, teaching them the values of industry and thrift, obedience to law and respect for authority. No longer could children be ignored or left to gain their initiation into society and the public house, in the street, or in the juvenile gang.[32] Bad habits or dangerous opinions once formed would be difficult to change. Education therefore became of primary importance to the proponents of change, and with energy they turned their attention to the schools—"the very places for cultivating self-restraint, order, decency and a regard for all the proprieties of life."

The reformers all shared the conviction that the schools were not only to instruct their pupils in useful knowledge but "to look after their morals and manners." They were "to impress on their minds the principles of piety, justice, and a sacred regard to truth, love to their country, humanity, and universal benevolence, sobriety, industry and frugality, chastity, moderation and temperance." Upon the schools fell the duty of inculcating "habits of application, respect to superiors, and obedience to law." For these were values "indispensable to the business man and the good citizen," and "the basis upon which a republican institution is founded."[33]

The Lynn citizens who voiced these sentiments would probably have agreed with the Massachusetts mill owner who also praised the services to industry rendered by the schools. He found that "it is a fact that the class of help which has enjoyed a good Common School education are the most tractable, yielding most readily to reasonable requirements. He was also convinced that "there is a connection between education and morals, and . . . our Common Schools have been nurseries not only of learning, but sound morality."

The needs of the Lynn shoe industry were similar, and they found expression in the educational policies set forth by the town's school committee. Tardiness was inexcusable, whether in the pupil or in the cordwainer, and should be replaced by punctuality—"a habit, invaluable to individual credit, successful business, and general tranquility." Children in Lynn should be "docile, modest, cheerful, courageous, self-possessed." They ought also to be taught the importance of "having a place, time and order for everything, and everything in its order, time, and place."[34] These virtues were not only conducive to learning but to productive labor as well.

In seeking to establish these values in the local schools, reformers in Lynn gained enthusiastic support from men in the Massachusetts legislature who shared their views and sought to use the power of the state to advance them. In 1826 they passed a law that required school committees "to obtain evidence of the good moral character of all instructors." Shortly afterward, a State Board of Education was formed; its first annual report appeared in 1838, and in its pronouncements on all aspects of educational policy, established standards to which many towns in Massachusetts aspired. State normal schools and teachers' institutes were formed, and legislative support was enlisted by the State Board to implement changes that were desired in the local school districts. One important change secured by the reformers was a transfer of power from the neighborhood to the town school committee.

Prior to 1838, the neighborhood prudential committee held responsibility for constructing and maintaining schools, adopting the curriculum, and hiring and firing instructors. The decision to retain or release an instructor usually depended on the students' performance in the oral examinations given at the end of the school year. The prudential committee attended the examination and if pleased retained the instructor; if not, the teacher was released. The law of 1838 affirmed the prudential committee's duty to maintain the schools, but transferred hiring power to the school committees.[35] Although the town could by special act, valid only for the year in which it was granted, give the prudential committee the right to select teachers, the selection was only advisory. "It is not legally possible for the prudential committee to make an absolute, unconditional contract with any person for keeping a school. He cannot appoint a *teacher*; he can only nominate a *candidate for teaching*."[36] Any appointment by the prudential committee, without ratification from the school committee, was legally void. A critical right thus passed from the neighborhood prudential committee to the school committee. In the following decades, the school committee preempted additional prerogatives until the prudential committee disappeared entirely.

In seeking to tighten discipline in the schools and inculcate values compatible with those of an emerging manufacturing society, the school reformers encountered resistance. It frequently took the form of truancy. In 1838, an average of one-third of the students enrolled in the state public schools were absent during the winter. In the summer months, this figure increased to 40 percent.[37] In Lynn, the situation was worse. Of the 1330 children in the town between the ages of four and fourteen years of age, 1130 were enrolled in the common schools. Average attendance was 'not over 650.'[38] If the malleable minds of the young were to be shaped in the manner desired by the reformers, a means was needed to compel enrollment and attendance. The wish sired the action; in 1851 Massachusetts made school attendance compulsory.

The reformers also encountered the obstinate cultural legacy of the eighteenth century. If they sought to instill in children the virtues of self-disciplines, respect for law, obedience to authority, and self-imposed restraints on "natural impulses," they encountered the progeny of an age that had, at best, been indifferent to those values or, at worst, had encouraged their opposites. The task of the teacher in gaining respect, maintaining attentiveness, stimulating interest and teaching children to curb their impulses is difficult enough for the instructor whose efforts are duplicated and reinforced by others. The task is infinitely greater if the instructor is seeking to change habits of behavior and values that the student shares not only with his peers but with his parents and much of the society in which he lives. This clash of values was evidently at the root of the conflict between school reformers and teachers, on the one hand, and a significantly large portion of the people of Massachusetts on the other.

In 1838, about 150 or more schools in Massachusetts were "broken up by the insubordination of the scholars." Six years later, in the school year 1842 to 1843, this figure dropped sharply to 2. In the following year, 7 schools in the state closed because of insubordination on the part of students. Although the Secretary of the Board of Education failed to explain the nature of the insubordination, he at one point used the term "insurrection," suggesting collective action on the part of students. There is no explanation offered for the sharp decline in the number of schools shut down because of insubordination between 1838 and 1844. The Secretary merely expressed "heartfelt congratulations that this class of cases is reduced to so low a number."[39]

A probably cause for the closing of scores of schools was the inability of the teacher to maintain order and impress on the students a code of disciplined behavior that was foreign to their experience outside the classroom. The law of 1826 required school committees to obtain evidence of good moral character of all instructors.[40] A decade later, the hiring prerogative shifted from the neighborhood prudential committees to school committees, which in many instances seemed to reflect views of education similar to those held by educational leaders in the state. The sharp increase in cases of insubordination may, therefore, have resulted from the efforts of the reformers at the levels of state and town to impose standards of behavior on people who neither shared their values nor saw the necessity for a strong emphasis on punctuality, obedience, and docility.

The problem for the teachers and their employers was enforcing compliance to habits that the students had not acquired in the home or in other social institutions, habits such as sitting attentively in the same seat for hours, refraining from coarse or vulgar expressions, responding with alacrity to commands, and conforming to the dictum of "everything in its time, order and place." In Lynn, for example, the school committee in the 1830s praised teachers "who had assiduously inculcated moral instruction in their schools, by which much of that profane and vulgar talk, and of that spirit of tale-bearing and falsehood . . . has been checked."[41] But to perform that admirable function and to meet the standards set for them by school committees, teachers were frequently compelled to use corporal punishment.

Those who formulated educational policy in Lynn were reluctant to concede that force was necessary to maintain order and gain obedience to the code of conduct they believed desirable. They preferred "a kind and paternal discipline," one that relied on methods of persuasion or if necessary punishment that stopped short of actual violence. Yet how could they deal effectively with students who set "bad examples of rudeness, immoral and disorderly behavior?" Despite the presence of "these backward, truant and disorderly pupils, who too often put the rules at defiance and give great trouble to the female teachers," the school committee of Lynn maintained that corporal punishment should be a last resort.[42] And when administered, there should be no "blows at the head, no hair pulling, and no boxing of ears." The committee also recommended that, to spare the student additional humiliation, the punishment be inflicted "after school is dismissed."[43]

Despite these guidelines, force was used to punish refractory students: the incidents caused bitter controversy in Lynn between the reformers and their opponents. In 1850, a boy in ward four was flogged by his teacher Samuel W. King. Two years later, an Irish boy in ward six was beaten by the Reverend Mr. Richards, a member of the school committee. In the following year, Josiah Hand was flogged with a wooden stick, two feet long and half an inch thick, for refusing to sweep the class room. And in 1857, the whipping of a student by Samuel King led to his dismissal by the school committee.[44]

Some people in Lynn viewed corporal punishment as an innovation used to foster obedience to values they did not share. The cultural legacy of the preindustrial eighteenth century evidently did not foster discipline. Many children never attended school, and those who did were neither punctual nor regular in their attendance. Teachers, who also shared the values of their pupils, showed no great concern to change habits that had been acquired in the home. Truancy and tardiness, therefore, were often ignored. Students who went off to Nahant for a day at the beach or went berrying in the woods did not meet a stern reprimand on returning to the school room. Some teachers punished disobedience and disruptive behavior with methods designed to evoke ridicule from other pupils, but they rarely seem to have inflicted corporal punishment. Samuel Collins, a Lynn teacher in the first decade of the nineteenth century, sometimes made a student stand in a corner or hold his arms extended outward for a short period of time but refrained from use of bodily force. Collins may have been exceptional, yet the problem of maintaining order seems to have become increasingly difficult as teachers and reformers sought to tighten discipline and punish forms of behavior that were generally tolerated outside the classroom.

Members of the Lynn school committee recognized the source of a good deal of the intransigence encountered by the teachers in the classroom. "Right control at home," they observed, "will generally secure obedience at school. Its want is often the true cause of the child's ill conduct and punishment." To justify the use of corporal punishment by the teacher, they argued that "the duties of a parent are devolved upon the teacher."[45] The instructor was not only justified in using force, they argued, but was bound by the duties of his role as substitute for the parent to apply punishment. However, this reasoning assumed an identity of values and outlook between parent and teacher that often did not exist. The committee, therefore, felt compelled to request that parents of children who had been punished address their grievances to the committee. The teacher "should not be assaulted, nor his schoolhouse be entered, either to accuse, or reprimand him." "Some of our teachers have thus be uncourteously visited."[46] Others were neither as diplomatic nor as deferential towards the rights of parents. They argued that too many parents were "total strangers to all discipline, whether mental or moral," and could not be relied upon to delegate disciplinary power to the teacher. Once the child entered the classroom, the authority of the parent ended. Although one ought not to overestimate the conflict between teachers chosen by the school committee and parents, there evidently was in Lynn, and in other towns of Massachusetts, resistance to the methods used to enforce discipline and punish "deviant" behavior.

In the process of social disciplining, the lax sexual practices inherited from the eighteenth century also came under attack. An example of the contrast between the laxity of the past and the new emphasis on self-control is found in Sylvester Graham, ordained minister, physiologist, and dietary reformer, who sought to change the sexual practices of his generation. Although Graham is known to the present generation primarily because a type of cracker bears his name, he was chiefly concerned with the disastrous effects of sexual stimulation on the human body. His concern with the human diet arose from his belief that meat, spices, sweets, coffee, tea, and alcohol "were the substances which intensified the sexual drive." But Graham's notions about sex contrasted sharply with forerunners in the eighteenth century who had also studied the subject. The difference is most clearly shown in their views toward sexual desire. Whereas the eighteenth century author of a pamphlet on the evils of such sexual practices as masturbation, fornication, and adultery assumed that such forms of sexual activity should be regulated, he also assumed that sexual desire was "a wholly natural feeling which must and should be indulged." Graham, on the other hand, rejected this notion and sought to prevent sexual desire with a rigorous regimen of physical activity, bland foods, and a tremendous exertion of will power. The energy conserved in suppressing sexual desire could, in the words of an interpreter of Graham, be expended into the world "with a single-minded determination that was sure to be effective at both the production and the acquisition of worldly goods." How great an influence Graham exerted in his lifetime would perhaps be impossible to estimate. Yet one may note only that as early as 1832 Oberlin College had forbidden the consumption of "tea, coffee, highly seasoned meats, rich pastries and all unwholesome and expensive foods." A devoted follower of Graham, Mary Gove of Lynn, opened a "Graham Boarding School" in 1838. If the Grahamite disciple is "suggestively close to the figure of the archetypical Jacksonian in all his forms, from rural frontiersman to urban entrepreneur,"[47] it is not surprising that he should appear in the manfacturing town of Lynn.

The attempt to establish a rigid code of sexual morality also appeared in the program of the school reformers. The Massachusetts Board of Education, in listing the duties of the prudential committees in maintaining schoolhouses, demanded that the committees construct privies. Indecent exposures would lead to unchaste thought, which would, in turn, nature into an unchaste life. Boards of Education in other states sought to implement the same reform. The Superintendent of Schools in Connecticut asked rhetorically, "who can duly estimate the final consequences of the first shock given to female delicacy, from the exposures to which the girls in the public schools are necessarily subjected? What quenchless fires of passion have been kindled within the bosoms of the young of both sexes by these exposures?" The fires kindled would lead "to the destruction of personal character."[48] Although the Boards were not empowered by law to compel the construction of privies, they conjured a chamber of horrors to overcome local indifference and provoke immediate action.

The school reformers, in an effort to prevent intimacy and immorality, also sought to segregate the sexes. They did not possess the legal power to order local prudential or school committees to comply with their wishes, but they did, by subtle means, encourage them to do so. One method was to include in their annual reports diagrams and floor plans of "model" school buildings, complete with descriptions of their enlightened, progressive features. Some of these "models" were the newly constructed state normal schools, which perhaps most accurately embodied the values of the Massachusetts reformers headed by Horace Mann. Other model schools were selected from towns with school committees composed of men much like themselves. The floor plans of the "model" schools showed the extent of segregation by sex. There were separate entrances, separate stairways, separate cloakrooms, and separate playgrounds. Segregation practically abolished contact between the sexes except in the classroom under the watchful eye of the instructor.[49]

The proponents of these changes based their position on several assumptions, which may or may not be valid. They assumed, for example, that the exposure of the sexual organs would provoke sexual stimulation. The same notion motivated the passage in Lynn of a town ordinance that made punishable by fine any profane or obscene utterance. It is in this period that the term "profane" began to lose its originally sacrilegious meaning and became nearly synonymous with obscene. Although it is questionable whether use of a common slang expression for sexual intercourse would actually encourage the act, the assumption that it would was the underlying cause for the appearance of legislation proscribing such expressions.

Tightening of the moral code also led to condemnation of bundling, a custom commonly practiced in areas of the Northeast during the eighteenth century. According to custom, courting couples would lie together in bed, sometimes fully clothed but more often divested of outer garments and with only under clothes. Parents of the girl not only countenanced the practice but defended and encouraged it, frequently doing their part in assisting the couple in their preparations for retiring to the bed. Although parents would not have admitted to encouraging fornication, premarital sexual relations were commonly the result. Church records containing confessions of sin by persons owning the baptismal covenant suggest the prevalence of premarital relations. Of 200 persons owning the covenant in Groton, Massachusetts between 1761 and 1775, "no less than sixty-six confessed to fornication before marriage." The entries themselves are significant. At first, the words "confessed and restored" were affixed in full to the offender's name. In 1763, the entry became "Confessed Fornication." In 1765, it is reduced to "Con. For.," and then is further abbreviated to "C.F." And during the three years 1789, 1790 and 1791, of sixteen couples admitted to full communion, nine had the letters "C.F." inscribed after their names in the church records.

Decline of the custom after the Revolution cannot be adequately explained by material improvements in living conditions. Larger homes with ample room, separate beds for each member of the family and for guests, plentiful fuel for heating and light, and more dense settlements that would allow a suitor to return to his own home in the evening, are partly valid, accounting only for the custom's decline among people possessing these improvements. More imporant was the moral assault on bundling and the conviction of critics that bundling promoted fornication and promiscuity. One poetic opponent of the practice stated the principal objection in his description of "a bundling maid":

> She'll sometimes say when she lies down,
> She can't be cumber'd with a gown,
> And that the weather is so warm,
> To take it off can be no harm;
> The girl it seems had been at strift;
> For widest bosom to her shift,
> She gownless, when the bed they're in,

The Spark [lover] nought feels but naked skin.
But she is modest, also chaste,
While only bare from neck to waist,
And he of boasted freedom sings,
Of all above her apron strings.
And where such freedoms great are shar'd,
And further freedoms feebly bar'd,
I leave for others to relate,
How long she'll keep her virgin state.

Criticisms of bundling intensified in the following years, losing the satirical levity of the above selection and becoming harsher, adopting such phrases as "rank disgrace and scandal base," "burning shame," and comparing practitioners of bundling to pigs and whores.

Most alarming, it seems, to the moral vigilantes were the damaging social consequences of promiscuity and the free, guiltless expression of sexual impulses. It signified the lack of self-control and the inability to deny oneself the pleasures of physical gratification. It meant also—as did drinking, gambling, or prolonged festivities—the expending of energies in unproductive activities. Enjoyment, merriment, and pleasure consumed time and energies that could better be employed in the endeavors that resulted in material improvement to the individual and to the entire society. A few reformers like Graham went further and maintained that sexual activity was harmful to the body, taxing the nervous and circulatory system and causing palpitations of the heart. And what was damaging to the individual was also detrimental to the society, depriving a collective entity of the productive talents and energies of a member.

The cultural legacy of the eighteenth century and its incompatibility with the emerging values of early industrialism becomes clearer if one notes the indifference the moral reformers confronted. Why did the people of Massachusetts, Connecticut, New York, and Wisconsin not conscientiously construct privies, one for males and one for females, adjacent to school houses? Were they not alarmed by the "grossness and brutality" perpetrated on young girls by exposure to a male urinating? Why, instead, did they either neglect to build privies or construct rough buildings that sheltered one from the weather but did not hide one from the view of others? It appears that a large portion of Americans were largely indifferent to the evils and immoralities that outraged the reformers. Many families simply saw no connection between exposure of the body and sexual promiscuity. In Lynn, for example, people were accustomed to bathing in the nude in the ponds and ocean. By 1828, that practice was banned and made punishable by a fine of one dollar for each offense.

The attack on bundling also reveals both the extent of the custom and an acceptance so broad that it found acknowledgement in common law. In a suit brought by a father against a young men for impregnating his daughter, a New York judge in 1804 acquitted the defendant. He found that the plaintiff and his wife knew that "she and the defendant slept together at their house, without forbidding or discountenacing the intercourse." The plaintiff and his daughter were angry only because the defendant failed to marry the girl. Although the judge condemned the premarital relations as "criminal intercourse," the father was equally guilty for encouraging or permitting the activity. The judge also made it clear that he was aware that bundling was a common practice in certain parts of New York: "We lay out of view the custom which it is agreed prevails in that part of the county, for young people, who are courting, to sleep together."

A generation later, in 1830, a Methodist preacher was charged by the Methodist Conference for "upholding whoredom." It seems rather that he had expressed neither shock nor disapproval of a young man "lying with a young woman all night," and added that "he used to do so himself when he was a young man." The minister defended himself with the observation that "young men and women lie on the same bed together at camp meetings."

In a similar case in New York in 1846, a man accused of seduction called to his defense several witnesses—"among them three married women, who were mothers, and wives of respectable farmers in the neighborhood." They testified that bundling "was the universal custom of the country," and that a girl's sleeping with a young man did not adversely affect her character. Although the custom may have persisted longer in upstate New York than in New England, there is little doubt of its popularity in Massachusetts during the eighteenth century.[50]

The tightening of the moral code gave rise to a vigorous assault on popular holidays that, in the eyes of the reformers, were conducive to promiscuity and other corrupting vices. Most objectionable was 'Lection Day (Election Day), which was celebrated in Massachusetts on the last Wednesday in May from the mid-seventeenth century until 1831. For nearly two centuries, the day marked the election of the governor and the choice of representatives to the opening sessions of the General Court. Festivities began on Wednesday and continued for several days.

In fact, "the entire week partook of the flavor of a holiday." Tamer diversions included visiting friends, gathering spring flowers, and eating 'Lection Cake, a pastry made of molasses, wine, fruits and spices and covered with a sugar glaze. But these were not the activities that came under the scrutiny of critics.

'Lection Day was also a time of heavy drinking, gambling, wild and bawdy dancing at taverns. Young men from the Salem area journeyed to public houses on the Danvers Road or to Putnam's tavern on the Danvers Plain and indulged in an assortment of drinks: egg-pop, beer, punch, flip, and toddy. There were also athletic contests like jumping and wrestling, as well as games of chance like pitching coppers, throwing props, and shooting dice. Adults took time from their tippling and gathered at the Danvers Plains for horse racing and betting. On the Boston Common hundreds of people gathered around the shanties and gaming tables that were erected for the holiday. Lynn people journeyed to old Willis's tavern on the Boston road to drink rum and muddy beer, hustle coppers, and enjoy the revelry of dancing and singing.

There is evidence that 'Lection Day was an important holiday for the black population of Massachusetts: the holiday was sometimes referred to as "Nigger 'Lection." One historian maintains that the day derives its name from a custom practiced by the slave owners of the Commonwealth. On 'Lection Day in May they gathered in Boston for the opening of the General Court, giving their slaves a holiday from their usual labors. The slaves assembled on Boston Common and over the years developed a ritual of electing their own rulers, celebrating their achievement, and mimicking the manners and idiosyncracies of their masters. In the Lynn area, a slave of Thomas Mansfield, Pompey, a man of regal bearing and according to legend a former African prince, was installed on a throne fashioned from an arm chair and made ruler in a ceremony conducted in the Saugus section of Lynn. In Connecticut and Narragansett, the blacks selected a governor from their ranks and celebrated the occasion with "much gayety and considerable feasting." The festivities and merriment that became predominant features of 'Lection Day in Massachusetts thus seem to have originated with the blacks. Paw-paw, a game of chance popular in Boston, is said to have been introduced by blacks from the West Indies.[51] And although slavery in Massachusetts ended with the Revolution, blacks continued to celebrate the day in much the same manner as before. At taverns and drinking spots in the vicinity of Salem visited by Robert Rantoul in his younger years, "the fiddler was a negro, in almost all cases." Blacks and whites danced to the same music, but there seems to have been no "intermixing in dancing."[52] It seems blacks in Boston eagerly awaited the chance to gather on the Common for their annual celebration: in 1817, an enraged Negro seaman who had been confined to his ship and deprived of his right to attend 'Lection Day, blew up the ship, the Canton Packet. In 1831, 'Lection Day as an actual election day and for the opening session of the General Court, was abolished. But as an occasion for merriment, it continued to evoke celebration from some who resisted the ban on "lewd and lascivious behavior." In the same year in which the day was legally abolished, a Lynn historian wrote a revealing poem commemorating an occasion that epitomized the life style of the eighteenth century:

> And is Election Day no more?
> Good Old 'Lection. . . .
> No more shall we go up
> To see "Old Willis!"
> He has hung up his fiddle
> On the last peg.
> The days of old 'Lection are over,
> The glorious days of "Landee John!"
> When "Gid" used to hustle coppers,
> And the niggers play "paw-paw,"
> On Boston Common.
> No more shall we eat "Lection cake,"
> Or drink muddy beer,
> Misnomered "ale,"
> At "Old Bly's."
> The days of dancing "Suke" are done,
> And fat "Bet" shall shake her jolly sides no more
> To the merry "winding about
> Of linked sweetness, long drawn out,
> From old "Pompey's fiddle!"
> No more shall "the Governor"
> Sit in his great arm-chair,
> To encounter the stare
> Of the idle mixed multitude,
> "Black spirits and white,
> Blue spirits and grey,"
> Barefoot and booted,

Maudlin and merry.
Yes, 'Lection is done
With all its paraphernalia
Of cocked-up-hats and fun . . .[53]

Equally distressing to the moral reformers was the manner in which unwholesome and indecent behavior had become associated with militia training days. Militiamen ordinarily assembled once or twice a year for marching, shooting, and mock warfare. Although the intent was to prepare the militia for fighting, the disappearance of an imminent foreign threat after the war of 1812 seems to have helped convert training day into a rollicking, fall festival. One observer reported that "the scenes of riot and drunkenness usually witnessed in the neighborhood of our parades, are disgusting and harmful, and were yesterday carried to an extent seldom equalled on similar occasions." He was particularly disturbed because "men and boys were seen in a brutal state of intoxication, and even larger numbers of females were to be observed mixing with the motley crowd."[54] The militia units attracted a large crowd of camp followers who gathered about "the numerous shanties that were located around the muster field." Their enterprising proprietors dispensed "ardent spirits of a base and poisonous quality," which, in the view of another critic, encouraged "tumults and riots." The occasion also attracted "pickpockets, gamblers drunkards, profane swearers, with many others of a similar stamp." The excitement of parades, cannon fire, and soldiers in uniform also enticed "innocent children and youths" to the field. They were youngsters "whom curiosity brought together, but whom nothing but night [would] send home more corrupted than they went." The critic concluded with the warning that "more mischief is here done in one day, more vicious inclinations here take root, than home, or the pulpit, can eradicate in a year."[55] Military commanders worsened matters by treating their men to draughts of rum from barrels hauled to the training field.[56]

Although the abolition of 'Lection Day can be explained by a desire to change the schedule for selecting legislators and the decline of the militia system by the disappearance of any threat to the security of the state, one cannot ignore the objections to these customs from moral reformers. These holidays, lasting for several days, fostered an array of corrupt habits that violated every tenet of the emerging industrial code of behavior. On each occasion there was drinking and gaming, horse racing, self-indulgence, and uninhibited behavior of every sort, including intimate and unchaperoned relations between young men and women. There was a complete disregard for the values of sobriety and frugality, self-denial and self-control, and the ability to overcome desires for physical gratification and pleasure. The celebration on 'lection and training day thus constituted a standing rebuke to the architects of a new society.

Perhaps no single aspect of early nineteenth century culture underwent such thoroughgoing change as the drinking customs of Americans. The tracts, pamphlets, learned essays, and scientific treatises inspired by the issue would fill a large place in any depository. The illicit consumption of alcohol probably sent more men to jail, settled more political contests, caused more court cases and suits, enlisted more supporters, and produced more polemical literature than any other single moral issue.[57]

The origins of the temperance movement in the United States cannot be understood apart from the social context in which it arose or without a consideration of the particular evils that its advocates sought to extinguish. Temperance reform must be viewed as an integral part in the larger process of social disciplining, the tightening of the moral code, and the creation of a system of values compatible with the needs of an emerging industrial society. The link between temperance and other reforms is especially close in the early years; drinking seemed conducive to every vice that obstructed the emergence of the new order—poverty and pauperism, debauchery and promiscuity, idleness and dissipation, self-indulgence and physical gratification, brawling and civil disturbances. It also incapacitated men for productive, efficient labor and wasted their wages. Drinking not only harmed the physical constitution but consumed precious hours of one's time in totally unproductive leisure. For a society that was becoming increasingly cognizant of the opportunity for material improvement, drinking was in every particular an enormous evil. The task that lay before the reformers was to root out all vestiges of a practice that made human beings unfit to seize the opportunity for material improvement.

The temperance movement in America spans the period from approximately 1830 to 1930. It did not begin in 1650 or in 1750. True, one can locate in the first two hundred years of settlement a number of voices raised against the heavy consumption of ardent spirits. Massachusetts had licensing laws restricting the establishment of taverns and inns that dispensed alcoholic beverages. It also attempted to control chronic tippling and frequent visits to public house. But it was not until the second or third decade of the nineteenth century that isolated voices began coalescing in an organized movement to revive and strengthen its injunctions against drinking that had fallen into disuse during the eighteenth century.[58] The evangelical churches that proliferated in the Second Great Awakening ultimately became the engine of reform for the temperance movement, establishing temperance or abstinence as a requirement for membership.

Some students of the subject maintain that the movement arose in response to a sharp increase in alcoholic consumption in the late eighteenth and early nineteenth century. Alice Felt Tyler cities an increase in per capita consumption from two and half gallons in 1792 to four and a half gallons in 1810 to seven and a half gallons in 1823.[59] Joseph Gusfield and John A. Krout also report the spread of heavy drinking as the condition that precipitated the organization of temperance forces fearful of the threatening social consequences that would result from a tippling, drunken population. Statistics on the production of ardent spirits may, in fact, suggest a trend towards an increase in per capita consumption. But although comparable figures for a half century earlier are lacking, observers seemed to agree that Americans at the time of the Revolution were a hard drinking people.

The lamenting refrain of soldiers at Valley Forge was "no pay, no clothes, no provisions, no rum." Workmen at Trenton building ships for the state of Pennsylvania consumed between two and three hundred gallons of whiskey a week. In 1780, in order to meet the demand for liquor from American troops, the Continental Congress levied a requisition on the various states. Connecticut's share was over 68,000 gallons. At an ordination in Beverly, Massachusetts in 1785, one third of the funds appropriated for the celebration went for liquor. Beer, ale, wine, cordials and ardent spirits were made from nearly every form of fruit and grain—apples, peaches, grapes, cherries, barley, wheat, rye and corn. In the early eighteenth century, New Englanders began distilling rum from West Indian molasses, producing the drink that seemed "capable of satisfying so many human needs." It is, thus, hard to accept an estimate that puts per capita consumption of ardent spirits at two and a half gallons in 1792, the first year in which an unpopular tax was levied on alcohol. The American troops, who received a ration of one half pint of rum per day, were probably consuming an amount equal to or less than the daily ration to which they were accustomed; a half pint was the daily amount a workingman or laborer ordinarily received from his employer, thus totaling nearly two gallons a month. On any special occasion he was likely to consume several times that amount of rum or whiskey. The average adult male probably consumed between fifteen and twenty gallons of hard liquor a year in the late eighteenth and early nineteenth centuries.

Drinking customs inherited from the eighteenth century continued into the nineteenth. "Spiritous liquor," according to John Krout, "penetrated deeply into the social life of Americans,"[60] and this was as true of Lynn as elsewhere. There were grog shops in every part of town and "it was not a rare sight to witness the apprentice, and even the school boy, laying his change on the counter, and receiving his evening dram." To every visitor to one's home, the decanter, the tumbler, and the sugar bowl were always offered as a gesture of welcome. The schoolmaster and teacher took their brandy and water at the bar of the Lynn Hotel and the parson his glass of punch at the Deacon's sideboard. "Even the poor parishioner felt herself bound to make an apology of regret if she had not 'a little spirit in the house for the Minister,' when he made his customary call." No storekeeper could survive if he did not sell liquor by the dram and occasionally treat his customers to a drink.[61] One grocer in Saugus kept several barrels of rum in his dimly lit shop and was careful to see they were not exhausted before the start of the day's trade. In the shoe shops, many cordwainers drank their daily pint of "white eye," and there were some "who went the whole quart."[62] And eleven and four each day, a boy went to the rum shop with a two-quart bottle for a supply of "black strap," a popular drink made from rum and molasses.[63] One young man who worked in the shop of Theophilus Burril recalled seeing a man preparing the day's supply of black strap for the shop's crew. He mixed the molasses and rum in a tub and stirred the ingredients with a four foot stick, insuring a plentiful supply for all.[64] The worker who made the best shoe treated his fellows to drinks, and he who made the worst one also paid the "scot." "Every birthday of each operative was a 'treat,' every holiday was a regular 'blow out'—and every 'raising,' training, election of civil or military officers, and even the ordination, was an occasion for the circulation of the pail of punch."[65] The man who reached "his majority," age 21, was attended by his neighbors, and the host customarily laid in a supply of the choicest liquors. Shoemakers who went to Nahant for an outing "would as soon think of sailing on dry land as of having a 'good time' without plenty of punch."[66]

"It was a common belief that a man could not do a good day's work without liquor," recalled Nathan D. Chase, a Lynn shoe manufacturer, who learned first hand the strength of this conviction. Upon hiring carpenters to construct a central shop for him in 1823, Chase was told they would quit if he did not provide them with spirits.[67] Robert Rantoul of Beverly noted that "it had been an universal custom in this town, that when a mechanic or laborer was hired by the day, he should be supplied with not less than half a pint of rum daily if he chose to drink so much." As a temperance advocate and a rising entrepreneur, Rantoul broke with custom and informed his workmen that he would not provide liquor. His action "was attended with much unpopularity for some time." An elderly member of Beverly's Board of Overseers of the Poor resisted Rantoul's attempt to withdraw spirits from paupers who labored on the poor farm. Mr. Wood "entertained the opinion at that time very prevalent, that persons who labored hard ought to be furnished with spirituous drinks, and he had always acted in conformity with this opinion in all his transactions."[68]

Drinking was integrated into nearly every aspect of the social life of Americans. Alcoholic beverages were consumed in abundance at birthdays, weddings and funerals, militia training, elections, shopping trips, picnics and outings, house raisings, husking bees, auctions, independence celebrations, ordinations, pig killings, and meetings of fire companies.[69] There were, in addition, regular "breaks" in each working day for draughts of beer, ale, rum, cordials, or wines. It was a custom practiced by ministers, lawyers, doctors, and teachers as well as by clerks, artisans, and workingmen; by young and old, male and female. These drinking patterns were inherited from the eighteenth century, a period that did not stress self-denial, self discipline, or an exclusive orientation toward productive labor.

Self-sacrifice requires the conviction there will be some reward, temporal or spiritual. The religious and secular values of the eighteenth century did not foster that notion. The eighteenth century gave a prominent place in its culture to enjoyment and pleasure. These were as necessary to human existence as were the material benefits that resulted from productive labor. The eighteenth-century individual thus demonstrated a view of life in which no single aspect of human endeavor was stressed at the expense of others. The level of expectation for the material rewards of work were so low that regular drinking and frequent holidays could be indulged in without creating a sense of loss, failure, or deprivation.

The temperance movement arose in the early nineteenth century because economic activity quickened, bringing a fundamental reordering of values. Extension of markets, improvements in transportation, and in Lynn a demand for shoes, meant an opportunity for material improvement. But this was an opportunity that was available to other towns as well, and in the competition for the rewards afforded by trade not all would triumph. Success would go chiefly to those who fitted themselves for the tasks demanded of them in competition with others. Lynn, in other words, was feeling the pressures of an emerging competitive market economy.[70] The town's experience of hard times during the depressions of 1816 and 1819 to 1820 had confirmed the necessity of rooting out vestigial cultural remnants of the past that contributed to hardship. It was thus imperative "to wean the mind from those scenes of festivity and amusement which at the present day are too prevalent among us." The temperance movement stemmed from this impulse.

One's life under the new order would be oriented towards work; whatever intervened to distract one from this duty or to diminish the will to work, became objectionable. The criterion for evaluating any activity, whether individual or social, was its conduciveness to industry and frugality. The entire moral reform movement derived its existence from the application of that tenet to customs inherited from the eighteenth century. It is thus common in the period before the Civil War to find advocacy of temperance combined with support for one or all of the reform measures discussed earlier. Temperance in itself is less important than its crucial place in a constellation of values which together constitute the basis for the culture of industrialization.

The temperance advocate invariably saw a close link between drinking and a large array of socially destructive practices. The pioneer moral reform organization in Lynn was the Society for the Promotion of Industry, Frugality and Temperance, formed in 1826. It became evident in the following years that industry and frugality were the Society's primary goals, while temperance was viewed as the means to those ends.[71] The citizen of Lynn, who wrote under the name of "Civis" and outlined the town's new policy toward the poor, was also a strong proponent of temperance. As mentioned earlier, Civis had suggested that the community ostracize relief recipients and levy a two-dollar fine on any manufacturer who employed a citizen who took out-of-the-house support. To speed the adoption of temperate habits among cordwainers, he urged also that bosses employ no worker who drank to excess.[72] "You alone," he stated, "must take the bold, manly and decisive measures to make all your workmen temperate, industrious, punctual and faithful in their business."[73] The temperance advocate also saw a similarity between drinking and the reading of novels, "a habit like intemperance." Indulgence in both leads to addiction: "the mind becomes disordered and craves more." "Total abstinence from all exciting stimuli of a hurtful nature should be the watchword of every christian, and every scholar."[74]

The growth of the temperance movement in the 1830s can be attributed, in part, to the conviction that "the use of intoxicating liquors is the source of more disturbance, pauperism, crime and misery, than all other causes together."[75] Clear evidence for this notion came from a Lynn reformer who noted: "The effect also produced by the temperance cause in the public at large is happily visible by the diminished number of paupers in these establishments [poor houses]."[76] Samuel Cheever, the young clergyman in Salem, convicted of slandering the owner of a distillery, defended himself with the contention that ardent spirits filled the Commonwealth "with brawls, riots, poverty and anguish." Drinking tended "to break up all social order, prostrate all barriers of law, set fire to all violent human passions, and whelm all institutions of blessedness, domestic, civil and religious, in one blasting, fiery tide of ruin." Robert Rantoul of Beverly, in many ways typical of the rising middle class, agreed that "intemperance is the most fruitful source of pauperism." He found that half the inmates of the workhouse since 1804 were intemperate. Rantoul's antidote for pauperism and his own prescription for a successful and happy life was "habits of punctuality, order and diligence—the determination to concentrate the mind and power on one object at a time, to persevere and . . . to being earnest about every worthy object, great or small." Intemperance was destructive to each of these.

The conviction that Lynn's prosperity "must come from industry and frugality and temperance of its citizens" speeded the progress of the temperance movement.[77] Membership in the Society for the Promotion of Industry, Frugality and Temperance increased from 143 in 1826 to 450 in 1830. In March 1833, the town meeting requested that selectmen not approbate "any individuals as retailers of spirituous liquors for the current year." Citizens entrusted with advancing the material and moral well being of the town gave their support to the reform movement.[78] As mentioned earlier, doctors decided not to attend any family whose head was a drunkard. Young girls were urged not to receive favors from men who drank.[79] Employers were implored to deny employment to tipplers. Nathan Breed, one of Lynn's largest manufacturers, prohibited his workmen in the central shop from imbibing alcoholic beverages. To stay their temptation and satisfy their thirst, he kept a large barrel of ginger beer in his central shop. In the central business district that Isaiah and Nathan Breed owned, the pious temperance advocates leased property only on the condition that no alcoholic beverage be permitted on the premises.[80] Militia captains agreed to dispense with ardent spirits at trainings and use only cider and beer.[81] Some fire companies also consented to insert a temperance clause in their bylaws and ban spirits from the meeting house.[82] Dozens of temperance societies appeared in the years from 1830 to 1860 and enrolled hundreds of members who pledged themselves to either temperance or abstinence. The Sunday Schools furnished a thousand or more young people for the "Cold Water Army."[83] Doctors in Lynn went so far as to renounce the use of ardent spirits for medicinal purposes and to adopt, instead, the cold water theories of Preisnitz's hydropathy.

In combatting drinking, gambling, lax sexual practices, or profane language, the moral reform movement vacillated between moral suasion and legal coercion.[84] School reformers preferred to advance changes in the educational system without resort to force, yet found it necessary to employ corporal punishment. The same was true of the temperance movement. The tension between moral suasion and legal coercion endured throughout the entire history of the movement. In each case legal coercion required machinery for enforcement producing a significant change in the constabulary of Lynn.[85]

Prior to the conversion of moral values into a legal code, the constables performed a minor function in the affairs of the town. Their main task was to canvass the town before the town meeting and read to each citizen the warrant explaining the order of the business. They also served as sergeants-at-arms, lending official authority to the chair, helping keep emotions in check, and maintaining order. The constables were chosen annually by the selectmen, received no pay except a share of the fine levied for an infraction, wore no uniforms, and carried no weapons. The badge of their office was a long staff ringed at the top with alternating bands of colored stripes. But the role of the constables gradually changed as they were called upon to enforce the standards of conduct that accompanied the early stages of industrialization. An illustration of the change that occurred is found in the constables' badge of authority, the staff. In the late 1840s, John A. Thurston, deputy police chief, cut the staff into pieces and made billy clubs. The need for a corps of trained, experienced, and armed police arose from the conflict engendered in the imposition of a moral code, which a portion of the population did not accept.[86] A survey of arrests made in Lynn during the late 1850s shows clearly that the vast majority were for such offenses as illegal sale of liquor, drunkenness, and disorderly conduct; not for capital offenses or robbery.

Social disciplining was as much a part of early industrialization as the extension of markets, division of labor, and increases in production. Economic advance in a competitive market economy required a reordering of values: an emphasis on industry, self-denial, frugality, temperance, and self-discipline, and the disapproval of their opposites. It required also the selective repudiation of eighteenth-century customs, which were incompatible with and thus subversive of the new social order. The dominant features of the moral code called "puritanical" originated not in the seventeenth but in the nineteenth century. Although evangelical religion served effectively as a vehicle for implementing the new morality, this particular brand of piety itself reflected values identical to those of the emerging social and economic system.

The Lynn shoe manufacturers were the leaders and strongest supporters of the movement for social disciplining. Yet it would be erroneous to view industrial morality solely as a bourgeois or middle class way of life that was imposed on the rest of society. There was, in fact, legal coercion and the use of force against the recalcitrant.[87] But there seems to be a logic inherent in the early stages of industrialization that compels compliance from those who either choose to accept its demands or are born into the system and comply out of their need to survive. Thus one can discern in the behavior of the Lancashire mill owner, the Lynn shoe manufacturer, the Bolshevik, or the Chinese Red Guards a similar strain of asceticism, self-sacrifice, and frugality. Many of the dominant features of this system of values and code of conduct together form what can be termed industrial morality—that extreme orientation toward work, maximum productivity, and material accumulation. Yet the system of property relations within which this tightening of the moral code occurs invariably produces a class bias, particularly in the selective process of weeding out some customs and values from the past, while encouraging others. So too is the bias in capitalist economic growth evident in the implementation and enforcement of the new code. In Lynn, for example, pauperism became a humiliation, but the exploitation that often produced pauperism evoked little moral outrage. Profanity was punishable by a fine of two dollars, two day's wages for a cordwainer; an hour's profits for a large shoe manufacturer. The cordwainers in Lynn perceived the class bias of the moral reform movement and the duality or contradiction in the value systems of its members. The results were profound. Moral issues became enmeshed with emerging class antagonisms. Alignments on social issues began to reflect the conflict between journeyman and boss, thus lending a class tone to the moral reform movement. It led, on the one hand, to outright rejection by some workingmen of nearly every aspect of the movement and, on the other, to the evolution of a unique and distinctive class morality, which if bearing a resemblance to the dominant features of the moral code of the middle class, was nonetheless different in several important respects. The response of workingmen to this cultural dimension of social change is, therefore, indicative of an experience that included far more than their place of work. Lynn itself must be viewed as an immense manufactory in which a whole cultural apparatus is created to foster habits that facilitate production. If economic change brought a deterioration in their status as wage earners and skilled workingmen, the tightening of the moral code by a movement led by their employers was clearly a part of the same process. Their response was manifested in the grog shop and the class room as well as in the meeting hall of the cordwainers society.

# 8. Patterns of Mobility and Property Ownership

In recent years sociologists and historians have offered a number of hypotheses to explain the behavior of social groups undergoing the experience of economic change. An important part of many of these hypotheses is social mobility, both geographical and occupational. The first is concerned with the movement of people either from one country to another, from farm, village and small town to the city and factory, or from one town to another. The second deals with the movement of people either upward to positions of greater prestige and higher income or downward to jobs of lower status with less remuneration. The lack of movement, geographical and occupational, is also offered to explain social behavior and to characterize a particular society. In the field of labor history, the ultimate intent of these theories is to explain the absence or prevalence of social discontent and to account for the ways in which workers respond to economic change. In some instances there may be persistent protest, rebellion and revolutionary activity; in others, passive acquiescence in the face of conditions that elsewhere evoke resistance.

Economic change often produces social disruption in the form of an accelerated movement of people. Several studies of nineteenth-century America have noted the large number of labor transients that appeared in northern cities. There is evidence that these migratory laborers were present in considerable numbers during the antebellum period, at least in the burgeoning city of New York.[1] But it was in the post-Civil War period that the "tramp problem" grew to alarming proportions, causing many cities and towns to pass laws to curb vagrancy and allay the fears of apprehensive citizens.[2] An exhaustive study of the labor troubles of 1877 gave a prominent role to transients in the looting and burning that accompanied the disorganized upheavals of the late 1870s.[3] But vagabonds are the most extreme form of transiency, a symptom trace-able to roots within the economic life of "stable" communities.

Nearly every detailed examination of a particular manufacturing town or industry has stressed the high rate of labor turnover. Stephan Thernstrom's study of unskilled workers in Newburyport, Massachu-setts, found that "less than half of the unskilled laborers listed in the city on the census of 1850, 1860, or 1870 remained there for as much as a decade."[4] Two thirds of the 171 common laborers employed in Newburyport in 1850, for instance, had disappeared by 1860. A recent study of the payroll records of the Boston Manufacturing Company of Waltham, largest cotton textile firm in the Bay State, produced even more striking figures. For the years 1850 and 1855, in the months be-tween January and August, the turnover rate was 39 percent for 1850 and 34 percent for 1855. In other words, slightly more than a third of the persons named on the payroll were missing eight months later. Over a longer period it becomes evident that the labor turnover was characteristic of the entire workforce and not restricted to a constantly changing minority. Of the 583 individuals on the 1850 payroll, only 3 were included on the roster of 1865.[5] An examination of the 1853 payroll of the Pepperell Mill in Biddeford, Maine showed a gross turn-over rate of 100 percent.[6]

Important conclusions are drawn from evidence of a rapid turnover in the workforce. A high rate of transiency may account for the absence of concerted efforts by workers to organize to resist their employers. Shunted from job to job, constantly moving from one town to another, they were rarely in one place long enough to establish ongoing organi-zations that could bring about social change. They developed the out-look of the hitchhiker: each job and abode was a temporary one, and any improvement gained by sacrifice and risk would be lost by the act of moving.[7] The lack of organization among migrant agricultural workers or casual laborers is partial proof of this notion. Furthermore, migrants were open to the charge of being outside agitators, thus per-mitting opponents to externalize the source of trouble and attribute the cause of protests to a foreign source.[8] Blaming outsiders effectively di-verts attention from the conditions that evoked the dissatisfaction and crystallizes a rigid alignment between members of the community, re-gardless of their differences.

Among Lynn shoemakers, the rate of transiency was relatively small (see Table 1).[9] Three-fourths of the shoemakers remained in the town for at least ten years and a majority stayed for twenty. Yet it is impor-tant to note that there is a slight increase in the number of those who were unlisted in the directories ten and twenty years later. A trend toward increased geographical mobility in the thirty years before the Civil War foreshadowed the transiency that became so marked twenty years later. Observers in Lynn noted as early as 1849 the influx each summer of more than 500 seasonal workers. And police reports in the late 1850s recorded an increasing number of destitute, jobless men whom city officials lodged in the city jail: 18 in 1855, 77 in 1859, 218 in 1860, and 354 in 1861.[10] In the 1870s, these figures would reach into the thousands. But figures on the shoemakers do not corroborate those of Thernstrom: the persistence rate is twice as high for the Lynn shoemakers as for the common laborers in Newburyport. It appears, then, that most cordwainers were settled, long-term residents of the town and not transients.

Table 1. Shoemakers Who Remained in Lynn*

|             | 1832 | 1841 | 1851 | 1860 |
|-------------|------|------|------|------|
| 1832 Sample | 100  | 79   | 76   | 67   |
| 1841 Sample |      | 100  | 76   | 64   |
| 1851 Sample |      |      | 100  | 70   |

*These figures include shoemakers who died. Deceased are included with those who remained in Lynn. For the 1832 sample, by 1841 six had died, by 1851 fourteen had died, and by 1860, nineteen had died. For the 1841 sample, by 1851 eleven had died, and by 1860 thirteen had died.

Length of stay or the duration of residency in a town may also be important as a factor of social behavior. A comprehensive study of the textile manufacturing town of Lawrence, Massachusetts, scene of a famous strike in 1912, found that the length of stay in the town was the main determinant of one's response to the conflict.[11] The Yankees and Irish, long-time residents of the city, almost unanimously opposed militant protests against wage cuts and speedups. This was true even of Irish workers in the mills who were subject to the same conditions that from other workers evoked intense dissatisfaction and a refusal to comply. The strikers were mainly recent immigrants: Italians, Poles, Franco-Belgians, and Syrians. The French-Canadians, a numerically large portion of the working population, were divided. Those who had arrived in the years shortly after the Civil War tended to oppose the walkout, while the most recent migrants from Quebec sided with the strikers. Members of the "older" ethnic groups were subject to the social controls of voluntary institutions that had grown up over the years;

the newcomers were a rootless, floating labor force that was hostile to agencies of law and order. Duration of residency, then, was apparently the primary determinant of alignments on critical social issues. The process of establishing roots in a community and becoming socially integrated into the life of a town seems to have acted as a conservative influence.

Length of stay in the community also appears to have been a factor in the response of Lynn shoemakers to the unfavorable consequences of economic growth, but not as important a factor as Cole found in his study of Lawrence.[12] The men who were most active in organizing to defend themselves against exploitation were more likely than the rank and file to have been born outside the town. Yet comparative figures do not indicate so great a discrepancy as existed in Lawrence. Of the 49 leaders of 1830–34, 45 percent were born in Lynn, compared with the 56 percent of shoemakers in general. Of the 112 leaders in the affairs of the Journeymen Cordwainers Society in the 1840s, 36 percent were born in Lynn in contrast to the 54 percent of the entire population of shoemakers. But in 1860, the year of a strike that was as crucial an event in the life of the town as was the conflict of 1912 to Lawrence, the gap between leaders and followers disappeared: by then, 26 percent of the leaders, and 27 percent of all the town's shoemakers, were born in Lynn. (See Table 2.)

Table 2. Nativity of Shoemakers

|  | 1832 | 1841 | 1851 | 1860 |
|---|---|---|---|---|
| Born in Lynn: | 56% | 54% | 38% | 27% |
| Shoemakers |  |  |  |  |
| *Leaders | 45% | 36% |  | 26% |
| Born and/or |  |  |  |  |
| married in Lynn: |  |  |  |  |
| Shoemakers | 85% | 80% | 61% | † |
| Leaders | 88% | 67% |  | † |

*Number of leaders in study: 49 for 1832–34; 112 for 1844–45; and 84 for 1860.
†The vital records terminate in 1850. No figures, therefore, are included for 1860.

There is also evidence that duration of residency influenced the behavior of some shoemakers, yet it is difficult to determine why. There was, for example, a lack of continuity in the leadership of the journeymen's organizations. Of the 49 men active during the 1830s, about

63 percent were present in Lynn a decade later, and 70 percent were still shoemakers. But only 6 of the 23 shoemakers were among the 112 men active in the affairs of the journeymen during the 1840s. The same was true a decade or more later. Roughly half of the 112 leaders of the 1840s were present in Lynn in 1860, and 44 percent were shoemakers. But only 4 were among the 66 men who made up the leadership of the strike movement. Length of stay may affect social behavior, but not to the same extent or in the same way in Lynn as Cole found to be true in the "immigrant city."

Transiency, turnover in employment, and duration of settlement are aspects of geographical mobility; another is immigration and ethnic background. The emphasis on race and nationality derives mainly from the importance attached to immigrants in American economic growth, the particular ways different groups respond to similar conditions, and the conflicts within the workforce caused by racial and cultural differences. English historians E. P. Thompson and Eric Hobsbawm have shown that people of diverse cultural background reacted differently in the face of conditions that were essentially the same.[13] Each group, in its own way, used the cultural legacy of the pre-industrial past—with its religion, customs, traditions, and folklore—to interpret its experience and to find ways of legitimizing resistance. In the United States, foreigners played a crucial role in economic development because they made up a large portion of the laboring population. Oscar Handlin maintained that in the "two decades after 1845 the Irish energized all aspects of industrial development in Boston by holding out to investors magnificent opportunities for profits from cheap labor costs."[14] Rowland Berthoff assigned to British immigrants an important role in the rise of American industries that had long suffered from a lack of skilled workers able to produce goods of a quality equal to the best made in England.[15] Both note the effect of successive waves of immigrants on occupational mobility, with the newcomers thrusting natives and older immigrants upward into positions as skilled workers or supervisory personnel.[16] In addition to these efforts to measure the economic impact of immigration, there have been numerous attempts to ascertain the significance of cultural background as a factor in the behavior of workers.

As yet there is no greater agreement among historians than among people of the nineteenth century in deciding whether foreigners constituted a conservative or radical force in American life. Handlin contended that peasants, possessing little more than the shirt on their backs and their labor power, showed no inclination to risk the little they had for a grand dream of a new society. David Brody reached a similar conclusion in his study of the steel industry: the terrible conditions of employment were, for the most part, passively accepted by the East European workers because almost anything was better than what they had known in the old country.[17] Thernstrom's examination of unskilled Irish laborers produced the same conclusion: the Irish had low expectations and thus accepted as adequate their low wages as laborers.

Evidence on the other side is equally impressive. Just as Americans externalized the most distasteful and baleful effects of industrial growth, so too did they hold the foreigners responsible for strikes, riots, collective action, and violence in general. They were seen as agents of subversion, immorality, and radicalism, the originators of ideas and practices that could not have arisen from indigenous sources. Historians give credence to a number of points in this general indictment: foreigners were active in radical political movements; they did occasionally riot and strike; and they often did look askance at the moral reformers who wanted to take away their beer, wine, and whiskey.

But the ethnic factor was of little consequence among the Lynn shoemakers. The bulk of the cordwainers were born in America; a large portion were born in the town. In 1832 and 1841 more than half its shoemakers were born in Lynn: 56 percent in 1832 and 54 percent in 1841. (See Table 2.) This figure declined to 38 percent in 1851 and to 27 percent in 1860, demonstrating that in two decades of rapid growth large numbers of young men from outside the town were moving in to take jobs in the shoe industry. By 1851, less than half the shoemakers in Lynn were natives; by 1860, nearly three-fourths of the shoemakers came from other areas. It should also be noted that a large portion of the outsiders came as young men and married in the town: 68 percent of the 1832 group married in Lynn, 57 percent of the 1841 group, and 37 percent of the 1851 sample. It appears though that the trend was toward an influx of either older men who had married before coming to Lynn or men who remained single.

Foreigners only began to make their appearance in Lynn before 1860. In comparison with other towns in eastern Massachusetts, especially those engaged in textile manufacturing, the percentage of Irish was low. In 1850, there were 1,497 foreigners in Lynn, 1,073 of whom were Irish. By 1860, there were 3,047, most of them born in Ireland (2,284). If one compares the figures for Lynn with those for the textile-making town of Lawrence, one finds that in 1850 10.5 percent of Lynn's population was foreign born, compared with 30 percent of the population of Lawrence. By 1860, the number of foreigners had increased to 16 percent in Lynn and 41.9 percent in Lawrence.[18]

The first Irish immigrants came to Lynn as railway construction laborers in 1836, and most appeared to have remained laborers during the next twenty-five years. The place of the Irish in the occupational structure of the town is especially evident if one examines how the structure changed. (See Table 5.) The number of laborers grew from 26 in 1841 to 182 in 1851 and to 321 in 1860. The Irish were also strongly represented in the morocco-leather industry. The number of morocco dressers increased from 24 in 1841 to 125 in 1851 and to 225 by 1860. Yet some Irish did make their way into the shoe industry. By 1860, approximately 12 percent of the shoemakers were Irish.

If the shoemakers from outside Lynn were not foreign born, where did they come from? Although the data for the period before 1850 is fragmentary, there are traces of relevant information in the marriage records. It appears that most were from the surrounding towns of eastern Massachusetts—Salem, Marblehead, Reading, Danvers—as well as from New Hampshire and Maine. The population balance between Lynn and the seacoast towns became reversed in the nineteenth century. The movement of population was no longer from Lynn to Salem and other port cities, but rather from the declining ports to rapidly growing manufacturing towns like Lynn. A second important source of new population was the declining farming area of upper New England that sent part of its migrant population westward and an equally important segment south to the industrial towns of Massachusetts. In 1850, for instance, 75 percent of the people in Lynn were born in Massachusetts, 15 percent were born in other states, and 10 percent were foreign born. Most of the newcomers from states other than Massachusetts were from New Hampshire (844) and Maine (792). Young women from outside Lynn bore most of the children born in Lynn. In 1853, there were 542 births: 137 to mothers born in Lynn, 137 to mothers born in Ireland, and 245 to mothers born in other towns of the United States, mainly New England towns.[19] That a large portion of the migration out of upper New England should go to Lynn is not surprising in light of the organization of the shoe industry. Under the putting out system large quantities of shoe stock went into the countryside to outworkers who made shoes for Lynn employers. It appears that new settlers in Lynn were acquainted with the town through their earlier contacts with the shoe bosses. A young man who was eager to leave New Hampshire would often emigrate to Lynn and resume work for his old employer. The channels of trade between Lynn and the hinterland to the east and north were the same avenues along with young men traveled in their migration from the country to the city.[20]

Thus the pattern of geographical mobility among the Lynn shoemakers is largely different from those of other groups. The rate of transiency and labor turnover in the period 1830 to 1860 was low but, nevertheless, on the rise. For the most part, the shoemakers were settled, long-term residents of the community and not seasonal laborers. Although the number of foreigners was small, their prominence in the town's population became more marked. More important, however, than the Europeans were immigrants from neighboring towns of eastern Massachusetts and from the countryside of upper New England.

An inquiry into the subject of occupational mobility brings one to perhaps the most potent and frequently used explanation for social behavior. It is difficult to overestimate the importance of variations on this theme for labor history. It offers the view that upward mobility has enabled the United States to escape the serious and prolonged social conflict along class lines that has plagued other nations. Despite gross exceptions to the promise of unlimited opportunities, the actual fulfillment of that promise is presented as the principal reason for the absence of a definable working class, of a radical labor movement, and of any serious challenge to capitalism.[21] From Tocqueville to Louis Hartz, interpreters of our past have stressed the importance of personal liberty, equality of opportunity, and material abundance as distinctive features of the American experience and the secret to social harmony.

Occupational mobility is in good part dependent on the number of opportunities available to those who compete for them. Table 3 gives a statistical resume of the growth of the shoe industry in Massachusetts, in Essex County, and in Lynn, the principal center in the state for the manufacture of ladies' boots and shoes. Unlike Newburyport, Lynn showed steady and, at times, dramatic growth in population. Table 4 gives an overview of that growth from 1790 to 1870. As mentioned in an earlier chapter, Lynn grew slowly in the eighteenth century, making little progress since its founding in the late 1620s. The first great spurt in population growth came in the decade of 1800 to 1810, despite the trade embargo that Congress passed in 1807. The 44 percent increase in population came "after it had become decidedly a shoemaking town." The decade of most rapid growth was 1845 to 1855, when the town's population nearly doubled from 9,367 to 15,800.[22] With no other industry of any great consequence, it seems evident that Lynn's growth was due to the expansion of the shoe industry. The two went hand in hand. This can be seen in the employment figures for the

Table 3.  Boot and Shoe Industry—Production and Employment

| | 1837 | 1845 | 1850 | 1855 | 1860 | 1865 |
|---|---|---|---|---|---|---|
| *Massachusetts* | | | | | | |
| Boots | 1,672,808 | 3,768,160 | | 11,892,329 | | 7,249,921 |
| Shoes | 15,016,969 | 17,128,152 | | 33,174,499 | | 24,620,660 |
| Value | $14,642,520 | $14,799,140 | $24,102,316 | $37,501,723 | $46,230,529 | $52,915,243 |
| Males | 23,702 | 27,199 | 29,252 | 45,001 | 43,068 | 42,626 |
| Females | 15,366 | 18,678 | 22,310 | 32,826 | 19,215 | 12,534 |
| *Essex County* | | | | | | |
| Boots | 104,364 | 1,288,170 | | 4,893,519 | | 283,932 |
| Shoes | 7,861,612 | 8,380,769 | | 17,342,118 | | 12,419,985 |
| Value | $5,399,992 | $4,876,534 | | $12,190,936 | $14,540,606 | $18,011,197 |
| Males | 8,980 | 9,867 | | 15,104 | 17,191 | 13,519 |
| Females | 7,027 | 8,975 | | 19,595 | 8,542 | 7,845 |
| *Lynn* | | | | | | |
| Boots | 2,220 | 2,000 | | 3,274,893 | | 5,359,821 |
| Shoes | 2,543,929 | 2,404,722 | 4,561,400 | 6,000,700 | | |
| Value | $11,689,793 | $1,468,000 | $3,421,300 | $4,165,529 | | $8,817,711 |
| Males | 2,631 | 2,719 | 3,779 | 4,545 | | 6,984 |
| Females | 2,554 | 3,209 | 6,412 | 6,476 | | 4,984 |

period from 1845 to 1855. The number of shoemakers increased from 2,719 to 4,545, the binders from 3,209 to 6,476, in both instances the increase approximating the population growth of nearly 100 percent.[23]

Table 4. Lynn Population Growth

|      | Population | Percentage Growth | Amount of Increase |
|------|-----------|-------------------|--------------------|
| 1790 | 2,291     |                   |                    |
| 1800 | 2,837     | 24                | 546                |
| 1810 | 4,087     | 44                | 1250               |
| 1820 | 4,515     | 10                | 428                |
| 1830 | 6,138     | 36                | 1623               |
| 1840 | 9,367     | 53                | 3229               |
| 1850 | 14,257    | 52                | 4890               |
| 1860 | 19,083    | 34                | 4826               |
| 1870 | 23,233    | 48                | 9150               |

Table 5 provides an occupational breakdown of the adult male population and changes in the occupational structure from 1832 to 1860.[24] The importance of the shoe industry is revealed by the large portion of males directly involved in the business either as makers, cutters, or manufacturers. Only one step removed were the morocco dressers, who prepared leather for the shoe industry. Their numbers increased from 15 in 1832 to 125 in 1851 and to 225 a decade later. Sixty-four percent of the adult males gave their occupation as that of shoemaker in 1832. This figure declined to 47 percent in 1860. Thus in the period from 1832 to 1860, anywhere from one third to two thirds of the males employed in Lynn were shoemakers.

The changes in the occupational structure give a rough indication of the opportunities for upward mobility. The number of shoe manufacturers more than doubled between 1832 and 1842, increasing from 60 to 144. And this growth was continuous throughout the next two decades, rising to 152 in 1851 and to 191 in 1860.[25] More marked expansion of occupational opportunity is apparent in the increase in the number of shoe cutters, the skilled workers who cut the materials for the binders and shoemakers. The number of cutters grew from 79 in 1841 to 148 in 1851 and then doubled again by 1860, reaching 298. And for shoemakers who sought advancement in occupations outside the shoe industry, the opportunities seemed equally promising. The number of skilled craftsmen jumped from 63 in 1832 to 213 in 1841. In the same period, the number of carpenters went from 43 to

84, a 100 percent increase. Lynn was a rapidly growing town with an economy based on an industry that showed evidence of continuous expansion. Furthermore, there was an increase in entrepreneurial opportunities for new shopkeepers, shoe manufacturers, and merchants as well as for entrants into the skilled trades. For the shoemaker who was dissatisfied with his lot and desired to try his hand in a line of work that promised higher status and greater remuneration, Lynn seemed to offer attractive opportunities.

Table 5. Occupational Structure of Lynn

|  | 1832 | 1841 | 1851 | 1860 |
|---|---|---|---|---|
| Carpenters | 43 | 84 | 141 | 146 |
| (masters included) | | | | |
| Clerks & managerial | 7 | 27 | 72 | 223 |
| Craftsmen | 63 | 213 | 243 | 290 |
| Farmers | 56 | 83 | 69 | 76 |
| Fishermen | 58 | 93 | 40 | 28 |
| Laborers | 22 | 26 | 182 | 321 |
| Mariners | 6 | 18 | 35 | 39 |
| Merchants | (see shopkeepers) | | 105 | 127 |
| Morocco dressers | 15 | 24 | 125 | 225 |
| Professionals | 28 | 52 | 85 | 126 |
| Service | | | 35 | 54 |
| Shopkeepers | 100 | 184 | 277 | 355 |
| | (includes merchants) | | | |
| Teamsters | 9 | 20 | 61 | 103 |
| Traders | | | 41 | 44 |
| Shoemakers | 840 | 954 | 1,200 | 1,790 |
| | (64%) | (46%) | (39%) | (40%) |
| Shoecutters | | 79 | 148 | 298 |
| Shoe manufacturers | 60 | 144 | 152 | 191 |
| Gentlemen | | | | |
| Textile | 12 | 23 | 32 | 27 |
| *Total | 1,320 | 2,071 | 3,090 | 4,463 |

*Some listed as "no occupation" or "gentleman."

But Table 6 showed that the great majority of the Lynn shoemakers who remained in Lynn remained shoemakers. Of an original sample of 100 shoemakers taken in 1832, occupational data on 73 of the 100 is available for 1841. Of the 73, 59 were shoemakers, while 7 were shoe cutters and another 7 were listed in such positions as teamster, farmer, laborer, painter, and fishmonger. Ten years later, in 1851, there is oc-

## Table 6. Occupational Mobility Among Shoemakers

### A. *Shoemakers of 1832:*

|  | 1832 | 1841 | 1851 | 1860 |
|---|---|---|---|---|
| Shoemakers | 100 | 59 (81%) | 42 (68%) | 30 (63%) |
| Shoecutters |  | 7 (10%) | 6 (10%) | 7 (15%) |
| Shoe manufacturers |  | 0 | 3 (5%) | 2 (4%) |
| Died |  | 6 | 8 (+6) | 5 (+14) |
| Not listed |  | 21 | 24 | 33 |
| Other |  | *7 (10%) | †11 (18%) | ††9 (19%) |

| *teamster | †2 teamsters | ††trader |
|---|---|---|
| laborer | 2 farmers | laborer |
| fishmonger | painter | salesman |
| farmer | cabinet maker | stonemason |
| painter | stonemason | gluemaker |
| 2 no occupation | fisherman | shopkeeper |
|  | clerk | painter |
|  | sole dealer | eating house owner |
|  | no occupation | no occupation |

### B. *Shoemakers of 1841:*

|  | 1841 | 1851 | 1860 |
|---|---|---|---|
| Shoemakers | 100 | 48 (74%) | 32 (63%) |
| Shoe cutters |  | 2 (3%) | 7 (14%) |
| Shoe manufacturers |  | 2 (3%) | 0 |
| Died |  | 11 | 2 (+ 11) |
| Not listed |  | 24 | 36 |
| Other |  | *13 (20%) | †12 (24%) |

| *2 farmers | †2 fishermen |
|---|---|
| 2 shopkeepers | 2 shopkeepers |
| carpenter | silk dyer |
| laborer | ice dealer |
| fisherman | yeoman |
| yeoman | fishdealer |
| mariner | 2 retired |
| peddler | teamster |
| silk dyer | farmer |
| teamster |  |
| nursery |  |

*C. Shoemakers of 1851:*

|                     | 1851      | 1860      |
|---------------------|-----------|-----------|
| Shoemakers          | 100       | 53 (77%)  |
| Shoe cutters        |           | 6 (9%)    |
| Shoe manufacturers  |           | 1 (1%)    |
| Died                |           | 1         |
| Not listed          |           | 30        |
| Other*              | 9 (13%)   |           |

| * 3 clerks          | laborer   |
|---------------------|-----------|
|   2 morocco dressers| mariner   |
|   ice dealer        | teamster  |

cupational data for 62 of the 100 shoemakers in the original sample: 42 were shoemakers, 6 were clickers, and 3 were manufacturers. Eleven others were employed in such jobs as teamster, sole dealer, stonemason, fisherman, and farmer. By 1860, nearly a generation later, 48 of the original sample were employed in Lynn: 30 were cordwainers, 7 were shoe cutters, 2 were manufacturers, and 9 others held a wide array of jobs from laborer and stonemason to salesman, glue maker, painter, and eating house owner.

A similar pattern of modest change in occupation is evident also in the experience of a sample of 100 shoemakers in 1841. Of the 65 who were employed in Lynn ten years later, 48 (74 percent) were shoemakers, while 2 were shoecutters, two were manufacturers, and 13 of the original 100 shoemakers had moved into occupations outside of the shoe industry. By 1860, 51 of the original sample were employed in Lynn, with 32 (63 percent) as shoemakers, 7 as cutters, and 12 in other occupations. A sample of 100 shoemakers from the city directory of 1851 also showed only modest change. In 1860, a decade later, 69 of the 100 were employed in Lynn, with 53 (77 percent) still laboring at the bench as cordwainers, 6 as shoecutters, one as a manufacturer, and 9 in other occupations.

In the absence of comparable figures for other groups of workingmen in other cities in the same period it is difficult to evaluate the extent of occupational mobility among the Lynn shoemakers. What is a significant degree of mobility and what is a negligible one? The cordwainers show a greater upward mobility than the unskilled laborers of Newburyport for whom Thernstrom found practically no evidence of mobility. But it is understandable that skilled workers should be more upwardly mobile than the unskilled. Yet it seems equally clear that there was a permanent wage earning class in Lynn before the Civil War. Despite the absence of machines and factories, the men who fashioned shoes with their own hands and their own tools generally remained shoemakers. In the first decade after the year for which a sample was taken, the figure for occupational continuity ranges from 75 percent to 85 percent. That is, seven or eight of every ten shoemakers in Lynn were still shoemakers a decade later. After the second decade, the range is from 63 percent to 68 percent. And for those shoemakers who did change occupations, it was more likely that they move into employment outside the shoe industry than that they were to become cutters or manufacturers. Thus as Lynn grew in population and its economy became more diversified, the shoemakers obtained a share of the new places. This was especially true in the service sector, where former shopkeepers appeared as teamsters and shopkeepers.

The process of mobility within the shoe industry can be approached from another direction. Table 7 provides the geographical and occupational backgrounds of the men who became shoe manufacturers in the years 1832 to 1860. The table also includes figures on the occupations of the fathers of the new men. Tradition has it that the typical manufacturer rose from the bench to the central shop. The data does not support this view. It is true that in 1841, for example, most of the new men had listed their occupation in 1832 as "shoemaker" but nearly two-thirds of them were the sons of manufacturers or merchants. The capital needed for a start in manufacturing under the putting out system was indeed small when compared with the funds needed for the purchase or rental of machinery twenty years later. But at a time when payment of one's poll tax required a 25 percent reduction in the cordwainer's weekly budget, the capital that came from one's personal savings was difficult to acquire. Clearly the advantage lay with the sons of the manufacturers and of men who were clickers: the first ordinarily possessed the capital, while both had first hand experience in the vital phases of the business that took place at the central shop—shoe design, preparation of stock, bookkeeping, and marketing. This hypothesis is borne out by the figures on the new men who became manufacturers in the period from 1841 to 1851. Nearly as many new men had been shoe cutters as shoemakers even though shoemakers outnumbered cutters eight to one. And the same is more markedly clear for the next decade: 37 of the new men had been shoemakers, while 57 gave their former occupation as cutter. The importance of one's father's occupation for gaining access to the rank of manufacturer is indicated in the data in Table 7. Of the 35 fathers whose sons became manufacturers in the period 1832 to 1841, 20 were manufacturers or merchants. In the next decade, there was only a slight reduction in the importance of birth. Occupational data on 44 fathers whose sons became manufacturers by 1851 indicates that 26 (59 percent) of the 44 were shoe manufacturers or merchants and only 6 (14 percent) were shoemakers. But a significant change appears in the figures for the next decade. The number of fathers who were shoemakers increased to 24 (36 percent) while the portion who were manufacturers dropped to 32 (48 percent). At the same time that there was a decline in the number of new manufacturers whose previous occupation had been shoemaker (down from 43 percent in 1851 to 31 percent in 1860), there was an increase in the number who had been cutters (up from 38 percent in 1851 to 47 percent in 1860). It thus appears that a position as a cutter at the central shop would compensate for the lack of parental backing from a manufacturer father. One should note, nonetheless, that a sizable portion of the new manufacturers were former cordwainers whose fathers had also been cordwainers. The highly decentralized shoe industry seemed to provide some opportunity for a few shoemakers to make a modest start as entrepreneurs. Like most manufacturers, of course, they failed in business, and the large number of manufacturers conceals the fact that a handful dominated the trade. When the total number of shoemakers is considered, ranging from 840 in 1832 to 1770 in 1851, with a turnover of approximately 20 percent each decade, it is evident that only a small minority could become manufacturers. If, in other words, 37 shoemakers became bosses in the decade from 1851 to 1860, 2000 did not.

Despite the absence of much upward social mobility, the Lynn shoemakers did apparently obtain a modest share of the wealth that accrued to Lynn as a result of the town's growth as a manufacturing center. Table 8 provides an outline of real property ownership in Lynn from 1832 to 1860.[26] At no time in the approximately thirty-year period did a majority of adult males own any real property. This variation in property ownership seems to be tied to the business cycle in the shoe industry. In 1832, for example, 61 percent of the ratable polls in Lynn were propertyless, but after five years of relative prosperity in the shoe industry this portion declined to 56 percent. During the depression that began in the spring of 1837 and lasted into the mid-forties, the gains of the preceding five years were eroded, leaving 61 percent of adult males without real property in 1842. But with the recovery of the shoe business in the mid-1840s, 5 percent of the polls were able to acquire real property. Thus by 1849, 44 percent held real property, while

Table 7. Occupational Mobility—Shoe Manufacturers

| | 1832–1841 | | 1841–1841 | | 1851–1860 | |
|---|---|---|---|---|---|---|
| Number of New men | 86 | | 103 | | 179 | |
| Born in Lynn | 44 (51%) | | 60 (58%) | | 78 (44%) | |
| Born or married in Lynn | 70 (81%) | | 82 (80%) | | 100 (56%) | |
| Average age | 32.3 | | 33 | | 34 | |
| How many listed in former directory | 36 (42%) | | 37 (36%) | | 121 (68%) | |
| Fathers listed in former directory | 35 (41%) | | 44 (43%) | | 67 (37%) | |
| Occupations: | New Men | Fathers | New Men | Fathers | New Men | Fathers |
| How many listed | 36 | 35 | 37 | 44 | 121 | 67 |
| Shoemakers | 32 (89%) | 11 (31%) | 16 (43%) | 6 (14%) | 37 (31%) | 24 (36%) |
| Shoe cutters | (shoe cutters not listed in 1832 directory) | | 14 (38%) | 1 (2%) | 57 (57%) | — |
| Shoe manufacturers or merchants | — | 20 (57%) | — | 26 (59%) | — | 32 (48%) |
| Other | 4 (11%) | 4 (11%) | 7 (19%) | 11 (25%) | 27 (22%) | 11 (16%) |

56 percent were propertyless. And in the next decade or so, an additional 3 percent acquired property, bringing to the highest point in nearly 30 years (47 percent) the portion of adult males with real property.

Table 8. Extent and Distribution of Real Property Holdings

| Year | 1832 | 1837 | 1842 | 1849 | 1860 |
|---|---|---|---|---|---|
| Population* | 7,200 | 9,323 | | 12,606 | 19,083 |
| Polls | 1,571 | 2,219 | 2,571 | 2,809 | 3,933 |
| | (25%) | (24%) | | (22%) | (21%) |
| Polls having no real property | 966 | 1,234 | 1,570 | 1,560 | 2,097 |
| | (61%) | (56%) | (61%) | (56%) | (53%) |
| Polls having real property valued at $1–$300 | | 227 | 217 | 230 | 194 |
| | | (23%) | (21.7%) | (18.4'%) | (10.6%) |
| $301–$400 | | 96 | 85 | 68 | 62 |
| | | (9.7%) | (8.5%) | (5.4%) | (3.4%) |
| $401–$600 | | 134 | 176 | 137 | 206 |
| | | (13.6%) | (17.6%) | (10.9%) | (10.7%) |
| $601–$800 | | 121 | 126 | 183 | 147 |
| | | (12.3%) | (12.6%) | (14.6%) | (8%) |
| $801–$1000 | | 89 | 96 | 112 | 156 |
| | | (9%) | (9.6%) | (9%) | (8.5%) |
| $1001–$1500 | | 116 | 110 | 151 | 296 |
| | | (11.8%) | (11%) | (12%) | (16.1%) |
| $1501–$2000 | | 68 | 48 | 116 | 236 |
| | | (7%) | (4.8%) | (9.3%) | (12.3%) |
| $2001+ | | 134 | 143 | 252 | 539 |
| | | (13.6%) | (14.3%) | (20.2%) | (29.4%) |
| Totals | | 985 | 1,001 | 1,249 | 1,836 |
| | | (44%) | (39%) | (44%) | (47%) |

*Population figures for 1832, 1837 and 1842 are estimates from contemporary sources. See Lynn Directory, 1832; Lynn Mirror, January 3, 1837; Lynn News, July 13, 1849.

Yet one should also note a slowdown in the rate at which the propertyless gained real property. In the five years from 1832 to 1837, for example, about 5 percent of those without property acquired either a house, land, or both. In the interim of depression the portion of propertyless rose to 61 percent, but in the seven years from 1842 to 1849 6 percent of the adult males acquired real property. Yet in the next eleven years there was a gain of only 3 percent in the ranks of the property holders. The acquisition of property, therefore, seems to have become more difficult than had been true ten or twenty years before. The slowdown may in turn be related to a reduction in the availability of small properties, which were ordinarily the first purchase of people moving into the ranks of property owners. As will be shown in the next chapter, the shoemakers readily conceded that some cordwainers acquired small homes of their own, but argued that they had to work too hard to do so.

Table 8 also indicates the changes that occurred in the distribution of real property. In each of the categories of persons owning property assessed at values from $1 to $1000 there was an almost uninterrupted decline, while in the categories from $1000 to $2000 and more, there was steady growth. In other words, not only did more adult males own real property, but the average property owner tended to hold real estate valued in excess of $1000. This was especially true in those sections of Lynn dominated by manufacturers and merchants rather than by shoemakers, and characterized by business establishments rather than by working-class residences.

Table 9 gives a breakdown of real-property ownership by ward for 1860. Ward 4 encompassed lower Broad Street (then Front Street), and included it in the homes and places of business of Lynn's most prominent manufacturers. Ward 4 was not only the most populous ward in the city, but had one of the largest portions of propertyless people (59 percent) as well as the largest portion of persons with property valued in excess of $2000 (45 percent). The cleavage between rich and poor was clearer in Ward four than in any other neighborhood in Lynn. There apparently was little real estate in Ward four that could be purchased for less than $1500. If one moved at all from nothing to something, it most likely entailed a leap over the categories of small parcels to ownership of property valued in excess of $2000.

In contrast to Ward four is Ward three, the traditional stronghold of Lynn shoemakers. Not only did more people own real property (51 percent in Ward three compared with 41 percent in Ward four), but the parcels of real estate were smaller in size and more equitably distributed. In each of the five categories up to $1000, Ward 3 had a portion of owners twice as large as Ward 4. But for the two highest categories of wealth holding, the ratio is reversed: Ward 4 had twice the portion of wealthy real estate owners with property valued in excess of $1500 and $2000.

Complete evidence for property ownership among the mass of shoemakers is lacking, but it is possible to advance tentative judgments based on fragmentary data. The inquiry into the extent of property

Table 9. Extent and Distribution of Real Property Holdings, by Ward, 1860

| | | | | | | | | |
|---|---|---|---|---|---|---|---|---|
| Population | 348 (2%) | 864 (5%) | 3500 (18%) | 4500 (24%) | 4224 (22%) | 4815 (25%) | 830 (4%) | 19083 |
| No. polls | 64 (18%) | 191 (22%) | 746 (21%) | 975 (22%) | 915 (20%) | 892 (19%) | 150 (18%) | 3933 (21%) |
| No property | 39 (61%) | 83 (43%) | 365 (49%) | 572 (59%) | 495 (54%) | 462 (52%) | 81 (54%) | 2097 (53%) |
| $1–$300 | 3 (12%) | 20 (19%) | 52 (14%) | 30 (7%) | 47 (11%) | 33 (8%) | 9 (13%) | 194 (11%) |
| $301–$400 | 0 | 8 (7%) | 20 (5%) | 7 (2%) | 8 (2%) | 13 (3%) | 6 (9%) | 62 (3%) |
| $401–$600 | 5 (20%) | 16 (15%) | 54 (14%) | 26 (6%) | 33 (8%) | 59 (14%) | 13 (19%) | 206 (11%) |
| $601–$800 | 1 (4%) | 14 (13%) | 36 (9%) | 22 (5%) | 26 (6%) | 37 (9%) | 11 (16%) | 147 (8%) |
| $801–$1000 | 6 (24%) | 15 (14%) | 40 (10%) | 20 (5%) | 31 (7%) | 42 (10%) | 2 (3%) | 156 (8%) |
| $1001–$1500 | 2 (8%) | 16 (15%) | 71 (19%) | 52 (12%) | 74 (18%) | 76 (18%) | 5 (7%) | 296 (16%) |
| $1501–$2000 | 3 (12%) | 5 (5%) | 32 (8%) | 64 (16%) | 69 (16%) | 56 (13%) | 7 (10%) | 236 (13%) |
| $2001+ | 5 (20%) | 14 (13%) | 76 (20%) | 182 (45%) | 132 (31%) | 114 (27%) | 16 (23%) | 539 (29%) |
| Totals | 25 (39%) | 108 (57%) | 381 (51%) | 403 (41%) | 420 (46%) | 430 (48%) | 69 (46%) | 1,836 (47%) |

holding among workers is tied to the notion that possession of property acts as a conservative influence on social behavior, discouraging the risk-taking inherent in any movement against the status quo. Stephan Thernstrom offered the view that the acquisition of land and small houses by unskilled laborers in Newburyport probably accounts for the absence of manifest discontent. The process of acquiring property lent support to the promise that hard work, thrift, and self-sacrifice would be rewarded by material improvement. Thus the system would function as its defenders maintained.

If this hypothesis is correct, expressions of social discontent should diminish as property ownership increases. Secondly, those workers most actively engaged in radical politics should be worse off economically than those who give tacit consent or remain passive. Table 10 suggests that property holding is a factor of questionable value in explaining the social behavior of the of the Lynn shoemakers. Without elaborating, suffice it to note at this point that the level of protest among the cordwainers mounted in extent and intensity from 1832 to 1860, culminating in the great shoemakers strike of February 1860, the very year in which property ownership was most widespread. Equally doubtful is the importance of property ownership in explaining involvement of shoemakers in the various organizations and activities that represented a heightened class consciousness. Of the 49 shoemakers involved in the Journeymen's Society of 1830 to 1834, 44 were listed in the tax records for 1837. Of these, 23 (52 percent) possessed real property, most of which ranged in value from $400 to $800. In the same year within Lynn as a whole, only 44 percent of the entire population owned real property. Although the officers and committeemen of the Society were better off materially than the vast majority of the other 800 shoemakers, their propertied status did not deter them from activities that signified a dissatisfaction with the status quo.

It is also questionable whether in the upsurge of activity between 1844 and 1845, property holding accounts for the involvement of the 112 men active in the Journeymen Cordwainers' Society. Of the 112 men, 89 (79 percent) were named in the tax lists for 1844: 21 (24 percent) owned real property, while the remaining 68 (76 percent) held nothing. These figures can be compared with a random sample of 100 shoemakers whose names were taken from the city directory of 1841. Of the 100, 79 percent were listed in the tax records of 1842: 28 (35 percent) owned real property and 51 (65 percent) were propertyless. Thus there is 11 percent more property ownership among the shoemakers in general than among the leaders. But the extent of property holding among both groups is less than in the adult male population of the entire town, suggesting a change away from the tendency of the respectable, propertied journeymen mechanics to occupy most of the leadership positions as they had in the 1830s.

Table 10. Real Property Ownership Among Shoemaker Leaders
and Sample of Shoemakers

| | | Leaders | Sample of Shoemakers | |
| | 1832−34 | 1844−45 | 1841 | 1860 |
|---|---|---|---|---|
| Number in Study | 49 | 112 | 100 | 84 |
| Listed in tax records | 44 (94%) | 89 (79%) | 79 (79%) | 60 (71%) |
| Real property | 23 (50%) | 21 (24%) | 28 (35%) | 27 (45%) |
| No real property | 21 (48%) | 68 (70%) | 51 (65%) | 33 (55%) |
| Unlisted and no real property | 24 (51%) | 91 (81%) | 72 (72%) | 57 (68%) |
| Distribution of real property | 23 | 21 | 28 | 27 |
| $1−300 | 3 (13%) | 3 (14%) | 11 (39%) | 3 (11%) |
| 301−400 | 0 | 8 (38%) | 2 (7%) | |
| 401−600 | 7 (30%) | 1 (5%) | 4 (14%) | 3 (11%) |
| 601−800 | 7 (30%) | 5 (24%) | 3 (11%) | 5 (19%) |
| 801−1000 | 2 (9%) | 3 (14%) | | 2 (10%) |
| 1001−1500 | 1 (4%) | 1 (5%) | 6 (21%) | 8 (30%) |
| 1501−2000 | 3 (13%) | | | 4 (15%) |
| 2000 or more | 0 | | 2 (7%) | 2 (7%) |

The figures for 1860 are no more helpful in establishing the impotance of property as a factor influencing the behavior of workingmen. Of the 84 men active in the strike of 1860, 60(71 percent) were listed in the tax records of the same year. Of the 60, 27 (45 percent) owned real property, while 33 (55 percent) did not. With the partial exception of the men most active in the movement of the 1840s, it does not appear that real property ownership influenced the behavior of the shoemakers one way or the other, at least not in any way that is discernible from the statistics alone. One must note that for no decade in the period from 1830 to 1860 does property ownership characterize any group of shoemakers, whether leaders or followers. Journeymen mechanics with property and without consistently joined together to provide leadership for organized movements that periodically appeared in Lynn in the thirty years before the Civil War. If one were compelled to evaluate the significance of real property as a force in determining one's view of the status quo it would be that the leadership of the shoemakers, with the partial exception of the movement in the 1840s, came disproportionately from the propertied mechanics rather than from the propertyless. Yet it is also possible that the acquisition of forms of property other than land and houses constituted an avenue of material improvement for the Lynn cordwainers.

Thernstrom found that unskilled laborers who remained in Newburyport were able to build small savings accounts in local banks. These personal savings were often the first step to property ownership. One might, therefore, expect to find among Lynn workers a similar pattern of accumulation through patient, systematic savings at a local bank. The men who founded the Lynn Institution of Savings in 1826 had adopted as one of their purposes the creation of a bank that would accept, protect and reward the small savings that accrued to workers as a result of moral self-disciplining. A similar concern motivated the philanthropist-businessmen who founded a savings bank in New York in the same period, and a careful examination of their records showed that workingmen and working women were, in fact, a considerable portion of the depositors.[27]

Table 11 provides figures on the number of new accounts opened each year at the Lynn Institution for Savings from 1826 to 1860.[28] The variation in the number of new accounts from year to year is another index of the cycle of prosperity and depression in the shoe industry. A high of 153 new accounts in 1835 marks the peak of prosperity in the boom of the 1830s. This figure was not equalled again until 1847. One can also discern the impact of the downturn of 1857 in the sharp decline in the number of new accounts.

The bank records suggest several observations on the identity of the depositors and their use of the savings bank. First, most of the depositors were women, a group difficult to identity by family and occupation because of the sexual bias of sources, which either do not list women at all or list them only by name of their husband. As wives and daughters they may have assumed the responsibility of saving for themselves and for the male head of the household or they may have been independently employed, depositing in the bank their own savings. Whatever the reason, females were the principal depositors in the Lynn savings bank. Of the first 100 depositors, for example, 74 were women. And of the 57 persons who opened new accounts in 1842, 40 were women. A second feature in the savings patterns of the depositors, whether male or female, was that they were not systematic, habitual savers who customarily took a dollar or two to the bank each Wednesday afternoon. The typical depositor placed about forty dollars in the bank, made additional deposits on an average of less than once

Table 11. New Accounts Opened at the
Lynn Institution for Savings, 1826–1860

| 1826 | 1–57 | 57 |
|------|------|-----|
| 1827 | 58–112 | 54 |
| 1828 | 113–154 | 41 |
| 1829 | 155–179 | 24 |
| 1830 | 180–225 | 45 |
| 1831 | 226–293 | 67 |
| 1832 | 294–389 | 95 |
| 1833 | 390–470 | 80 |
| 1834 | 471–536 | 65 |
| 1835 | 537–690 | 153 |
| 1836 | 691–778 | 87 |
| 1837 | 779–821 | 42 |
| 1838 | 822–869 | 47 |
| 1839 | 870–940 | 70 |
| 1840 | 941–985 | 44 |
| 1841 | 986–1060 | 74 |
| 1842 | 1061–118 | 57 |
| 1843 | 1119–1193 | 74 |
| 1844 | 1194–321 | 127 |
| 1845 | 1322–1429 | 107 |
| 1846 | 1430–1535 | 105 |
| 1847 | 1536–696 | 160 |
| 1848 | 1697–1836 | 139 |
| 1849 | 1837–1994 | 157 |
| 1850 | 1995–2219 | 224 |
| 1851 | 2220–2494 | 274 |
| 1852 | 2495–2852 | 357 |
| 1853 | 2853–3316 | 463 |
| 1854 | 3317–3703 | 386 |
| 1855 | 3704–4083 | 379 |
| 1856 | 4084–4454 | 370 |
| 1857 | 4455–4793 | 338 |
| 1858 | 4794–5192 | 398 |
| 1859 | 5193–5632 | 439 |
| 1860 | 5633–6000 | 367+ |

each two years, and closed the account after five years. Depositors perhaps used the bank for the security it provided. Savings patterns among the Irish were slightly different. Among Irish depositors, also mainly women, the initial deposit for new accounts in 1849 was sixty-one dollars. The accounts were open as long as the non-Irish accounts, but depositors made more additions, an average of one per year. The infrequency of deposits by both Irish and non-Irish depositors was probably due to the lack of regular wage payments. When the wage earner settled accounts with his employer for four or six months' labor, he or she placed the sum in the bank for safe keeping. The systematic, habitual saving of small sums probably does not occur until the appearance of equally regular wage payments. Thus, one does not find much evidence in Lynn before the Civil War of the disciplined, patient saving of a few dollars per week by workers preparing for entry into the ranks of the propertied.

The statistical summary of Lynn and the shoemakers warrants a few concluding remarks. First, the cordwainers tended to be settled, long-term residents in the community and not transient workmen who left after a short stay. Yet there nonetheless was a growing tendency toward a large turnover in the workforce, a trend that foreshadowed the accelerated geographical mobility that became more apparent in the post-Civil War period. The same trend was evident in the nativity of the shoemakers. Although a majority in 1832 and 1841 were born in the town, there was a steady increase in the portion of shoemakers who were outsiders. By 1860, about 75 percent of the cordwainers had been born outside the town. Although outsiders constituted a large and growing portion of the working population, they were not foreigners. The number of Irish steadily increased in the two decades before 1860, but most newcomers to Lynn were born in America and from eastern Massachusetts, especially the declining port cities, as as well as from the countryside of upper New England, particularly the areas to which Lynn bosses sent stock.

The great majority of shoemakers who remained in Lynn remained shoemakers, yet there was modest occupational mobility. With each decade, a portion of the shoemakers moved into other occupations: a few as cutters and manufacturers, most in occupations outside the shoe industry. This occupational mobility seems tied to Lynn's continuous growth as a manufacturing town, changes in the shoe industry, and the expansion of employment in the construction and service sections of the economy. Although at no time in the three decades from 1830 to 1860 did most shoemakers own real property, a significant minority, probably about one third, did own a plot of land and a small home. But whether a shoemaker owned real property or not, this single factor does not account for behavior that signified either an acceptance or rejection of the status quo. The groups of men most active in the workingmen's movement in Lynn cannot be identified, or their behavior explained, by the amount of property they possessed. Personal property in the form of small savings accounts seems to have been of little importance, depositors typically placing small sums in the bank, making additional deposits on an average of less than one per year, and closing the account in five years.

Theories of social behavior based on mobility may be adequate explanations for the response of workers in other communities to the experience of social change, but they are of limited value in the case of the Lynn shoemakers. The data presented here either sharply contradicts the evidence for other groups, and thus calls for an alternative mobility thesis, or suggests the necessity for a different approach. The changes in areas of society that cannot be adequately gauged by statistics and yet which were crucial to the experience of the cordwainers indicate that a different approach is warranted.

# 9. The Formation of Class Consciousness: Experience and Ideology

Lynn's history from the Revolution to the eve of the Civil War shows many notable features of change. From an obscure and stagnant agricultural village, far overshadowed in nearly every respect by its more prosperous neighbors along the coast, Lynn emerged as a vibrant manufacturing center. Stagnation gave way to rapid growth, with population doubling every twenty years or less, a rate of growth that exceeded most communities in the state. Swampy lowlands were filled and cow pastures were criss-crossed by scores of new streets dotted with homes and shops. Transportation vastly improved with the construction first of turnpikes and then of railroads. New markets for Lynn shoes in the South and the West stimulated enormous increases in production, raising total output from 800,000 in 1810 to 2,541,929 in 1836 to 9,275,593 in 1855. Expansion of production brought evidence of prosperity: property ownership became more widespread than a half century before, and there appeared scores of shopkeepers and merchants to cater to the tastes of more people with more money to spend. At the same time, the moral reform movement that accompanied economic change seemed to make Lynn and its people more disciplined, more orderly, and, some would say, more enlightened and civilized. An elderly Lynn citizen looking back on a half century of change must have been impressed; the town's achievements had indeed been great.

Yet beneath the surface of material wealth, the facade of new streets, stately homes, and the multitude of shops and stores, there were other forces at work. In the same half century or so significant changes took place within the social structure of Lynn and in the patterns of social relationships. The journeymen cordwainers, whose praises the town's spokesmen so often sung in verse and song whenever they paused to explain the town's good fortunes, increasingly showed signs of restiveness. And restiveness gave way to an agitation that grew steadily in the

164

years between 1830 and 1860. At first weak and amorphous in the 1830s, more clear, articulated and sustained in the 1840s, and aggressive and assertive in the 1850s, the movement finally culminated in the great shoemakers' strike of 1860. The conflict that flared in the spring of 1860 may have shocked many citizens who nostalgically recalled the harmony of an earlier era, but the antagonism had been building for years. The editor of the *Lynn News* reacted with stunned anger in 1860 when shoemakers refused to allow him to enter their meeting.[1] He could not understand what had happened. The reason, if one can be briefly stated, was a sense of class. The shoemakers had come to feel, as a result of a shared experience as wage earners, more in common with one another than with any other group. The great divide in society was between workingmen and their supporters on the one hand and employers and their allies on the other. Thus, along with Lynn's rise as a prosperous manufacturing center went the formation of class and class consciousness among the Lynn shoemakers.

Class is used here to mean a relationship that evolved among the Lynn shoemakers as a result of a common experience that was largely determined by their position as wage earners. "And class happens," according to the historian Edward Thompson, "when some men . . . feel and articulate the identity of their interests as between themselves, and as against other men whose interests are different from (and usually opposed to) theirs." Furthermore, "the class experience is largely determined by the productive relations into which men are born—or enter involuntarily."[2] Class consciousness is used here to mean the way in which the class experience is expressed in ideas, traditions, folklore, and institutions. The form of expression that a particular people use derives chiefly from the culture that they bring to the class experience.

The emergence of class consciousness was a process, a tendency, and not something that simply happened at a particular point in time. There was no dawning of a revelation among the shoemakers, no immediate severing of old ties with their employers, no sudden repudiation of solidarity between master and journeymen, and no dissolution of deference to their employers. For some shoemakers the old ties remained nearly as strong as they had been a generation before. To them the employers were virtuous men whose status and power attested to their thrift, skill, and hard work and not to exploitation. Yet over a thirty year period this point of view was clearly in decline as were the way of life and patterns of social relations it expressed.

The major cause of the cleavage, which progressively deepened between the journeymen and their employers, was an alteration in their productive relationship. The stimulus to this change was external in origin: an extension of markets that increased the demand for shoes and thus provoked new methods of organizing production. The outstanding feature of the new phase of production in the shoe industry was the physical separation of journeymen from employer at the work place.[3] The master who either sold directly to the consumer or produced for the market, was replaced by the shoe manufacturer. Despite their similarities as employers of labor, there was one fundamental difference, the one that mattered most to the journeymen: the employer no longer took part in the productive process. Whatever other functions the master had performed (purchasing the materials and selling the finished product) he did work alongside the journeymen who regarded him as a mechanic like themselves.

Under the putting out system a new phase in capitalist development was reached. In its most refined form, the system functioned under the direction of the shoe manufacturer who may or may not have been a former shoemaker. The manufacturer directed operations from the central shop, typically a one or two story wooden frame structure where the raw material was cut up and put out in parcels to the binders and shoe makers. Here too the manufacturer inspected the finished product, supervised packing, and sold the shoes to regional wholesalers, who visited the central shop to place orders. There were deviations from this model, depending on the size of the firm. The larger manufacturers withdrew entirely from the central shop and delegated supervisory work to a trusted assistant, while others withdrew from one phase yet retained a hand in another. William D. Thompson, for instance, conscientiously tended shop for his fellow Quaker Nathan Breed, while Breed attended to his many other affairs.[4] Christopher Robinson, on the other hand, personally inspected and packed most of the shoes at his central shop.[5] There were dozens of small employers whose operations were too limited to release them entirely from labor. Some, therefore, continued to make shoes or concentrated on cutting patterns from rolls of leather. But the trend for employers was definitely away from the place where the shoes were actually produced.

As the manufacturers withdrew to the central shop, the shoemakers were left in the small shoe shops, which as mentioned before were commonly called ten-footers because they often were ten feet square. The ten-footers were physical remnants of an earlier phase of the business when both master and journeymen labored together under the same roof. But with the demise of the masters and their replacement by the manufacturers, the masters either became journeymen and remained in the shop to work in the customary manner or abandoned the ten-footer for the central shop. Journeymen often purchased or rented the small shops from the departed masters or cooperatively constructed their own ten-footers. In any case, the physical separation of worker from employer was nearly completed with the refinement of the putting out system presided over by the boss at the central shop. This separation was crucial for several reasons.

First, separation was the first step in destroying the dual role of the master as part worker and part employer. Secondly, separation meant the removal of the employer from a place that served as more than a shop for making shoes. The ten-footer was the center of the shoemaker's life. Here as a boy he gradually gained admission to the craft and to the social world of the journeymen, first performing menial tasks such as running errands, waxing threads, or stitching seams, finally taking his place as a full-fledged member of the craft. The sedentary manner of shoemaking, with the journeymen seated at the bench, encouraged frequent discussions of political and religious topics as well as the exchange of gossip. Peddlers, preachers, and politicians stopped occasionally to enliven the routine with a flow of chatter, while delivery-men brought the latest newspapers from Boston, leaving the jours with a full agenda of discussion topics for the day. If a shop's crew worked into the night during the winter, the shoemakers remained at the shop at quitting time and shared an evening meal before returning home. On weekends and holidays crews of journeymen went on fishing trips to George's Banks, dug clams at the Point of Pines or Lynn Beach, or walked to the peninsula of Nahant for a picnic. On Saturday the men returned their finished shoes, fetched the week's supply of groceries, and spent the afternoon sharpening their tools. In short, the ten-footer was the center of shared experience, a source of group loyalty, and a place for the formation of opinions and a sense of identity.[6] But with the withdrawal of the employer from the ten-footer, what had once been the cultural inheritance of both became limited to the journeymen. Employer and worker no longer shared at the place of work the common experiences that often reduced antagonisms and mitigated differences. The distinctiveness of boss and worker that derived from an experience unique to each became built into the very structure of the shoe industry.

It should not be thought that the physical separation of employer and journeymen immediately produced open antagonism between the two and the reorganization of social relations along the lines of the cleavage within the shoe industry. Far from it. There were several conditions that temporarily compensated for a division between the owner of the means of production and the workers he employed.

One condition that served to perpetuate a sense of unity between manufacturer and journeymen was the highly decentralized nature of the shoe industry. In the absence of machinery, a small amount of capital and perhaps some skill in shoe design or cutting enabled a large number of persons to start in a small way as entrepreneurs. Easy admission to the rank of manufacturer is evident in the large number of manufacturers in Lynn throughout the first half of the nineteenth century. In 1829, there were 66 manufacturers, in 1841, 110, in 1851, 145, and in 1860, 179. The directory of 1832 designated as manufacturer anyone who worked his own stock. Although the author undoubtedly relied too heavily on the former role of the master in choosing his definition, there were manufacturers who continued to take part in production. The margin of profit was too meager to enable a man employing several journeymen to do nothing. If a boss did not actually make the shoe he probably did perform the cutting. The continued presence in the Lynn shoe industry of small employers who resembled the former master undoubtedly delayed the evolution of class consciousness among the journeymen.

But in addition to the separation of journeymen from employer at the work place, there was a steady increase in the power and influence of the larger manufacturers. Their rise to power was the catalyst that precipitated an agitation among the shoemakers that grew in extent and intensity in each decade between 1830 and 1860. The shoemakers began using the pejorative term "grinders" in the 1840s to describe such large employers as Isaiah and Nathan Breed, Joseph W. Saunderson, Micajah Pratt, and Daniel Farrington.[7] They numbered less than a dozen. They were mostly Quakers from Pudding Hill. They resided in imposing homes on the hill and kept shop along "Grinders' Row" at the foot of Broad Street in a depression, which the shoemakers called "Extortion Hollow." Pious in a way that evoked ridicule, they were stern, shrewd, and self-righteous, the pioneers in the shoe business, former bag bosses grown big. The sons of small merchants and landowners, they were well equipped by training and endowment to seize the opportunities that an expanded market for shoes undeniably provided. They also profited from their far-flung contacts with Quaker businessmen well-placed in trading communities along the Atlantic seaboard. If there was a pattern in the dissemination of entrepreneurial methods in the Lynn shoe industry, it would be from the Quaker bosses to their small competitors.

From hindsight it appeared that the Quakers were merely the first in Lynn to discover the surest way to success in the shoe business. But at the same time they played a crucial role in the formation of class consciousness among the journeymen. It was the grinders who were the harbingers of the new emerging order that first evoked from the shoemakers apprehension and then resistance.

First, the Quaker bosses created the immediate issues that inspired the wrath of the shoemakers, and as their power increased so too did the extent and intensity of the opposition from the shoemakers. Secondly, the Quakers, by virtue of their success, compelled other manufacturers to copy their methods in order to survive in the highly competitive business. And lastly, the Quakers foreshadowed for the shoemakers a definite though incomplete image of the capitalist employers, who, if past and present anticipated the future, would dominate the shoe industry. In other words, the grinders represented the new, while the small bag bosses, who resembled the old master mechanic, stood for a dying system.

In their critique of their employers, that is, in the grievances they expressed, and the alternatives they offered, the journeymen of Lynn provide an insight into the sources of popular discontent among workingmen in the pre-Civil War period. They also suggest some of the sources of an indigenous American working-class radicalism. They were especially incisive in describing what was happening to them and in identifying the conditions and practices that they found most objectionable. And in so doing they reveal their own identity and the values that they felt were in greatest danger of destruction.

The shoemakers complained long and bitterly against the various forms of exploitation the bosses used in augmenting their profits. One of the most objectionable was the order system of wage payments, which the larger bosses were the first to use on a large scale. Under this system the employer made it a condition of employment that workingmen take their wages in the form of orders drawn on a store that a combination of bosses jointly owned. The Union Store, Lynn's first combination store, opened in 1829 under the ownership of Isaiah and Nathan Breed, James Pratt, and later, Micajah C. Pratt. Another combination store, the Mechanics', followed a year later, signaling adoption of a practice that lasted for nearly twenty years.[8] There were several reasons why the manufacturers introduced the order system.

One was the chronic shortage of specie and paper money. Another was the desire of the larger manufacturers to rid themselves of the need for stocking groceries and dry goods in the central shop. Instead of paying the shoemaker in flour, cloth, coffee, and other items, the larger boss merely issued the worker an order that he could exchange for goods at the boss's combination store. The system might not have been objectionable if the bosses had paid the shoemakers in orders whose purchasing power was equal to the same amount in cash. But instead, the bosses compelled the shoemaker to accept orders that the combination stores discounted at anywhere from 25 to 33 percent.[9] A shoemaker, for example, who turned in an order of $10 from Micajah Pratt might receive $6 or $7 worth of goods, often of inferior quality. The smaller bosses, who were unable to establish their own stores, either rented the services of the Union and Mechanics' stores or issued orders drawn on local retail establishments. The shopkeepers in turn gave the bosses kickbacks of 8 to 10 percent of their trade with shoemakers bearing the orders.

The system was almost universally unpopular, particular when shoemakers violated the law by paying their debts in orders. Thus, the clergyman, doctor, or tradesman also received a taste of the practice. The *Lynn News*, a Whig paper, denounced the system as a "system of swindling; a curse to the working people and a shame to the capitalists," issuing this condemnation only after the system was in decline.[10] But the harshest words came from the shoemakers themselves. It is a way of "cheating them out of half or two-thirds of their earnings," "a means to oppress us, and to eat our substance."[11] A shoemaker had to pay $.50 or $1, a worker reported, to obtain the $20 in earnings that were rightfully his.[12] Another shoemaker, in a poem entitled "The Grinder's Lament," drew on his personal experience in portraying the bosses:

> The bosses here have many forms
> By which to oppress their men;
> For they are beasts of many horns,
> And ever thus have been.

> For there's orders and trash,
> Low wages, no cash,
> And fraud of every hue;
> Oh, are they not a tyrant crew
> As ever a mortal knew?

> The bosses, too, are very sly,
> Deceivers from the first;
> They'll crush you down until you die,
> Then cry because you're crushed.[13]

The "frauds of many hue" included the practice of paying shoemakers in depreciated paper money, the detested "shin plasters," that were worth less than their face value and in the view of the shoemakers, were used for that very reason as wage payment.[14] Workers cashed the "shin plasters" at local "shaving mills" where they took a heavy discount. A shoemaker from Marblehead experienced another form of fraud. He worked for a Lynn "friend" (Quaker), made "good shoes" at $.125 a pair, and took his pay in salt pork at the inflated price of $.22 a pound.[15] Some women who bound shoes from an inventive employer took their wages in pickled mutton from a vat which the boss constructed beneath his central shop. One of the angered recipients vented her anger in a poem that ended with the boss being pickled in his own brine.

Sometimes fraud gave way to a tyranny that was equally offensive to the shoemakers. On one occasion a shoemaker who had attended a workingmen's convention in Boston returned to the central shop of his boss to obtain more stock. "He had no sooner entered his shop, than he was told by his Boss that he could have no more work. This was his destiny, without a why or wherefore." Another shoemaker who succeeded in obtaining higher wages from a new employer, found himself faced with eviction from his house if he did not return to his former employer and landlord and labor at the old rates. The journeymen also resented threatening inquiries into their political views and loyalties or their opinion on the money question.[16] A journeyman warned the bosses that "the insulted laborer will visit a terrible retribution on the head of those who dare thus call in question his right of free thought, and speech, and ballot."

Chronically low wages in the shoe industry fed the shoemaker's resentment and deepened his conviction that he was fast losing ground as a mechanic. His real wages declined between 1830 and 1860. In flush times rising prices ate up wage increases, while the depressions that frequently followed an over-expansion in production forced the shoemaker to spend most of the money he had managed to save. In addition, the stimulation of extended markets invariably set into motion the forces that increased competition in the labor market. Large numbers of young men migrated to Lynn to seek employment in the industry, while the bosses sent larger amounts of raw stock into the countryside to tap an immense supply of cheap labor.

Exploitation became intensified as the journeymen worked longer and harder to keep their real income at a stable level. Shoemakers saw themselves spending most of their waking hours, day in and day out, struggling for an existence and killing themselves in the process. In

1844 William Frazier, a Lynn shoemaker, described his condition in the following manner, "for where we have to sit on our seats from twelve to sixteen hours per day, to earn one dollar, it must be apparent to all, that we are in a sad condition."[17] And if anyone doubted the toll exacted by prolonged and constant labor, another cordwainer invited the skeptic "to visit the workshops of our town . . . and let them visit our grave yards, and read the tombstone inscriptions there."[18] In 1850 the Lynn Board of Health reported that the life expectancy of shoemakers was nearly twenty years less than the life expectancy of farmers in the Commonwealth.[19] As a group, the shoemakers were "compelled to work every day, and some of them from twelve to sixteen hours in each day that they may be enabled to discharge that highest of all other obligations they are under, the maintenance of their families." Another shoemaker expressed a similar view: many shoemakers were forced "to work throughout their lives, until exhausted nature and dimness of sight compels them to desist, and in many instances with nothing left to support life, as all they got for their labor has been given to the support of their families."[20]

Such an exacting regimen of labor was oppressive; the journeymen were losing their humanity. In their view, the uniqueness of humankind, the feature that distinguished human beings from animals, was his possession of higher faculties which work alone could never satisfy.[21] Although the sedentary work process permitted him some opportunity to exercise and satisfy the faculties of the mind, prolonged labor was debilitating. He needed time for recreation and pleasure, for reading and contemplation, and for the free expression of his needs outside and apart from work. Prolonged labor for twelve, fourteen, and sixteen hours a day exhausted his body and mind and made him unfit for any other exertion. He would merely spend the interim recovering his strength and preparing for another round of labor on the morrow. In the shoemaker's view, he was becoming a dullard and a brute, more like a beast of burden, a draft animal, than a human being. In addition, a preoccupation with labor made him little more than a laborer; he was losing both the will and the capability to carry out his responsibilities as a citizen in a republican society.

Workingmen also believed in what they called a "competency." In their view, a workingman when young, strong, and hearty should be able to earn enough for the maintenance of himself and his family, and a portion for savings. The small amounts, which he would regularly set aside during his working life, would constitute his "competency," a fund he could draw upon when too old and feeble to support himself

by labor. Without a competency he would become utterly dependent on
the employed young, hating himself for his dependence and being
hated by those who supported him. Even worse, he might become a
pauper. From 1830 to 1860, workingmen found that a competency was
becoming impossible. They were earning barely enough to subsist, with
nothing to set aside for "the evening of life"—"a portion of our time
which was never intended for a season of labor."[22] A shoemaker observed that "we find but a few individuals of fifty years of age, who
have arrived at a competency; and these have obtained it only by a long
series of unparalleled exertions. And the prospect for the future is not
more flattering." To end one's years at the Alms House among paupers
and criminals was a fear that haunted many mechanics, a clear sign of
the utter degradation into which the respectable mechanic was sinking.

An equally important reason for the shoemaker's discontent with his
economic plight was the sharp contrast between his condition and his
employer's. The journeymen were becoming increasingly aware that
the bosses prospered, while they suffered. Low wages, a corrupt order
system, and prolonged labor harmed the journeymen and helped the
bosses. They frequently pointed an accusing finger at manufacturers
who were also landlords, describing them as "those who have grown fat
upon the earnings of the toil worn laborer; men who, after having retired with their thousands, which have been scraped together by the
suffering and privations of the poor, still are not satisfied, but stick,
leech-like, unto him, until the foundation of life is dried up, and the
green sod is closed over him."[23] By what strange alchemy did a system
produce paupers and princes except by the one profiting at the expense of the other? Shoemakers cast their eyes toward their employers
and, as they said, saw "the gaudy palaces in which they now reside . . .
erected upon the very ruins of those cordwainers who have been sent
to an untimely grave by this same system of grinders." They also saw
the opulent manufacturer "frequently give parties that cost $1,000 each,
and furnish his daughters with bridal dresses, at an expense of several
thousand each."[24] While the bosses enjoyed luxury and pleasure, they
saw themselves as having "the unspeakable privilege of being sent to
the poor house with the reputation of being a poor creature, who did
not know enough to take care of himself . . . to die among pauepers
and criminals." Wealth and poverty seemed to operate in a close causal
relationship, so close in fact that one shoemaker warned his fellow to
watch for a cut in wages if the boss purchased a new carriage to attend
the yearly meeting in Boston, an obvious reference to a Quaker boss.

The prolonged fatiguing labor that brought such meager returns to the shoemaker did provide handsome profits to the boss. Deprivation was not due to a natural calamity that befell all parties and caused equal suffering, but rather was partial and grossly unequal, the result of deliberate, calculated exploitation. The bosses purposefully designed ingenious methods for maximizing their profits at the expense of a decent income for the cordwainers.

One practice that proved more enduring than the order system and far more crucial in the history of Lynn and the deteriorating relationship between the journeymen and the manufacturers was the growing presence of outworkers in the labor market. As early as the 1830s, the Lynn bosses were employing people in surrounding towns to make shoes in competition with the Lynn shoemakers. In 1832, for example, there were in Marblehead 582 men employed in making shoes, either full time or part time. Of these, 150 worked for local bosses, while 432 worked for Lynn manufacturers.[25] In the next few decades this practice increased, became better organized, and covered a far larger area, until by 1855 the outworkers were making nearly three fifths of the shoes sold by Lynn bosses. The employers used the cheaper labor of the outworkers in the countryside to keep down the wages of the Lynn shoemakers. In the mid-1840s, for instance, as the business began to recover from the long depression that had begun in the 1830s, shoemakers anticipated increases in wages. But when they approached their employers and requested raises, the bosses refused, informing them that outworkers would make the same shoes for 10 cents a pair less. The Lynn shoemakers learned that bosses were using the same technique with the outworkers, informing them that they could obtain shoes at cheaper rates from the Lynn jours.[26] The problem of labor competition with a pool of workers in the countryside became increasingly acute in the 1850s, and was the principal cause of the great shoemakers' strike in the spring of 1860. The extent of support that the striking shoemakers managed to evoke from the community suggests their success in portraying the shoe manufacturers as selfish profit seekers who placed their own interests above the best interests of the community. But in the 1830s, the magnitude of the competitive threat was slight, barely felt by most shoemakers. By the 1840s Lynn shoemakers were citing the practice as an illustration of their employers' perfidy and avarice.

The journeymen also blamed the bosses for causing a deterioration in the quality of shoes. To augment production, they adopted the practice of hiring young men, training them to make a single type of cheap shoe, and paying them low wages. These novices became an additional source of competition for cordwainers, who thus lost a measure of control over the admission of new men to the craft. The bosses also cheapened the product in an effort to cut costs. In this respect, as in others, they showed extreme ingenuity in augmenting their own profits at the expense of the shoemakers. They required that cordwainers insert paper stiffenings into the shoes instead of real leather, giving the shoes a porosity that ruined them in a short time.[27] The low prices that the bosses paid also pressured the shoemakers to maximize their production at the expense of quality. They became contributors to the decline in craftsmanship by using fewer stitches per inch, using the cheaper but softer neats leathers in the upper part of the shoe, and generally sacrificing care for speed in their work. A decline in the quality of the product brought with it a decline in the reputation and status of the shoemakers. His status suffered because customers continued to hold the maker responsible for upholding the standards of the craft. "The bosses are the ones that should bear this burden," a shoemaker insisted, "but they have fathered it on us, and is this not oppression? when we are doomed to bear the scoffs and jeers of the public that ought to be fastened on the brazen faces of our oppressors." Too many people considered the Lynn cordwainer "to be the lowest class of mechanics that inhabit the globe." The cordwainer was as ashamed of a shoddy shoe as a hostess might be of soiled linen or dirty china at her banquet table. The shoemakers, therefore, blamed their employers for causing them to be held up "to scorn, ridicule, and contempt."[28]

If there is a key to comprehending the ideological basis for the shoemakers' response to capitalist development in the shoe industry, it is their belief in the labor theory of value. In this respect they were much like workingmen spokesmen elsewhere of whom one author has noted: "The solid rock on which their idea of the good society rested was their belief that labor created all wealth."[29] The journeymen were not the originators of this notion. It figured prominently in English agrarian radicalism, and for this reason led conservatives to denounce American radicals in this period as "agrarians." John Locke, in his *Second Treatise on Government*, based much of his theory of property ownership on the labor theory of value, though he practically negated the principle with his introduction of money into political economy. It was fundamental to the classical economists, particularly David Ricardo, and formed the core of Marxism and most socialist thought in the nineteenth century.[30] That thinkers of such diverse views as Locke and Marx should rely heavily on the same principle indicates both the pervasiveness of the idea and the extreme diversity of conclusions it permitted. The manner in which the journeymen used the labor theory of value as the underlying value in both their evaluation of their experience and the foundation for an alternative suggests stages in their ideological growth.

The labor theory of value took deep root in Lynn as the town turned to the manufacturing of shoes. It formed the cardinal tenet in the mechanic ideology of both journeymen and masters who formed the bulk of the town's population.[31] The validity of the labor theory of value seemed self-evident; value derived from the application of human labor to raw materials. The cordwainers with their simple tools transformed raw leather into fine shoes that extricated Lynn from economic stagnation and formed the foundation of material prosperity. Having arisen and taken root in a manufacturing town of skilled craftsmen, the idea was sharpened and clarified in the citizenry's consciousness during the course of their rivalry with other towns in an area whose economy was predominantly mercantile. The labor theory of value took on broader meaning as the rising manufacturing interests sought a definition of the good and just society.

Society should reflect the basic division between the producers and the nonproducers. The first included farmers, mechanics and workingmen, while the second was made up of aristocrats, merchants, middlemen of all types, lawyers, politicians, idlers, and vagrants. The right of the producers to social prominence and political power derived from their role in the production of goods that were essential to the maintenance of human life. Without food, clothing, and shelter nothing else was possible. All else was dispensable, for life would endure. The good society should acknowledge the essential role of the producers by rewarding them, if not with first rank, then at all times with respect. Most desirable would be the society governed by those who ranked highest in the particular craft or calling in which they plied their skill. It was assumed that skill, not wealth, was the prerequisite of status within the craft and that the preeminence of the masters was, therefore, justified both within the craft and in society as well.

But what of the relationship between the producers? The labor theory of value implied a prescription for harmony. The behavior of masters toward journeymen should at all times be decent and fair, deriving from their common membership in a craft whose practice, routine, and way of life gave them more in common with one another than with those outside the craft. If there was a single phrase that best captured the code of acceptable conduct, the system of rights and responsibilities, and the mechanics' notion of what ought to be, it is "the laborer is worthy of his hire." That a man labored for another and depended upon him for the right to apply his labor to something which the employer owned was no reason for inhumane treatment. He ought not to be cheated and robbed, intimidated or interrogated, humiliated, snubbed, or ridiculed merely because he labored. "The laborer is worthy of his hire": this is the standard the journeymen initially applied to their experience as wage earners through most of the nineteenth century.[32] Their expectation of decency and fair play rested on an estimation of their worthiness as craftsmen and producers. The disillusionment, anger, and sense of betrayal that underlies their criticism of the order system, the petty frauds and chicanery of the grinders, and the forced competition with "botches" and footloose apprentices is due to their growing awareness that for the bosses the laborer was no longer worthy of his hire. Yet if the phrase persisted well into the nineteenth century, it was because many workingmen continued to invoke it in a plaintive manner, requesting the manufacturers to remember their responsibilities.

In other words, there was not, in the opinion of many, an irreconcilable conflict between themselves and their employers but rather an estrangement that could be remedied through a reaffirmation of mutual dependence.[33] In 1829, for instance, there was an abortive effort by some manufacturers to establish an association for setting standards in the business.[34] The failure of the shoe manufacturers to seize initiative and take actions to preserve a semblance of order in the industry and harmony with their journeymen was one of the reasons the journeymen cited in the 1830s and again a decade later to justify their own efforts.[35] In the preamble to a statement that the Journeymen Cordwainers' Society issued in 1844, they noted that the bosses "have devised no plan of union or concert of action among themselves, whereby they might act justly towards us as citizens and seek honorable competition with each other." It was, therefore, incumbent upon the journeymen to assert "our just rights," for "then our employers will begin to see that it is time for them to be doing something towards elevating our condition."[36] The shoemakers were invoking the tradition of deference to reestablish their old rights and to remind the bosses of their obligations to regulate the trade.

But at the same time, the shoemakers' animosity toward the bosses deepened in the 1840s, prompting the conviction that they were so governed by greed and avarice as to be beyond redemption. Although the shoemakers invariably distinguished between good bosses—Christopher Robinson, Benjamin Spinney, James L. Alger, George

Keene, and others—and bad bosses—the Breed brothers, Micajah Pratt, Joseph N. Saunderson, Samuel Boyce, Nathan D. Chase—it became increasingly clear that the grinders possessed the power to set standards in the trade.[37] They were, in one man's estimation, "the very bloodsuckers of the shoemakers."[38] The grinders "seem to think that the jours were designed for no other purpose than to be their subjects; and if they assert their right, they will say that they are aspiring to a higher sphere than that to which they were born." A shoemaker labeled them "little stuck-up, self-conceited individuals, who have a little second-hand credit—that is they are backed up by somebody at the bank, and by that means are started in business, and soon they imagine themselves to be somebody of consequence—you must do as they wish you to do, or you are out of their books; they have no more employment for you."[39]

To a growing number of shoemakers, "so many of our manufacturers have become deaf to all noble appeals, and dead to all moral perceptions." They were, a shoemaker concluded, "men who are lost to every principle of justice and humanity—men professing great piety, with faces as long as any old horse in town—men who would sell their Saviour for less money than Judas did, for the sake of gain."[40] Another shoemaker warned that "if the devil stood grinning his approbation in their face while they were cutting down the wages of a poor journeyman, they would pull the broad brim over their eyes and continue his work."[41] Whereas "other men live by the sweat of their *brow* he lives by the sweat of his *soul*. What he lacks in labor he makes up in cunning. His deficiencies in virtue are atoned for by his acquirements in wealth."[42] One of the shoemakers who so characterized the grinders felt compelled to cite his sources: "This is no fancy sketch. It is not borrowed from a fruitful imagination. It is not the workmanship of an ingenious mind. It is not the diseased child of a morbid and misanthropic mind; but is drawn to the *life*. It answers to hundreds of *Lynn experiences*. Such manufacturers and such victims are known to you all."[43]

The waning of deference was due primarily to the actual experience of wage earners who labored for the manufacturers. Their experience prompted first the suspicion and then the conviction that the old relationship between worker and employer was dead or dying. The shoemaker had derived from the past an anticipation that his skill as a worker and his status as a man would gain the reward of respect. Instead he met exploitation. Ambition and avarice in his employer seemed more powerful determinants of behavior than any recognition of duty to his employees. The disillusionment that came from the experience of the cordwainer dawned in his consciousness and resulted in the repudiation of deference. Whereas he presumed that the manufacturer would be provident, considerate and fair, he experienced exploitation, petty fraud, and cunning. The transformation was neither sudden nor complete in a manner comparable with the conversion of the unbeliever. It was rather the slow outgrowth of a multitude of experiences which steadily touched the lives of a growing number of workingmen.

The delay in the journeymen's recognition that a change had occurred in their relationship to their employers was due to two factors. Many shoemakers instinctively transferred their old notions of deference to the manufacturer, despite the dissimilarity between the manufacturer and the old master. Secondly, the continued presence throughout the period from 1830 to 1860 of small bosses, "good bosses" as the shoemakers termed them, tended to justify the continuation of expectations derived from the past. These small manufacturers or bag bosses who employed a few workers, made a high quality shoe, paid higher wages, and often took part in the productive process themselves, closely resembled the old master mechanics to whom the journeymen felt an historic tie. But the bag bosses were in decline; they lost a larger and larger share of the trade to the grinders. As a result, the grinders, not the bag bosses, determined the experience of a growing number of shoemakers. In addition, smaller bosses intent upon surviving the competition of the larger manufacturers tended to imitate their methods, leading one writer to compare the contagion of competition to hydrophobia, which stimulated "one person to bite all under his influence, because himself has been bitten."[44] They too would accumulate a few thousand dollars by "grinding the faces of the poor, and defrauding the widow and fatherless." And to emulate the life style of the more opulent, they will "keep their families on bullock's liver and sawdust."[45] These trends strengthened the belief among shoemakers that the old ties were dissolving.

Only if the old relationship between master and journeymen is understood can one comprehend the shoemakers' response to their new position. They were fond of referring to themselves as mechanics, and in so doing they provide a clue to their identity. An historical analysis of the term "mechanic" would greatly illuminate the early history of American workingmen. Along with farmers and workingmen, the mechanics were a key group in that amorphous category of producers. Mechanics included skilled craftsmen and artisans such as carpenters, cordwainers, masons, and coopers. Membership in a particular craft, with its ritual of patron saints, holidays, unique customers, and special symbols gave master and journeyman a craft identity, while at the same time entitling all to the rank of mechanic. Perhaps because of America's birth in a period that witnessed the rise of the European bourgeoisie, the term was rich in favorable connotations of hard work, respectable wealth, audodidacticism, manliness, and dignity. Both master and journeyman alike laid claim to mechanic, and though they sometimes used the prefix master and journeyman for clarification, it seemed superfluous as long as harmony prevailed. For this reason it is hard to distinguish journeymen from master in the late eighteenth and early nineteenth centuries; in adherence to the labor theory of value, in politics and religion, as well as in life style, a sameness overshadowed what seemed insignificant: one worked for the other. American history is strewn with the remnants of institutions that attest to the mechanics' consciousness of a common identity and their rise as a group: mechanics institutes, militia units, newspapers, fire companies, banks, insurahce companies, and so on. And as shown in an earlier chapter, nowhere was this more true than in Lynn.

Yet if one examines these institutions more closely, it becomes clear that they were primarily the creations of entrepreneurs in the process of their emergence as manufacturers. Although many manufacturers were total strangers to the trade, having entered the business as merchants in anticipation of the profits to be had in buying and selling, others were former masters. Both persisted in retaining possession of the term mechanic, either because they still viewed themselves as mechanics and operated in the old manner or because they wished to preserve, if only in word, their old ties to the journeymen. But as the function of the manufacturer changed and he became more an employer of producers than a producer himself, the altered productive relationship caused a reinterpretation of the term mechanic.

The journeymen claimed the legacy of the mechanic and regarded themselves as the rightful heir, defending their claim against the manufacturers whenever they felt obliged to do so. This sentiment appears in 1845 in a journeyman's attack on the Mechanics Bank, Lynn's major lending institution, after it had fallen under the control of the town's largest shoe bosses. The author maintained that the original purpose in establishing the bank was to advance the business of this "then infant manufacturing village. Its very name the Mechanics Bank, indicates this." Instead it became a means by which a minority of manufacturers monopolized credit and discounts, set low wages, and enlarged the business operations of their own firms at the expense of both smaller manufacturers and journeymen. Their methods would "make even the engraved MECHANIC, if placed on the outward surface, blush with shame." "I solemnly protest," he concluded, "against your using in any form or shape hereafter, the Name or Emblem of the order, to which I belong."[46] Here was an outraged sense of betrayal that came from the realization that what was intended for the benefit of the many had become an instrument of oppression and a vehicle for the enrichment of a few.

The journeymen not only retained the word mechanic whenever they identified themselves; they also kept the traditional mechanic outlook with its Manichaean cast of heroes and villains. As they presented themselves as mechanics and producers they increasingly portrayed the manufacturers as aristocrats, the traditional foe against whom the mechanics had engaged in an epic struggle stretching back into the distant past. The larger manufacturers came to resemble the merchant aristocrats of the port cities—proud, arrogant, and parasitic, the same villainous element that was so prominent in the folklore of Lynn during its rise as a manufacturing center. The journeymen borrowed liberally from the past in building a case against the "purse proud aristocrats," casting themselves in the heroic garb of their forebears and relegating the bosses to the role of tyrants. In the process of using old ideas and values in a new context, they succeeded in fashioning a modified mechanic ideology that became the unique possession of wage earners.

The application of old ideas and values to new conditions prompted different and sometimes radical conclusions. An illustration of this process is the manner in which the Lynn journeymen applied the labor theory of value. In stressing their role as producers, the shoemakers used the labor theory of value in two ways. The first was as a plea for respect, a recognition from both employer and society at large of the workingmen's importance. According to this view, which is similar to the deferential outlook evident in the phrase "the laborer is worthy of his hire," the workingmen merely wanted a greater share of what they produced. An illustration of this view appears in the preamble to the constitution of the Mutual Benefit Society of the Journeymen Cordwainers of Lynn. "Believing labor to be the true basis on which happiness as well as riches, depends, and being ourselves dependent on labor, for both one and the other, we hold it to be our duty to sustain its value, that it may of itself be respectable, and the laborer be respected." It was further stated that one of the purposes of the organization was "to raise the standard of self-respect." The workingmen as a class were worthy of respect because they produced "something by which the world is made better."[47] And a writer in the *New England Operative*, in an article entitled "Labor is Wealth," stated emphatically that "labor, as the source of all value, is the only absolute value." Therefore, he continued, "let the laborer . . . receive the honor and influence of which he, and he only, is the source."[48] The author of a piece in the *Fall River Mechanic*, which the Lynn cordwainers journal also reprinted, sounded a similar appeal in 1844 when he asked "what class of men ought to be more respected than the mechanics and laboring portion of the community? Are they not the producers of all the real wealth?" In similar language a Lynn writer asserted that "labor is the creator of all wealth. It was ordained of God as a universal life condition. Yet, in civilized countries, only one third of our race are productively or usefully employed. Every laboring man is converted to a beast of burden, and compelled to carry two loafers through the world on his back."[49] Another Lynn citizen, in a letter addressed to a prominent shoe boss, asked "For who, I ask, is it, but the Mechanics and Laborers, who feed and clothe you; protect your property, till the soil, navigate the ocean, defend the country."[50] The frequency with which workingmen and others throughout America expressed this view, sometimes in language so similar as to suggest duplication, indicates widespread acceptance of the labor theory of value in the period before the Civil War.[51] Despite the indignant tone, the request was primarily for a more just share of what the workingmen felt was rightfully his. As one shoemaker put it:

> We are helping each other to get more good bread and meat (with the fixings) than we have usually had. We want plenty of good warm clothes, a plenty of nice, warm, clean beds, a plenty of coal and wood, to keep other people's houses warm, that we live in, a plenty of good books, and time to read them; and our children to be better educated. We do not like to work all the time; we want recreation, as well as them that don't work, who go, many of them, to Saratoga, and other watering places. In a word, we are trying to get our just share of this world's blessings.[52]

But a second conclusion was drawn from the labor theory of value, one that ran in a radical direction, prompting the formation of what became perhaps the core of working class radicalism. It is perhaps best summarized by the phrase: "The worker is entitled to the full fruit of his toil."[53] Whereas those holding the first view wanted more, those holding the second wanted all. Whereas the first maintained that the "laborer is worthy of his hire," the second wanted no hire at all, putting in its place producers' cooperatives owned and operated by the men who worked in them. Although there is a fundamental difference in the conclusions drawn from the labor theory of value, we should not see their respective adherents struggling for control of a workingmen's movement. The lines between the two were blurred, their differences muted or submerged in the immediate effort to build self-pride and create ongoing institutions capable of safe-guarding their common interests. In addition, one sometimes finds both views held simultaneously, the author unaware of the contradiction yet in his inconsistency attesting to the process of change and the transition from the old to the new. There is no hardened dogma or orthodoxy but a free flow of ideas, which reflected contradictions in the experience of the shoemaker: a mechanic yet a workingman, producer and wage earner, appeals to the conscience of men who sometimes showed no conscience, a plea for respect to men for whom labor was becoming a commodity.

An illustration of the process by which shoemakers evaluated their condition appears in a letter from a Lynn cordwainer. He noted first of the manufacturer that "he receives a large amount of wealth, while he renders but a *small* amount of labor; and as it is a generally received opinion, is it not clear, that the business man stands debtor to the world for all which he receives over and above the amount of labor given? And is it not equally clear that the mechanic, I mean particularly the mechanics of Lynn, receives *less* than a compensation for the amount of labor given? It appears, therefore, that the world stands debtor to the mechanic for this surplus labor."[54] Although the author recognized the source of the problem—the surplus labor—his solution was essentially a restatement of the popular view: a larger share of the surplus labor should go to the laborer or producer. Another shoemaker argued that the only share the worker received was a subsistence wage: workingmen were "robbed of all the fruit of their labor, except the beggarly pittance necessary to keep them in a condition to produce more for the men who first rob them of the wealth."[55] Others also saw the moral principle involved, and one can follow the direction of their analysis toward a different conclusion. "I think no man has a right," a shoemaker asserted, "to be satisfied with that which is wrong; and will any one deny that it is wrong for that part of the community who produce nothing to consume almost everything, and vice versa. Or will any one dispute that this is the case? Has not a man a right to that which he produces? And do not the laborers produce all the necessaries and luxuries of life, with the exception of those which nature furnishes us with?" When confronted with the ultimate question of what was due the nonproducer, he concluded: "Well, is not that just what St. Paul teaches when he says, that 'If any man will not work, neither shall he eat.' "[56] Another writer insisted that "every man is bound to do enough of productive work to support himself." Therefore the "countless herds of *pukes*, lawyers, priests, politicans, and capitalists, who feed on the labor of their neighbors, must be sent to get an honest living at work." At present, "they now eat all the laborer earns. They will pretty quick begin to eat him." If the writer had his way, the parasites would "go to work or go hungry, and dance to keep warm, for lack of clothes." He refused to grant that workingmen were rewarded in any way commensurate with their contribution. "Paid labor in civilization is a base lie. Labor is not paid. It is robbed."[57]

If there was a single condition that most provoked this response, it was the injustice of a system in which those who produced everything enjoyed little, while those who did little or nothing possessed everything. The workingman "pays for their libraries—but he can't have a spelling book for himself. He makes the most elegant furniture for them to loll upon, but he must sit upon his haunches. While labor creates all the wealth on the globe, it has to go a begging."[58]

Because the proponents of this view saw no vital role for the capitalist in the productive process, the alternative they proposed was the producers' cooperative. In 1844 and 1845, Lynn shoemakers established three jointly-owned shoe firms in which they purchased their own stock, made the shoes, and sold the product of their labor, dividing among themselves what they earned. Although the details of the arrangement are unclear, the purpose was not: the intent of the "Associated Labor Societies" was to "secure to themselves the profits of their own labor." As many as forty shoemakers were associated with each society, and during the firms' brief existence (about two years) they managed to pay wages comparable with the highest in Lynn as well as to return a share of the profits to their members.[59] In this Lynn experiment as well as in similar ones in the United States throughout the nineteenth century, there was one fatal flaw. Producers' cooperatives left the existing capital structure intact, while relying for capital upon whatever meager resources a handful of workingmen could scrape together. As one writer explained the projects, "there can be no sort of objection to this principle, when it proposes no opposition or prerogative to the existing laws of property." This flaw reveals a crucial missing link in the radical social theory that began to emerge among workingmen in Lynn and in other areas of the United States at this time. Starting with the labor theory of value and the supposition that labor creates wealth, they concluded, with Proudhon, that "property is theft." The capitalist, in other words, took his capital from the surplus labor that rightfully belonged to the producer; the capital structure was built upon past surplus labor. But the great majority of American workingmen, along with their European counterparts of the same period, did not then propose that labor seize what the capitalist had already taken. Instead, they resolved to write off what they had surrended in the past as an unfortunate but irretrievable loss and by various means to prevent its recurrence in the future. There were, of course, a few brave souls like Thomas Skidmore, the Connecticut sage and former Jeffersonian, who proposed outright confiscation, but this was an extremely unpopular view that sent paroxysms of fear through the rich and caused labor reformers to fall over one another in their efforts to disassociate themselves from Skimore. Thus the acceptance of existing property rights was the limit beyond which the ideological upholders of the labor theory of value did not go.

A second tradition upon which the Lynn shoemakers relied in interpreting their experience as wage earners was the republican heritage of the American Revolution. Unlike native-born American workingmen of the post-Civil War period who used Scriptures to comprehend what was happening to them, the Lynn journeymen used the secular tradition of the Revolution.[60] They occasionally used quotations from the Bible, but their world view and sense of history were not those of the evangelical Protestant. They compared their oppressors to George III and themselves to the patriots of 1776. At many points, they recognized a close analogy between the arbitrary, oppressive tyranny of the kind and the arrogant exploitation of their employers, between the heroic self-sacrifice and dedication of their forebears and their own emerging resistance to a monied aristocracy. They called upon workingmen "to rise unitedly in our strength, and burst asunder, as freemen ought, the shackles and fetters with which they have been chaining and binding us by an unjust and unchristian use of power."[61]

Was there any difference, they asked, in England's subjugation of the colonists, and bosses who "seem to think that the jours were designed for no other purpose than to be their subjects."[62] The "long train of abuses and usurpations" were like the petty frauds of manufacturers. "What matters it to us," a shoemaker asked, "whether he who oppresses us lives on this or the other side of the Atlantic Ocean, on the Island of Great Britain or on the Continent of North America." Nor was there any difference between an unjust system of taxation and the employers' use of superior power to deprive the workingman of the product of his labor. "What matters is whether our hard earnings are wrested from us to gild the palaces of southern monarchs, or to drop into the already overflowing coffers of Northern purse-proud aristocrats."[63] The Revolution was a struggle against oppression; its cry was "equality and justice," and its promise to freeborn Americans was the inalienable right to life, liberty, and property. It sought to abolish "the feudalism of former times [which] had recognized only serfs and dependents on the will of the crown or aristocracy."[64]

But equal rights were a fiction and a fraud as long as a small number of men possessed all the property and exacted heavy tribute from the their fellows for the privilege of working. Wealth was "rapidly accumulating in a few hands, the manufacturing population fast increasing, and becoming fixed and dependent upon the will of their employers." This process was tending to "annihilate those rights which the Patriots of '76 contended were inalienable."[65] The journeymen believed there was a close link between political and economic oppression, that political power flowed from the possession of wealth, which enabled some men to control and exploit others. They frequently pointed to the countries of Europe with their arrogant nobility and a mass of workers in "utter misery and wretchedness."[66] This was the fate that awaited the American mechanic. "In our own land," one man wrote, "similar results are beginning to show themselves, and must be seen as inevitable as like causes produce-like effects."[67]

The American Revolution, thus, provided a rich stock of metaphor, language, and parallel experiences that all Americans reared in the folklore of the Revolution could easily use and understand. The journeymen mechanics, having identified their oppressors and the source of their power, also used the heroism of the Patriots of '76 both to justify their own resistance and to evoke a similar response from others, who were also the heirs to the revolutionary legacy. Anyone who was a man and not a slave should resist: it was his duty as a citizen and a man. In the face of exploitation, "he cannot and will not stand that treatment; if he does not [resist] he is not worthy to be called a man. A man who does not assert his rights . . . is not worthy of the name of freeman."[68] Workingmen should, therefore, rise up and "purify this tainted atmosphere which we have endured altogether too long."[69] If they did not resist, they said, "a storm will inevitably gather over our heads, which may sink us with our boasted liberty and all those glorious privileges which our magnanimous and patriotic forefathers secured and transmitted to our hands for safe keeping; and we shall be reduced to the misery and degradation of our unfortunate brethen of other countries."[70] The journeymen were preempting the call to arms that master mechanics in Lynn had adopted in mobilizing all mechanics against the Federalist aristocracy of the trading towns. And the journeymen believed that they had a just claim to a heroic lineage; they were the direct descendants of the Patriots who were so often celebrated in American history. In 1845, for example, one journeyman proposed that cordwainers assemble on the fourth of July to erect a monument to the mechanics and laboring men who marched to fight the British on the nineteenth of April 1775.[71] He evidently intended to revive the spirit of '76, connect the struggle of 1845 to the Revolution, and strengthen the cordwainers' identification with the mechanics who fought the foreign oppressors. Thus, the American Revolution and the labor theory of value were the two traditions that form the basis of an indigenous working-class radicalism. Arguments based on these ideas would appear again and again throughout American labor history, whether in the columns of the *Awl*, the pages of Albert Parsons' anarchist *Alarm* in the Chicago of 1886, or the *Industrial Worker* of the IWW in the 1900s.

In looking back over the evolution of the journeymen's account of their experience, several features stand out. Although the means of production in the shoe industry remained the same, there was a fundamental change in the relationship between the journeymen and their employers. With the expansion of markets, the manufacturer in the central shop replaced the master cordwainer in the small shoe shop, thus physically separating worker from employer. Despite the continued presence in the industry of petty manufacturers, the larger ones increasingly dominated the trade and, in the process, withdrew entirely from the productive process. The large manufacturers or "grinders" adopted methods and practices which, though building their businesses, altered the experiences of the cordwainers and signified to them that something was awry. The shoemakers' resistance to the order system, low wages, shoddy goods, greater competition, and prolonged and intensified labor was based on values they derived from the past and applied to the present. These values determined the limits beyond which the journeymen would not be pushed.

The journeyman's resistance rested primarily on his identity as a mechanic and a producer. His high estimation of his own worth was the offspring of a conviction that he produced something indispensable to the preservation of life. Although he acknowledged his dependency upon his employer, he insisted that the injunction contained in the phrase "the laborer is worthy of his hire" ought to prevail, taking the form of justice and fairness in the relationship of journeymen and masters. The continual plea for respect stemmed from the notion, especially widespread in Lynn, that labor was the source of value and the creator of property, wealth, and capital. Most journeymen used the labor theory of value to justify their demand for a larger share of what they produced as well as for respect. But there were others, also drawing heavily from the past, who portrayed the larger employers as unproductive and worthless aristocrats, and used the labor theory of value to support their claim for the whole product of their toil. To implement these ideas in the shoe business they established producers' cooperatives which they owned and operated. These ideas were the outgrowth of the shoemakers' experience and form one aspect of an emerging class consciousness.

The second strand of support for resistance was the Revolutionary heritage that he claimed as a free born American. The Revolutionary struggle constituted in the journeyman's mind, the closest parallel to an experience, that was becoming increasingly harsh, exploitative, and intolerable. Like the king of England, their employers were arbitrary and tyrannical, treating the journeymen like subjects. Although the Revolution promised to all men the right to life, liberty, and the pursuit of happiness, the journeymen recognized that these rights derived from power, and power in turn sprang from either the ownership or control of property. A man dependent upon another man for the right to work, and thus to live, was vulnerable to exploitation. In the 1840s, the journeymen saw themselves slipping over the brink of a precipice, seeing below them a life of dependency, laboring for a subsistence while building the wealth and power of their employers. Here was the point at which the labor theory of value and the heritage of the revolution merged, leading them to comprehend the system they confronted: its source of power and powerlessness, of wealth and poverty, of rulers and ruled.

# 10. The Social Dimensions of the Class Experience

The growing distinction between boss and worker from 1830 to 1860 appeared in altered patterns of social relations beyond the cash nexus. Yet one should again note that this was a process or a tendency and not a sudden transformation. The changes took two forms. One was the increasing tendency of both journeymen and manufacturers, especially the wealthier ones, to establish voluntary institutions to meet their distinctive needs. The manufacturers, for example, founded fire clubs, a library, a private academy, lyceums, and a rural cemetery, while workingmen formed newspapers, mutual benefit societies, cooperative stores, and a reading room. A second form of change was the tendency for the class experience to influence the response of journeymen to political and social issues. Their hostility to the abolitionists, for instance, was due primarily to their hostility to abolitionists who were manufacturers and to the refusal of leading antislavery advocates in Lynn to recognize any similarity whatever between chattel slavery in the South and the wage system in the North. Independent political action, culminating in the cordwainers' takeover of city government in 1860, was a direct outgrowth of an experience that showed that only a workingmen's party could protect their political rights.

Signs of class distinctions in housing patterns began to appear as early as 1830. Although rich and poor, manufacturer and shoemaker, resided in every ward or neighborhood throughout Lynn, wealth was becoming a determinant of where one lived. The largest manufacturers resided on Pudding Hill, the Quaker settlement in Lynn, and kept shop at the foot of Broad Street near the railroad depot. In the 1840s, Ocean Street was laid out between Broad Street and the sea to the east. Ocean Street would become the "diamond district" of Lynn, home of the town's wealthiest citizens, who resided in Victorian mansions built with fortunes made in the shoe industry. In fact, the whole area between

189

Broad Street and the sea became the upper-class section of Lynn, indicating the link of the rich to a Quaker past.[1] There one could find the Quaker Meeting House and cemeteries as well as the Unitarian Church, which a number of Quakers helped found in the 1820s after their secession from the Friends Society in the Hicksite controversy. Further to the east, the peninsula of Nahant also showed signs of becoming the exclusive possession of the wealthy, many of whom were from Boston but with representation from Lynn as well.[2] Here one could find "the Boston Butterflies who fly up and down between Boston and Nahant during the summer, luxuriating on the money which . . . they have cajoled out of the people."[3] One critic described Nahant in the 1840s as the place "where the Boston aristocracy airs itself every summer and braces up for the dissipation of the coming winter."[4]

Shoemakers and others who had traditionally traveled to Nahant for picnics noted that the rich were establishing summer resorts and then permanent homes, converting what had been common land into private property, which they closed to outsiders. Lynn citizens resented this denial of their customary rights and the efforts of the rich to preempt for themselves what had belonged to all. The same was true of other parts of the town. One owner of a large estate on the outskirts of Lynn protected "his grounds from the profane step of Lynn shoemakers, by a pack of savage dogs."[5] The converting of common lands into private property was another sign that rights were coming to rest on property rather than tradition.

There also seemed to be unequal treatment of rich and poor in the eyes of the law. When a wealthy gentleman in Salem was murdered, the governor of Massachusetts, a Lynn article states, "comes forward in person, and profers them the resources of the state." But when assailants robbed and beat a Mr. Jones, a poor man, the same authorities ignored the incident.[6] The difference in response was due to the possession of political power by rich officials, who identified with the wealthy few rather than with the poorer many. If a poor man should "strike an insolent squire," a Lynn writer observed, "a fine of five hundred dollars, and six months imprisonment in the common jail, would probably requite him for his pains."[7] Such discrimination would continue, a man warned, "if you trust to men in power solely, to make laws, and to expound them. What can you expect, or what can you do to serve, but to make bricks without straw to the end of your days."[8] And what was the difference, a writer asked, between being robbed by a bandit and by one's employer. "The man who shaves a note and takes the advantage of his neighbor's necessities, is worse than a thief or a highway man, and should be punished accordingly."[9] To support his case, the shoemaker cited an instance in early Lynn history when the town fined and put in a pillory a wood dealer who overcharged his customers. Another form of class discrimination was the treatment of paupers. The bodies of the poor would go to the medical schools for dissection, while the corpses of those with money to pay the cost of burial would be interred in the town cemetery.[10] The equality that many shoemakers believed was the essence of a republican society was giving way to a society in which rights depended on wealth. This was the thought that crossed a shoemaker's mind when his employer told him that a poor man had "no right to have children" and no right to "hire help in his family during sickness." In anger, he asked "What impudence. Who made them judges and rulers over us?"[11] Money seemed to matter above all else in where one lived and played and in how high one stood in the eyes of the law.

The composition of social institutions began to reflect class. The typical form was the voluntary institution, which groups of citizens established to meet their particular needs. Although some of these organizations were based on the neighborhood or section and drew their members from a particular geographical location, they usually tended to reflect economic status. Sometimes they were exclusive, restricting their membership to a certain size. More often they resembled the joint-stock corporation, with the state granting a charter to a group of incorporators, who in turn sold shares to interested parties with the means to buy. One joined by purchasing a share or gaining admission by the consent of the members, not by being born as would be the case with the family, kinship group, established church, or even the neighborhood. Although there perhaps was nothing inherent in the voluntary institution to make it exclusively an organization of a particular class, they did essentially become such organizations largely because the interests they were designed to serve stemmed from wealth. In Lynn, one's wealth depended on one's relationship to the means of production.

The Lynn Academy was an example. A group of wealthy citizens in West Lynn, many of them merchants, obtained a state charter for an academy in 1805. Its purpose was to provide advanced education for the founders' children as well as for any others who could pay the tuition. The average cost of tuition in 1808 was $18.64, while a receipt for 1805 showed that thirteen weeks of instruction at the Academy brought expenses of $97.50 for one pupil. With the severe depression that followed the war of 1812, the Academy fell on hard times, and in 1817 there was a petition to dissolve the school. But the Academy limped through the next decade, and its fortunes brightened in 1832 when the rising Quaker manufacturers of East Lynn—Isaiah Breed, Daniel Farrington, John Lovejoy and John Alley III—joined with counterparts in West Lynn to place the Academy on a firm financial footing. For the next twenty years the Academy flourished as the town's sole institution of higher learning.[12] The Academy did not exclude shoemakers, but scarcely a single shoemaker in Lynn could afford to send his children to the Lynn Academy. Thus, the Academy's main function was to educate the sons of Lynn's bourgeoisie.

The Academy closed in 1852 with the opening of the Lynn High School, but the middle-class composition of the student body changed little if at all. Of the fifty boys enrolled in 1854 in the high school, only two were the sons of shoemakers.[13] Although education at the high school level was free and open to all, the sons of shoemakers continued to go into the shops to labor at their fathers' side. The manufacturers were the principal beneficiaries. They retained control of the school through the school committee, which set curriculum and hired and fired teachers, transferring to the public the cost of education. In addition, the former preceptor of the Academy, Jacob Batchelder, became principal of the high school. Although shoemakers wanted their children to attend school, they could not spare them. As one cordwainer explained, "How often do you see, in our shoemakers' shops, boys of from ten to twelve years of age, at work on shoes?—and when you ask the parents of those boys, why they put them to work at so early an age, the answer will be through necessity." He added that he knew of "more than a hundred families around men, whose children are ignorant of many of the common branches of education."[14] A free education at the high school would only have been free if the town had paid to the shoemakers what they ordinarily received from the labor of their sons, but this, of course, was never done.

A similar pattern evolved in the founding of a library in Lynn. In 1818 a number of citizens organized the Social Library for the collective purchase and circulation of books among the members. Membership depended upon the purchase of a share: by 1837 there were 73 who held shares in the social library and were entitled to access to its 206 books. Yet if one scans the impressive list of autodidacts one finds few shoemakers who could spare either the two dollars for a share or the time needed to read books that aroused their interest.[15] Although the Social Library became the basis of a Free Public Library, maintained with public funds and controlled by trustees that the town authorities appointed, the prolonged labor of the shoemakers gave them little time to use the library. Again, the manufacturers and professional people were the chief beneficiaries of the change. They made up the board of trustees and shifted onto the public the responsibility of providing funds to maintain and enlarge a collection of books used primarily by the middle class.

A middle-class orientation was evident also in other voluntary institutions. The Silsbee Street Debating Club sponsored stimulating discussions of metaphysics, political economy, slavery, and temperance. According to David Johnson, "many of the members had risen from the shoemaker's seat, and not a few even then worked at the time-honored craft." Yet if one examines the list of officers and about forty-five members, one finds only a bare handful of practicing shoemakers.[16] The Debating Club was primarily the creation of the manufacturing and professional men in Lynn and provided them with a means to sharpen their wits and forensic powers. The same could be said for the composition of other social institutions—the Franklin Club (founded in 1836), the Natural History Society (1842), the Social Union (1843), the Exploring Circle (1850), the Gnomologian Society (1849) and others.[17] The exclusion of the shoemakers was probably unintentional, yet their absence is evident.

If class differences seemed to determine the organizations to which citizens belonged and where one lived, they also began to determine where one would be buried. For more than two centuries Lynn citizens were buried in the limited space of five acres in the eastern and western burial grounds. Whether rich or poor, manufacturer or journeyman, all went into the same plot of ground nearest one's home. With the growth of the town's population and an increase in the number of persons who died each year, the small burial grounds became crowded. A number of citizens who recognized the need for a new cemetery were particularly disturbed to learn that congestion in the old cemeteries made proper interment difficult, sometimes pushing to the surface human bones that the keeper paid children to retrieve at so much per bone. A group of citizens united in the late 1840s to remedy this disgraceful overcrowding.

Once again the joint stock company prevailed and the results were predictable. On September 7, 1849, 7 men supported by a petition signed by 100 persons, voted to establish a rural cemetery. They obtained a charter of incorporation and sold shares at $10 per share to purchase a lot for $1800 on the outskirts of Lynn. Unlike the old cemeteries in which available space went to any citizen of the town, the

Pine Grove Cemetery gave lots only to those who paid for them.[18] Of the 173 subscribers to the stock of Pine Grove, the overwhelming majority were manufacturers, merchants, shopkeepers, and professionals, people who could afford a lot at the minimum price of $10. The names of 147 of the 173 stock subscribers appeared also in the directory of 1851. Inlcuded were 48 shoe manufacturers, 17 professionals, 55 merchants and shopkeepers, 8 shoe cutters, and 7 shoemakers.[19] One of the advantages offered to subscribers was that they received deeds for their lots, "in fee simple, securing to them and their descendants, exempted by law from taxation and attachment." And if a person so chose, he or she could purchase as many lots as wished, providing plentiful space for a tomb that would accurately symbolize his or her importance in this life and maybe insure a proper rank in the next. In addition, subscribers could also provide for cherished ones, who had died before Pine Grove opened. By 1852, the remains of 60 persons were transferred from the old cemeteries to Pine Grove.

The Lynn poet and historian Alonzo Lewis, by 1852 a fading voice from another era, explained what had occurred. He noted first that he "endeavored to have some provision made for the poor, but found no answer from a single individual." They replied that "if the town wants a graveyard, let them purchase one."[20] Two years later, Lewis observed: "The new cemetery will contain a portion but that is for the favored few. It is not for the people, for the poor, for the penniless widow and the destitute orphan. These must continue to be buried in pits that have been thrice occupied by the dead. . . . Nearly all the wealthy people in the town have secured their lots in the new cemetery, and left the poor to find their own graves as they can."[21] The rich put their new acquisition to good use. Their lots varied in size from 300 to 3000 square feet, with tombs appropriate to the lot size. They also further separated themselves from their fellows in death as they had in life. They enclosed their lots with "fences of a durable character" or with "neat and beautiful hedges."[22]

In the same way that the Lynn Academy and the Social Library became public, so too did the Pine Grove Cemetery. In 1852, the Pine Grove Cemetery Corporation offered the cemetery to the city, but only on the condition that the city accept certain stipulations. Among these were 1) that the city assume all liabilities of the corporation; 2) that the incorporators retain rights granted by the charter; and 3) that a board of commissioners, selected from owners of lots, control the cemetery. The owners also provided for the poor, but in a backhanded way. A portion of Pine Grove would be granted for free burial, "but no person shall be given control over that portion or a portion thereof." A year later, the city accepted the offer and granted the owners a profit on their investment as well as continued control. The owners had acquired 24 acres of land for $2000, made $4000, to $6000 in improvements (they said), and acquired $1000 in debts, yet the city paid them $15,000, or two thirds more than the original investment.[23]

A middle-class orientation also lent itself to the Lyceum, sometimes cited as a key institution in American popular culture during the pre-Civil War period. The Lynn Lyceum was organized in 1828 as a branch of the American Lyceum, with the purpose of broadening and enriching the knowledge of participants through lecture programs. Shoe manufacturers were prominent in the affairs of the Lynn branch. All four officers and most of the members in 1832 were bosses, and included the town's largest—Micajah Pratt, Nathan and Isaiah Breed.[24] Anyone who wished to attend the lectures either purchased a membership for $2 or paid an admission fee. For a program offered in April 1846, the fee was $.50, a nominal amount to some but half a day's pay for a shoemaker.[25] Lynn's Lyceum was probably more exclusive in the 1830s than in 1846. In 1832, a critic recalled that the first Lyceum failed in its broader purpose to enlighten because "the founders cooped up the lecturer with a select few." Although he promised that "none will be excluded for lack of money or membership," admission in the 1840s stood at $.50.[26]

Some supporters of the Lyceum wished to extend the influence of the institution to a broader audience, using it to shape public policy and morality. One advocate hoped that the Lyceum would prevent "mobs and riotous assemblies" by dispelling "the clouds of political and moral heresy, which has for several years enveloped many portions of our country." The upholders of this lofty purpose feared that "matters closely connected with the well being of society" would be "thrown to the popular breeze, institutions for the support of piety and morality . . . weakened, or scattered, and society left without compass or rudder." He was convinced that Lyceums would halt "those erroneous proceedings so often witnessed among a manufacturing people" and strengthen "religious, moral and political institutions."[27]

A similar intention motivated religious and business leaders to form the Lynn Young Men's Christian Association in 1856. It started with less than 100 members but claimed more than 200 members from 11 churches by 1857. Isaac Newhall, Jr., one of Lynn's largest manufacturers (in 1857 employing 1200 shoemakers), helped the YMCA immeasurably when he donated a hall for its varied activities. Its purpose was "to promise the moral and spiritual condition of young men in this vicinity by bringing them under the influence of Christian institutions." The threat was especially great in large cities—"the broad basins into which evil [was] pouring its turbid waters"—for there "the path of the youthful stranger [was] beset with countless snares and seductive arts" which apparently included the saloon and gambling house.[28] Benefactors like Newhall, who trusted in the Association to divert young men from the "countless snares," were probably disappointed when James Dillon, a "manager" or officer in the organization, emerged in 1860 as a principal leader among the striking shoemakers.

The process of institution-building signifies the maturing of the middle class and the formation of a social and cultural apparatus that fully complemented the appearance of the manufacturers as an economic group. The energetic entrepreneurs who transformed the shoe industry also reshaped nearly every other aspect of society. Both processes took place simultaneously and commonly involved the same men. If they created shoe firms, banks, insurance companies, railroads, and turnpikes, they also established the academy, library, lyceum, and temperance organizations. The typical form of organization was the joint-stock company, which enabled a group of individuals to fund, control, and guide an institution toward the achievement of a purpose that the subscribers desired. If the objective was broad in scope, for example, the moral regeneration of society—rather than limited as in the forming of a high school—the voluntary association was more appropriate. In either case, association meant the pulling together of men whose social experience gave them distinctive needs, which they sought to satisfy collectively rather than as individuals. Although the manufacturers were usually the prime movers in creating institutions, they were not a selfish interest group. It was a sign of the maturity of their class consciousness that they successfully fused their own interests with what they conceived as the best interests of all. They were leaders of all the people, spokesmen for timeless virtues and eternal truths, builders of a new order that would benefit everyone. The deference they gained from others, as well as the transformation from private to public of institutions that remained under their control, attests to their social hegemony.

Yet in the same period there were signs of rejection. The experience of the journeymen cordwainers produced needs that the existing society could not fulfill, largely because it bore the heavy imprint of their employers. The response of the journeymen took two forms. First, there was the creation of institutions that either paralleled those in the larger society or filled a place where no institution existed. Their newspapers—the *Awl, True Workingman,* and *New England Mechanic*—for instance, rivaled the existing political organs, while their cooperative stores competed with privately owned retail establishments. At the same time, the Journeymen Cordwainers' Societies gave formal expression to a sense of common identity that could nowhere else be found. A second aspect of the journeymen's response was their opposition to policies that were authored by the most disliked elements among their employers. In the area of temperance reform, for instance, they tended to oppose coercion and punishment of the drinker as both ineffective in reducing drinking and as a sign of the proclivity of middle-class reformers to rely upon laws that inevitably fell more heavily on the poor than the rich. They condemned as hypocritical a proposal for liberalized poor-relief measures from employers who paid the lowest wages. They also cast a jaundiced eye on the myopic abolitionists. Although in the controversy surrounding these issues it would always be possible to find journeymen on either side, there was a tendency for the alignment on social issues to reflect the growing cleavage between employers and journeymen.

From time to time in the years from 1830 to 1860, journeymen shoemakers combined to form societies to deal with problems unique to wage earners in the industry. The societies generally appeared in times of hardship and declined during periods of prosperity, lending credence to the view that the journeymen's difficulties were only temporary and would soon be remedied by an upturn in business. Depression in the trade served to give broader currency to views originally enunciated by a prophetic minority, while the return of prosperity cast them in the colors of malcontents. Yet one feature was clear: with each passing decade the societies became stronger, the membership larger and more determined, the leadership bolder and more aggressive. This was due partly to the sharp and frequent depressions in the trade and partly to the realization among a growing number of shoemakers that humble appeals to conscience were futile and should give way to sustained collective action.

The first society appeared in the summer of 1830.[29] The membership of the Mutual Benefit Society of Journeymen Cordwainers numbered about two hundred and was drawn from each section of the town, with considerable strength in Woodend, the center of the early shoe industry and still the home of a large portion of Lynn's journeymen. The immediate issues that precipitated formation of the society were low wages and the formation of combination stores. The purpose of the society, according to a friendly observer, was "to guard against any undue advantage being taken, in meting out to them the measure of their wages."[30] Yet the society was indecisive in determining precisely how they would achieve the objective of "preventing poverty or shielding misfortune," while obtaining "the full value of their labor." Convinced that "the weak must be combined in order to oppose the strong," they apparently resolved to build a reserve fund from membership subscriptions of one dollar to aid one another during hard times. They also extended support to the female shoe binders, many of them their wives and daughters, who had simultaneously organized their own society, The Female Society of Lynn and Vicinity for the Protection and Promotion of Female Industry. Employers had, they argued, "depressed the price of female labor, and reduced it down to almost nothing," harming both the binders and the shoemakers who often depended upon the binders to supplement the family income.[31] At a meeting at the Friends Meeting House in December in 1833, approximately a thousand binders resolved to draft a wage schedule and refuse to work for any boss who did not comply.[32] In the following month, the journeymen voted to support the binders by boycotting any employer who did not meet their demands. But this early attempt at a selective strike failed. In June of 1834, the Female Society was in a "deranged situation" because "more than three quarters who first signed its constitutions . . . [have] broken it."[33] The heavy demand for shoes caused a temporary suspension of the hated order system and probably raised wages to a level that made a strike less urgent.[34]

The second surge of activity came in 1844 as the trade began to emerge from the long depression that had begun in 1837. Once again there were persistent demands for unified action to raise wages and force employers to abandon the order system. The journeymen of the 1840s, like their predecessors nearly a decade before, viewed the society as primarily an instrument for bettering their economic lot. They intended to enroll in the Journeymen Cordwainers' Society a majority of shoemakers in Lynn and to work closely with cordwainers in other cities until they possessed sufficient strength to enforce a bill of wages on their employers. It made little sense, they insisted, to raise wages in Lynn alone, for shoemakers from surrounding areas would pack their kits and migrate to Lynn, increasing the supply of available labor and encouraging bosses to cut wages.[35] Although they succeeded in enrolling about a third of Lynn's 1500 journeymen, they did not feel confident enough to undertake a strike against the bosses, despite the demands of a significant minority for the attempt. With the gradual recovery of business in the mid-forties, the Society followed the path of its predecessor toward dissolution. The increased demand for shoes brought higher wages and more payments in cash, thus assuaging the grievances that the society originally sought to redress.

The sharp and frequent depressions during the 1850s, chronic low wages, and intensive competition with outworkers provoked a revival of collective action among the Lynn journeymen. As will be shown in the next chapter, the movement succeeded in winning support from the great majority of shoemakers as well as from thousands of outworkers in the countryside. Emboldened by a widespread determination to take action and confident that they could prevail over their employers, the journeymen struck in February of 1860. Thus a movement once modest in size, humble in tone, and erratic in its pattern of growth reappeared in 1860 on a scale never witnessed before in the history of Lynn. Yet it would be misleading if one concentrated merely on the efforts of the cordwainers to increase their wages. This was an important concern but not an exclusive one. The securing of better wages was not the limit of their activity; neither were the various societies the only institutions that they formed.

The journeymen established three weekly newspapers in the period between 1840 and 1860. *The Awl* was the official organ of the Society and ran for a little more than a year, July 1844 to October 1845. Its successor, the *True Workingman* edited by John Gibson, the leading orator among the shoemakers, spoke briefly for a remnant of the original society. A third publication, *The New England Mechanic,* had a brief existence, nearly a year as the official organ of the Lynn Mechanics Association, which commissioned Alonzo Draper, later a leader of the strike in 1860, to edit a journal on behalf of its members.[36]

The shoemakers founded these newspapers largely because the existing newspapers consistently opposed or ignored their grievances and excluded materials that their editors thought distasteful or inflammatory. In January of 1834, for example, Daniel Henshaw, editor of the *Lynn Record,* opted out of any further involvement in the struggle between the journeymen and binders, on the one hand, and their employers on the other. Although he complimented himself for carrying a letter on the subject one in a previous issue, he stated that the paper was "not anxious for any further discussion on the subject."[37] Three years later, Henshaw refused to publish an article from "A Genuine Abolitionist," who sought to show the essential similarity between the wage system and Southern slavery. Henshaw disagreed, arguing that white laborers in the North were not compelled to work; they could draw their pay and leave their employer. "There is," he observed of the relationship between boss and worker, "the most perfect liberty on both sides." Henshaw also detected in the letter an "evil tendency." That is, workers "would suppose some direct and immediate blame in the employer, and would wreak their vengeance on *him*, if anywhere."[38] Shoemakers a decade later found similar grounds for complaint when the editor of the *Lynn News* commended Horace Greeley, editor of the *New York Tribune*, who suggested that employers whose businesses suffered as a result of loco foco monetary policies were justified in firing workers who voted loco foco while retaining those who supported sound Whig policies.[39] In addition to the ideological bias that led some newspapers to oppose the journeymen, most of the papers were narrowly political in their coverage, trumpeting the virtues of their party, castigating the opposition, and giving little attention to anything else. For these reasons, shoemakers deemed it necessary to have a press that voiced their interests. The *Awl* was perhaps their most successful effort, gaining a claimed circulation of twelve hundred and reaching most of Lynn's shoemakers. Despite the impressive size of its audience, the *Awl* was dependent for revenue on the Cordwainers Society and, therefore, perished with the Society.

The Society also sought to expand its members' reading beyond the pages of the *Awl*. With the aid of a donation from a Lynn lumber dealer, the Society in 1845 opened a reading room and stocked it with materials relevant to the problems of workingmen."[40] The creation of a workingmen's reading room suggests the presence of a need that no other institution in society fulfilled.

With the demise of the order system of wage payments in the late 1840s and the substitution of cash, groups of Lynn shoemakers united to form cooperative stores. Most became affiliated with the New England Protective Union, which had several hundred or more branches. The Lynn shoemakers were the first to establish an N.E.P. store. New England Protective Union Number 4 on Union Street was the most successful of Lynn's half dozen stores, with a trading stock of nearly $500 in 1849; $2500 in 1853. N.E.P. Number 4, popularly known as the "Regulator," opened in 1846 in a barn. Fifteen shoemakers owned the store, each providing $3 to purchase supplies and each taking a turn tending the store. The store was open on Saturday afternoon and every evening to accommodate the working hours of its members. The "Regulator" purchased its stock from the wholesale house at the headquarters of the N.E.P. in Boston and sold to its members and others on a strictly cash basis. In 1850, N.E.P. Number 4 moved from William

Luscomb's barn into a new building and within a few years had a membership of seventy-five or more. The success of Regulator Number 4, according to the shoemaker David Johnson, "awakened an interest in the Protective Union plan, and other stores of a similar character were established in different parts of Lynn"; most of them, however, were in the Woodend area.[41] In 1863, the members of the cooperative sold out to a former agent who operated it as a private retail establishment. In the years from 1849 to 1853 anywhere from six to eight retail cooperatives did business in Lynn, most of them owned and operated by shoemakers, who used the cooperative principle to save on groceries, deal directly with other producers, and as the name of one implied to act as a yardstick or "regulator" for grocery prices.[42]

In addition to retail stores, groups of anywhere from ten to forty shoemakers with sufficient funds combined to form producers' cooperatives.[43] They established three associated labor societies in the mid-forties and another in the aftermath of the strike of 1860. These shoemakers were a few among many who were convinced that their grievances would never be remedied as long as they were dependent upon the employer for the opportunity to work on the materials he furnished. They desired also to have the pride that came with collective self-employment and to have the full product of their labor. Because they believed they could perform the function of purchasing materials, shoe design, and marketing the product, they were convinced that the employer was replaceable. Although the associated labor societies were short lived, they demonstrated the journeymen's desire to overcome the wage system by exerting their own control and ownership of the means of production.

It was also in the 1850s that the shoemakers began to establish links with workingmen in other towns, especially with other shoemakers. They began to recognize that Lynn employers were playing off one group against another, pitting one man against another in competition for employment at low wages. The New England Workingmen's conventions of the mid-forties were a means for establishing contact with other wage earners and for deepening the conviction that despite the difference of trade and location, their problems were essentially the same. The Lynn shoemakers sent a large delegation, ninety-six, to the 1844 meeting in Boston and another group to the 1845 meeting in Lowell. In the following year, the Lynn shoemakers were host to convention delegates from other cities throughout New England. At about the same time, they sponsored a meeting of shoemakers drawn from the surrounding towns of Essex County.[44] The Lynn journeymen also began corresponding with shoemakers in distant cities like New York and Philadelphia, inquiring into conditions of the trade and wage rates in those cities.[45] These tenuous ties were strengthened in the late 1850s with the formation of autonomous, but related, protective unions, which struck simultaneously in the spring of 1860. Concerted action signified a growing awareness among shoemakers in Lynn as elsewhere that their membership in a labor market hundreds of miles in area transcended the boundaries of place and linked their fate. As one Lynn workingman expressed it, "Brother laborers, be you united. Let not factions separate you . . . but remember, that the interests of all laborers is one and the same, here, there, and everywhere, and always will be."[46]

The volunteer fire companies seemed to have served an important social function in the lives of the Lynn shoemakers. Although the men of property in the town had originally provided the funds to purchase hand-pumped engines, the need for manpower resulted in the formation of companies made up largely of mechanics. The companies were dispersed throughout the town, with each neighborhood having a unit consisting of anywhere from forty to sixty men who hauled the engine from the engine house to the fire and operated the pumping apparatus. In 1837, there were eight engine companies in Lynn. The officers and membership of each were mostly journeymen cordwainers.[47] Eight of the eleven officers of Empire #5, for example, were shoemakers. The material benefits of membership were slight: refund of one's poll tax. Taking part in protecting the lives and property of oneself and one's neighbors was probably a factor that motivated men to join the companies, but more important it seems was the place the fire company held as a social center. Men gathered there for regular monthly meetings, which were followed with generous supplies of beverages, card playing, and discussion. The units periodically sponsored parties and dances for members and their wives and friends. On one occasion a newspaper editor who questioned the virtue of some females present at a fire company dance found his home besieged by an angry crowd of firemen demanding an apology.[48] The companies also resembled the modern athletic team. Before cheering crowds of several thousand, two units would compete to test their speed, strength, and accuracy. A contest in 1846, for instance, attracted 2000 viewers, while another two years later brought out more than 2500.[49] Support for the continuation of the hand pump companies was so strong in the town that there was widespread opposition to the acquisition of steam pumpers, despite the general agreement of their technical superiority. Yet by 1860 Lynn began to acquire the new machines, marking the beginning of the end for the volunteer fire units.

The fire companies also provide evidence of the deference that characterized the relationship of journeymen to middle-class citizens. If the general membership and most of the officers were shoemakers, the engineers were often manufacturers, who received the post because they donated funds for the purchase or maintenance of the engines. It is understandable that the largest property owners in Lynn would be ardent supporters of the fire companies, since their original purpose in founding them was to protect their homes and places of business.[50] For this reason, one shoemaker, who was also an engineman, announced in 1844 that he would no longer protect the property of the bosses. He noted that it was "the enginemen who are the laboring class which goes to their fires, and works like slaves to property, up nights, injure health, and liable to get sickness of them that will last for months. And whose property are these liabilities for? Are they for the benefit of those who do the work. No. It is for the rich, who care not one fig for the wants of those that do it, after they get their own ends answered." He then proposed a boycott of the fire companies, vowing that "I intend, for one, in case of fire, to look out for my health, as well as they for their property. And I do not intend to work at their figures as I have done, and I wish every man would do the same, till they are more liberal."[51] Yet it appears that few shoemakers followed his advice: the companies continued to draw upon the journeymen for the bulk of their enginemen.

If the fire companies were composed mainly of shoemakers, the manufacturers and merchants made up the fire clubs. There were two such clubs in Lynn, the Franklin Fire Club, in one part of town, and the Lynn Fire Club in the other. The clubs were limited to fifty members, each of whom equipped himself with two leather buckets, a bag able to hold three bushels, and a key. In the case of a fire, the members would rush to the dwelling, office, or store, or shop of a club member, whose membership was designated by a shield affixed to the door jamb, and assist him in rescuing his valuables.[52] Thus, in contrast to the fire companies which protected all property in a neighborhood, the fire clubs were truly private, extending assistance only to members. They acted as auxiliaries to the companies, providing further assurance to men of property that their possessions would be protected. The fire companies and clubs, therefore, illustrate how some institutions originally arose in response to a need to defend a group's interest, in this case the property of the shoe manufacturers. Yet it was largely because of the need for enginemen to operate the hand pumps that the fire companies' membership came to be made up of journeymen shoemakers, who in turn converted the companies into social centers. It is understandable, then, that fire companies throughout Essex County turned out in support of the striking shoemakers in 1860.[53]

In addition to their societies, newspapers, cooperative stores and shoe shops, reading room and fire companies, the journeymen also showed an increased tendency to form independent political parties. They showed a growing dissatisfaction with the deception and capriciousness of candidates from the existing parties, candidates who made pious declarations of their loyalty to the interests of workingmen but quickly forgot them. As one man asked, "where are all those *political demagogues*, with which our town was infested three months ago, who prated so long, and so loudly about the protection of the laborer?" Once the election was over, they "slid back into *their holes*, there to remain until the next *political clap of thunder*, when they will again crawl forth to dazzle the eyes of the people with their false colors, that they may bask in the sunshine of popular favor."[54] In 1840, a shoemaker recalled, one party promised "$2 a day and roastbeef" and, when elected, gave "a shilling a day and a haddock."[55]

Shoemakers argued that the principal source of their trouble was that they had mistakenly delegated power to persons who violated the trust vested in them, amplifying their own privileges at the expense of the people who elected them. As citizens, one man observed, "we are equal in rights, but of what use is this grant if we allow a portion, and a small portion too, of mankind to rule us, rod us, and degrade us."[56] The result was oppression and "legislation . . . all in favor of the rich." Such consequences were inevitable if workingmen continued to view themselves as their rulers viewed them. A shoemaker observed that "we have been willing to work and toil, reducing ourselves to mere machines, working hard and long, distrusting ourselves, practically believing that we were made expressly to work, and others to rule and govern."[57] Workingmen confessed that they had erred in entrusting the protection of their rights to others. "Our rights," one writer noted, "demand protection at our own hands. It would be folly in us to expect aid from any other source; past experience kills all hope of help from the rich and powerful."[58] In politics as in industry, the deference that presumed a system of reciprocal rights and mutual responsibilities between citizens of different ranks was breaking down.

The solution then, according to a view repeated again and again, was independent action. As one journeyman expressed it, "our redemption from oppression's grasp depends upon ourselves." The rich could not be relied upon, a writer asserted, for "self-interest forbids it," while the learned and educated "have questions of more importance to settle than anything apertaining to the goods of humanity." Therefore, "if you would preserve your rights, you must defend yourselves, fearlessly and independently."[59] Another shoemaker underscored a phrase which, with slight variation, rang loudly among workingmen's movements throughout the nineteenth century: "THE WORK-INGMEN IF EVER REDEEMED, MUST REDEEM THEMSELVES."[60] The time for action had come, another insisted: "It is high time that the workingmen took the reins of Government into their own hands."[61]

To prepare themselves for the task of taking power workingmen again turned to the labor theory of value and the republican heritage of the Revolution. The first they used to support their claim for a position of political power commensurate with their importance as the economic foundation of society. "You have the power of government and the laws in your own hands," a spokesman declared, "you pay all the salaries, fight all the battles, protect all the property and the lives of men, build all the cities, man all the vessels, work all the machinery, coin all the money, work all the mines, and in fact there is nothing done without you."[62] Power should abide with the producers, and the producers were the workingmen. In addition to their role as producers, makers of things, workingmen had "intellects which should be cultivated, genius which should be brought out, and . . . all that is requisite to improve, adorn, beautify, and elevate the condition of mankind."[63] The Revolution established the legitimacy of resistance to oppression and the defense of equality and justice for all. "Would it not prove that the noble blood that our ancestors poured out like water," one man asked, "when it was needed to defend their rights, or to water the tree of liberty, had, in their degenerate and contemptible sons, turned to dish-water, and become fit for nothing but to wash the furniture of their oppressors."[64] Workingmen should, therefore, said one, "throw off the yoke of bondage that now hangs upon the necks of our people." "We would like to see," another proposed, "a similar spirit manifested in 1845, that which was manifested in 1776, though different means used to redress them."[65] Yet to achieve the unity, self-pride, and confidence needed to achieve this end it was necessary to "put more confidence in each other," "assist one another," "look more at the reality or substance than to the mere outward show," and cease seeing oneself as the rulers see us.[66] These were the underlying ideas that motivated workingmen to assert politically their independence and distinctiveness.

206

In 1836, a group of mechanics hastily assembled a workingmen's ticket for the local election, evidently seeking to rally the journeymen shoemakers and to break the political stalemate that existed in Lynn. They polled only a handful of votes.[67] A decade later, workingmen who were members of the Society of Journeymen Cordwainers stood for election against candidates of the existing parties. Again they did poorly, winning less than 100 votes of the approximately 1300 ballots cast.[68] It seems clear from these early efforts that deference remained a powerful force; journeymen continued to support leaders whom they trusted for defense of their rights. But in the fall of 1860, party ties and deference momentarily dissolved. In the elections for local office, Lynn workingmen captured nearly every seat on the board of aldermen and city council, elected a shoemaker mayor, and placed their strike leaders in charge of the local police force.[69] If their victory was short-lived, it nonetheless brought to fruition in a massive way a course of independent action that mechanics had begun decades before.

The formation of institutions that bore the imprint of the class experience was only one indication of a reorientation in patterns of social relations and loyalties. Another was the tendency for the social alignments that arose around controversial issues of public policy to reflect class. These alignments were never clear-cut struggles, with employers entirely on one side and journeymen entirely on the other, and no attempt will be made to show that they were. Nonetheless, it is possible to discern a tendency for the emerging conflict between journeymen and their employers to carry over into other areas and to affect issues that seemed but little related to economic concerns.

In the area of moral reform, for example, temperance and then abstinence provoked a controversy that lasted for a half century or more. As noted earlier, the Society in Lynn for the Promotion of Industry, Frugality and Temperance, founded in 1826, was primarily the creation of the town's rising manufacturers. The first temperance lecturer appeared in Lynn in 1829, and in the following years the growing membership of the Society focused on temperance as the principal means to the ends of industry and frugality. The Society succeeded in persuading the town to request the county supervisors to license no retail liquor establishments in Lynn, despite the opposition from non-manufacturing elements in the western portion of the town.[70] Although the early temperance movement was largely middle class in membership, the movement succeeded in gaining some support from workingmen.[71] Yet in the years from 1830 to 1860 workingmen became aware of the class bias that governed the policies of middle-class temperance advocates. First of all, the early societies were in fact temperance organizations, seeking only to halt drunkenness.[72] Like their Puritan forebears, they would have agreed that "wine is from God, but the drunkard is from the Devil." The first societies in both Massachusetts and in Lynn believed that ardent spirits or distilled liquor were the principal cause of drunkenness. They, therefore, sought to ban the most potent of all intoxicating drinks, rum, which happened also to be the staple beverage among workingmen, largely because of its cheapness and accessibility to the population in the eastern half of the State. Although the temperance forces permitted the use of wine, beer, and cider, this too seemed like class discrimination. Yet it was the manner in which the temperance movement went about abolishing the use of rum that provoked a popular reaction in Massachusetts.

In 1835, the movement tried to pass legislation prohibiting the sale of rum in quantities of less than 28 gallons, an amount greatly in excess of any common man's ability to buy. Three years later, in April 1838, they gained passage of the fifteen gallon law, and immediately the cry of "class legislation" sounded across the state, setting off a revolt that welded together both the opponents of all restrictions and those who viewed the 15 gallon law as an upper-class imposition on the workingman. The critics might also have noted that members of the Massachusetts Society for the Suppression of Intemperance also voted in 1824 not to give liquor to workers they employed.[73] The furor among workers was undoubtedly the crucial factor in the election of Marcus Morton as governor of Massachusetts in 1839, an office the Democrats had consistently failed to win in several earlier attempts.[74]

A class bias of a different sort emerged in the following decade as the forces moved from temperance to total abstinence. The Washingtonian Total Abstinence Society reached Massachusetts in 1841 and enlisted the support of tens of thousands, many of them workingmen.[75] For the first time, the temperance movement struck deep roots in the working class. Several branches appeared in Lynn, and the town became the home of the *Essex County Washingtonian,* which Christopher Robinson, a Lynn shoe manufacturer popular among journeymen, published through most of the decade. The key to the success of the Washingtonians was their manner of promoting abstinence.[76] They dispensed with the stilted rhetoric and stuffy propriety of earlier societies and relied on the vivid, earthy testimony of reformed drunkards like Samuel Hayward, a popular speaker from Boston. "Many of the leaders," one historian of the movement noted, "were uneducated, and their addresses were not always of an elevated character. They chose to conduct their meetings in their own way, without dictation from any one."[77] Members signed a pledge to total abstinence, paid dues of $.25 to join, and promised $.125 cents per week to support the cause. Unlike the earlier societies, which relied on the law to enforce temperance, the Washingtonians went out among the drinkers, spoke kindly but firmly, recounted their own experiences and showed at all times a compassion that was noticeably absent in earlier efforts. They did not self-righteously condemn the drinker nor threaten the drinker with punishment, but instead depicted in the testimony of first hand experience what one ought to expect should one continue drinking. The Washingtonians also recognized that heavy drinking was often the result of poverty, frustration, and despair. They, therefore, sought to build pride by stressing the subject's strengths rather than his faults. They collected food and clothing and obtained offers of employment to help the drunkard recover self-esteem. This policy was largely the outgrowth of the personal experiences of men who were the outstanding orators in the movement. John Hawkins, for example, "was easily the most successful of the self-appointed orators." He was a hat maker from Baltimore, who lost his job during the depression of 1837 and, in the midst of his poverty, turned to heavy drinking. Another leader was John Bartholomew Gough, who spoke several times in Lynn to large crowds. He was a bookbinder from England who also suffered ruin during the depression of 1837, a trying period in his life that contributed to the death of his wife.

The leading figures in the Journeymen Cordwainers Society of the 1840s, founders and contributors to the *Awl*, were also prominent in the Washingtonian movement. William A. Fraser, William Skelton, John Gibson, and William Parker, for example, would often speak at temperance meetings on Friday and at Journeymen Cordwainers' meetings on Saturday.[78] It was probably in the Washingtonian Society that they acquired their experience in public speaking. Although some prominent citizens viewed outdoor public meetings in the streets of Lynn as improper, the Washingtonians were among the first to go into the streets for listeners. John Gibson, for instance, would speak to large crowds of journeymen from atop a lastings box on a wagon that young shoemakers dragged from Woodend to the common, stopping occasionally so that Gibson could shout his opening lines: "O Lynn! I love thy rocks, thy hills, thy running brooks! But what makes thy people have such haggard looks'"[79] There was a close tie between the Washingtonians and the Cordwainers Society. The Cordwainers' Tea Party or Social Gathering in 1844 was modeled after affairs similar to those the Washingtonians sponsored.[80]

Although the society contained abstainers from the ranks of both manufacturers and journeymen, a parting of the ways among Washingtonians came on the question of legal coercion versus moral suasion.[81] Temperate workingmen tended to oppose a resort to the law to compel drinkers to desist. Not only was the method ineffective in separating the drinker from the bottle, but the law typically fell more heavily on the poor than the rich. Critics noted a double standard in the application of laws prohibiting the sale of liquors. "There are some who are willing to have what is termed *low places* closed," one writer declared, "while such as are termed respectable should not be molested."[82] A poor man unable to pay a fine went to the workhouse, while the rich man paid his fine and went home. Furthermore, legal coercion would, in the words of one opponent, "paralyze our influence for good over the yet unclaimed inebriate." Customers also sympathized with the rumseller and viewed him as a persecuted man.[83] Instead, Washingtonians should rely on their "motto . . . never forsake a brother—if he fail once, twice, or even the third time, receive him again." Toward the drunkard one should "pity his sorrow, weep over his follies, commiserate his forlorn condition, and assist him to shake off his terrible load."[84]

The leading advocates of legal coercion, on the other hand, were William Rich, Jonathan Buffum, a former shoe manufacturer turned paint and hardware dealer, and William Diamond Thompson, the shop supervisor for Nathan Breed.[85] All were Quakers, closely tied to the "grinders" of "extortion hollow," who figured so prominently in the liturgy of the cordwainers society. One harsh critic of Thompson said that he was "a man justly despised by two thirds of our citizens—a man who does dog's work for 'Nathan,' i.e., barking and growling."[86] Nathan and Isaiah Breed, for example, were the circulators of petitions in Lynn during the 1850s that called upon city authorities to enforce the town's licensing laws and crack down on offenders.[87] In his own shop, Nathan Breed kept a barrel of ginger beer for his worker and refused employment to anyone who was known to drink.[88] The reformers' penchant for coercion, intimidation, or threats seemed related, in the eyes of many, to the way they treated their own employees, or "hands," as they were called. One temperance advocate testified that when temperance reformers attended meetings of workingmen, they were "condemned unheard because of either their occupations or their associations." It is not surprising that in the area of temperance workingmen showed hostility to men whom they had grown to dislike for other reasons.[89]

The journeymen's tendency to oppose the coercive efforts of middle-class moral reformers who used the law to impose their will on the public emerged again during the panic of 1857. City officials elected on a coalition temperance ticket put into law their conviction that Lynn's working people could best weather the depression if they practiced thrift and self-discipline. They resolved to end "rum and rowdeyism" and create the "morality, temperance, and good citizenship" needed to secure "a future of peace, order, quietness, and prosperity." They deemed it especially important to prevent workers from wasting their money on "low theatricals and circus exhibitions which drain so many hundred hard-earned dollars from our people."[90] They refused to grant licenses to "low amusements," which attracted "the idle, the dissipated, the unhappy, the profane, the spendthrift, the intemperate, the quarrelsome, the lecherous, the giddy, and the simple." The law was not designed to control the behavior of respectable people; they naturally avoided "so near an alliance with the above dregs of society." But young workingmen and working women were too often caught in the snares laid by the "vicious set of men," who sponsored the amusements. The coercive policy that city officials implemented in the year 1857 provoked a reaction from the populace. In December 1858, a "People's ticket" carried the city election, winning every ward in the town and electing a new mayor by a vote of 1188 to 911. According to one observer, "the recent election of city officials will inaugurate a new administration of men who are not disposed to oppress you, but whose motto is 'Live, and let live.' "[91]

The journeymen began to exhibit resentment and bitter opposition to the view of poverty that the moral reformers had impressed upon society. The reformers who drafted, implemented, and administered Lynn's poor laws explained poverty as the result of intemperance, laziness, moral corruption, and a lack of thrift and self-discipline. In their treatment of paupers in the Alms House and of those who collected partial relief, they sought to make pauperism so harsh and humiliating that citizens would do their utmost to avoid becoming paupers. The depressions that periodically paralyzed the shoe industry, destroying dozens of shoe firms and creating mass unemployment, caused all but a few citizens to abandon such a simplistic explanation for pauperism. They recognized that there were hundreds of respectable, temperate journeymen who were eager to find employment. To treat them as paupers would be disastrous, and to allow "the laboring poor" to go hungry would be dangerous. As the editor of the *Lynn Mirror* noted in May of 1837, those who demand bread "will speak in a voice that will shake the nation to its centre. The moment their children cry for bread, that moment is the cry of civil war threatened."[92] But despite this warning and the realization that a new approach was needed, the middle-class in Lynn could propose nothing more than a liberalized relief system. In 1837, one citizen suggested that the town purchase flour wholesale and distribute it to needy citizens.[93] In 1842, Isaiah Breed proposed that wealthier citizens supply funds for a soup house. During the depression of 1857, a meeting of middle-class citizens resolved that "honest poverty is no crime; and in this community suffering or destitution ought not to be, and shall not be permitted."[94] There were recommendations for the public purchase and dispensing of foodstuffs, sewing circles to make clothes for the needy, and the solicitation of donations for the unemployed.

Workingmen would have nothing to do with these suggestions. One contributor to *The Awl* ridiculed Isaiah Breed's pious declarations of concern for the plight of the laboring poor and his offer to help set up a soup house. "Who, I ask you, have always been the first in the day of prosperity to solicit the aid and labor of the 'jour,' and to extend their manufacturing beyond our limits. And who, when a slight reaction in business takes place, were the very first man to 'cut, sack' and 'turn off' their own townsmen. You, if I recollect right, adopted this course in the year of 1837, and in the winter of '42."[95] Respectable mechanics did not want a soup house; they wanted employment and decent wages. William D. Chamberlain, a former shoemaker and bag boss who had been arrested years before for burning in effigy a large shoe manufacturer, told a citizens meeting: "All we ask, as mechanics, is work." "A man will see his family suffer long," Chamberlain noted, "before he will go to a committee for relief." Another critic called upon Lynn's manufacturers to cease their offers of charity and instead dismiss their outworkers.[96] The debate over poor relief policy during the depressions of the 1850s revealed the cleavage between the journeymen and their employers. The bosses viewed the workers' poverty as unfortunate but unavoidable, a problem that could best be alleviated by grants of food and other necessities. The shoemakers, on the other hand, rejected the charity, blamed the bosses for causing their poverty by paying low wages and employing cheap labor in the countryside. The failure of leading citizens, acting as mediators between jours and bosses, to penetrate to the source of the journeymen's poverty, their inability to offer anything other than public relief, helped demonstrate to the Lynn shoemakers the need for independent collective action.

The journeymen's growing estrangement from their employers also conditioned their response to the slavery issue. The leading abolitionists in Lynn were middle class, largely Quaker, with close ties to the manufacturers most disliked by the journeymen. The most militant wing of the movement was made up largely of the sons and daughters of the well-to-do manufacturers. Known in Lynn as "Comeouters," the militant element directed their efforts primarily at the churches, demanding that the assembled Christians either condemn slavery and the racism that kept blacks in Lynn from white churches or segregated them in separate pews, or "come out" from such dens of apostasy.[97] The "Comeouters" included William Bassett, a Quaker, the son of a shoe manufacturer; James N. Buffum, a native of Maine, a lumber dealer and also a Quaker, and Lydia Estes Pinkham, also of Quaker background. Not all abolitionists were Friends, but most were. So prevalent was radical abolitionist sentiment among the younger, more intellectually inclined Quakers that Friends Meeting closed the Sunday School for several years rather than allow the abolitionist teachers to educate their children.[98] Although William Bassett repeatedly criticized the elder Friends for their moral cowardice, prominent Quakers were largely sympathetic to the abolitionist movement, standing aloof from direct action but lending financial support as well as verbal endorsement to the goal of ending slavery.[99]

The journeymen's hostility to the abolitionist movement derived from their hostility to manufacturers, who were abolitionists. As they said of the manufacturers in the preamble to the Cordwainers' Society constitution, the bosses were "noble and high minded philanthropists. But while they have been fighting against the slavery of the south, they have been grinding down the laboring men of the north, thereby enslaving them to a greater degree (in one sense) for the poor negro has a master, both in sickness and in health; while the poor white man is a slave as long as he is able to toil, and a pauper when he can toil no more."[100] Another writer noted, "when I see men who have never been known by a single act of benevolence, signing their names in the newspapers to long rigamaroles about slavery, I think it looks very much like fishing for notoriety."[101] And a Lynn shoemaker saw a similar contradiction in his own employer. His boss threatened him with eviction from the house he rented unless he made shoes at a price lower than the shoemaker could obtain elsewhere. "Now this man," he sneered, "is what is called a christian . . . and an abolitionist; and I think he is an abolitionist with a vengeance; he goes for emancipating the black slaves of the South while he is grinding his white slaves to the dust." If a Lynn citizen should "meet with him at an abolition meeting and hear him talk, you would think he had a soul large enough to contain the universe."[102] Another shoemaker also stressed the hypocrisy of "these men professing to be abolitionists, friends to the rights of man, and making slaves at home."[103]

If outspoken shoemakers were harsh in their denunciation of hypocrisy in their employers, their hostility did not push them to a defense of slavery. Racism was widespread in Lynn; most citizens for example referred to blacks as niggers, and it is doubtful if one could find a single shop in Lynn with a black cordwainer. Furthermore, shoemakers were most likely present in the mob that attacked George Thompson, the English antislavery lecturer, and drove him from Lynn.[104] They probably also participated in the destructive foray against the office of the *Lynn Record*—"that dirty *thee* and *thou* concern."[105] But one does not find in the letters of journeymen much evidence to support the view that racism was the principal clause of their hostility to the antislavery movement. They did not argue, as some in Lynn did, that slavery was an appropriate system for an inferior race or that if you "give a Negro his tambourine or banjo he is a happy man."[106] And unlike the loyalists of the Democratic and Whig parties, they were not terribly eager to prove their loyalty to the Southern slave holders by suppressing a movement that was likely to "tend directly to an insurrection of the negroes."[107]

They were most angered by the failure of most abolitionists to condemn wage slavery and grant that a similarity existed between chattel slavery in the South and the wage system in the North. One shoemaker, for example, insisted that most Lynn cordwainers labored under "slaving conditions." "I can call it by no other name," he said, "for we are slaves in the strictest sense of the word. For do we not have to toil from the rising of the sun to the going down of the same, for our masters— aye, masters, and for our daily bread, for a mere living."[108] And another journeymen informed his fellow mechanics that "our present condition and future prospect are not much better than the southern slaves. What can we expect to lay up for a day of want, when it takes all we earn, to provide for our daily wants."[109] It was especially galling for shoemakers to see manufacturers "enjoying the titles of honest, honorable, and benevolent men," while treating their workers "like so many old and broken down southern slaves."[110]

The journeymen also challenged the arrogance of manufacturers who exhibited such a sense of moral superiority in their view of the South, refusing to see in their own vaunted system of free labor features that paralleled chattel slavery. Although some workingmen came close to arguing there was no essential difference between the two, they never suggested that chattel slavery replace free labor or that white workingmen become slaves. Instead they sought to redirect the moral outrage of Northern opinion toward conditions in the north that were strikingly similar to the conditions of Southern slavery. They argued that slavery consisted "not in names, but in facts." It did not matter "what kind of lash is used, whether it be of leather, or the more potent lash of want and poverty, so long as any lash be used." Nor did it matter "whether the laborer be sold by another, or be forced to sell himself." In each case, slavery was "subjection to the will of another." "So long as one portion of the community labor for the other class, so long will the employers be slave-holders and the employed, slaves." Wage earners were thus slaves: "slaves to a monied aristocracy—slaves to an unnatural system of society."

When examined closely, the two systems were similar to many observers. "The southern slave's labor is bought for a certain sum during his life. The northern slave's labor is bought for a certain sum yearly." In each case, the wage earner and slave "receives but a subsistence, while the fact is indisputable that the hours of labor at the south are many less than at the north." In the south, "the poor negro must work or be whipped; the poor white laborer must work or be starved." In another respect, the position of the wage earner was worse than that of the slave. "The negro is like the farm horse, worked by his master and by him cared for; the white laborer is like the stable horse, worked by everybody, and cared for by nobody, and finally, when too old to work longer, is turned out on the common to die."[111] Thus, the failure of the abolitionist movement to win support among workingmen was due mainly to the prominence of certain manufacturers in the movement and the failure of all but a few abolitionists to condemn wage slavery as vociferously as they did chattel slavery.

If the shoemaker were suspicious of moral reform and hostile to abolitionism, they warmly embraced free soilism. Free soilism swept through Lynn in the late 1840s, attracting some abolitionists and conscience Whigs but drawing most of its support from the "free democrats." In the election of 1848, the Free Soil Party handily defeated its opponents, with Van Buren outpolling his rivals by a margin of 900 to 550 for Zachary Taylor, the Whig candidate, and 728 for Lewis Cass, the Democrat.[112] Many shoemakers undoubtedly remained in the Whig and Democratic parties, but for others free soilism meant the application of the labor theory of value in its pristine simplicity to the basic problem of land ownership. In the early 1840s, several years before the appearance of the Free Soil Party, journeymen shoemakers directed their attention to the western lands and developed a program similar to the one that George Henry Evans, the New York agrarian, popularized a decade before.

In the view of the journeymen affiliated with the National Reform movement, land was a gift that God bestowed upon man for his sustenance.[113] The American Revolution destroyed the notion that ownership derived from royal grants and established the principle that man possessed an inalienable right to life, liberty and property.[114] Life and liberty were meaningless without property. Because all citizens engaged in "the common struggle for liberty, all should share in the blessings of freedom, and, in the language of Moses, 'the land should be sold no more forever.' "[115] One gained rightful ownership of the land only by living on it and mixing one's labor with it; "hence the importance of throwing open the public lands to actual settlers; no one possessing more than enough for his subsistence, thus making our republic what it should be, a nation of freedom and freeholders."[116] And a report from the Committee of the Boston Mechanics and Laborers Association informed the Lynn shoemakers that "Universal Monopoly must give place to Societary ownership, occupancy, and use. The right of every human being to the soil whereon, and the tools and machinery wherewith to labor must be established; the right of every man to the production of his own hands must be acknowledged, and the law of God universally applied, 'If a man will not work neither shall he eat.' "[117] According to this view, no man had the right to take for himself what God intended for the use of all men. "The earth was given him for his inheritance," one shoemaker wrote, "and it should be inalienable." Yet, he noted further, "as soon as a man arrives to years of reflection, he looks around upon the earth, he sees the uncultivated fields, and saving pines, and sturdy oaks, he asks, whose are these? He is answered, Not yours, and should you dare to appropriate one or the other to yourself, yonder see a house of correction; hither you will be sent to atone for the crime."[118] And it was the ownership of these "natural gifts from God" that was the source of the monied aristocracy's power over laboring men. Without access to the property with which to mix his labor and possess the full fruit of his toil, the workingman was "doomed to drag out a life of servitude and want." Beholden to another man for the right to work, and thus to live, the mechanics saw themselves as "serfs and slaves."[119]

Although a number of historians have painstakingly demonstrated that the Western lands provided no safety valve for urban workingmen, unless perhaps by diverting emigration from the cities, there was a safety valve of the mind, a myth perhaps but one which became real to men who acted upon it as if it were true. The revival of the agrarianism of Evans in the 1840s was a step backward for men who dimly perceived the specter of capitalism, a system that demanded that workingmen sell themselves for a wage in order to subsist. "Wherever we turn our eyes," one man wrote, "we see unsurmountable obstacles presented to our view. Here we see a monied aristocracy hanging over us like a mighty avalanche, threatening annihilation to every one who dares question their right to enslave and oppress the poor and unfortunate." The question he then posed was "How shall we escape from a curse that we cannot avoid? The answer is self-evident," he asserted, "the improvement of the public lands."[120] Free soilism thus was partly a flight from an oppressive but invincible foe who was rapidly gaining in strength. "Where shall we go," a workingman asked, "but on to the land; deprive us of this and you reduce us to the condition of the serfs of Europe."[121]

There is also evidence that some workingmen in the free soil movement envisioned the possibility of linking producers on the land with producers in the manufacturing cities. At a National Reform meeting in January of 1845, for instance, participants discussed freedom of the public lands in conjunction with the creation of producers and consumers cooperative stores. They perhaps envisioned a system under which workingmen in Associated Labor Societies would exchange their products directly with producers on the land, taking in return the necessities of life that they would distribute through their Workingmen's Protective Unions. They would bypass the middle men, who extracted an exorbitant fee for their service. One man asked if it were not true that goods tripled in value as they passed through the hands of middle men in the cities.[122] For those who remained in the cities and did not pursue their claim to a share of the land, free soilism offered a possible means of insuring that life's necessities would at least remain with freemen and producers with whom they could enter an alliance bred of mutual dependence.[123]

There were some middle-class reformers who combined in their social philosophy an amalgam of temperance, abolitionism, free soilism, and evangelical protestantism and yet gained immense popularity among the Lynn cordwainers. An example of such a rare animal was the Hutchinson family of Lynn, a group of musicians and singers who put to verse and music the reform principles they upheld. The journeymen frequently invited them to their social gatherings. The following excerpt from one of their songs, "The Popular Creed," may partly explain their strong appeal to the Lynn shoemakers:

> Dimes and dollars! Dollars and dimes!
> An empty pocket's the worst of crimes!
> If a man's down, give him a thrust!
> Trample the beggar into the dust!
> Presumptuous poverty, quite appalling!
> Knock him over! Kick him for falling!
> If a man's up, oh, lift him higher!
> Your soul's for sale, and he's the buyer!
> Dimes and dollars! Dollars and dimes!
> An empty pocket's the worst of crimes!
>
> So get ye wealth, no matter how!
> No question's asked of the rich, I trow!
> Steal by night, and steal by day
> (Doing it all in a legal way!)
> Dimes and dollars! Dollars and dimes!
> An empty pocket's the worst of crimes!

In the area of regular party politics there is only fragmentary evidence to suggest the affiliations of the Lynn shoemakers in the years from 1830 to 1860.[125] Because of their numbers, no party could either win or compete effectively for power without the journeymen's support. But an examination of lists of elected officials who represented Lynn indicates that deference prevailed; shoemakers often voted but did not serve, and they selected their representatives largely from the ranks of popular manufacturers.[126]

Throughout most of the generation before the Civil War the Democratic party was the majority party in Lynn, maintaining power almost continuously from 1836 until the appearance first of the American and then of the Republican party. Lynn was the stronghold of the Democracy in an area of Massachusetts that was largely Whig, yet it is ironic that in the "Age of Jackson" the Democratic party did not gain the support of the Lynn shoemakers until Jackson gave way to Van Buren. In the elections of 1828 and 1832, Jackson suffered defeat, while Van Buren defeated his opponent 625 to 440 in 1836.[127] The new Democratic party resulted from the unification of the old Jacksonian group and the larger Anti-masonic Democratic Union, a sizable remnant of a once powerful movement that swept through Lynn in 1830 and for nearly four years thereafter dominated town government. The unified Democrats also seemed to obtain the larger share of the newcomers who settled in Lynn. The Whigs regularly challenged the Democrats, occasionally won a few contests in the late 1830s and 1840s, but more frequently retired from the hustings in defeat, causing the *Lynn News* to report glumly in 1848 that the Whigs were beaten "as usual."[128]

The Democrats inherited and wore ostentatiously the mantle of the anti-aristocratic party. They gave expression to the popular antipathy toward institutions like the Lynn Mechanics Bank, cheap paper money, and the "hocus pocus" of joint-stock corporations and insurance companies, all of which they portrayed as the creations of the monied aristocracy.[129] Furthermore, Lynn's largest shoe bosses were Whigs, a fact that did not go unmentioned by the Democrats or unnoticed by many shoemakers.[130] The Democrats traditionally opposed coercive reform that sought to impose a code of behavior on citizens who liked to drink, attend "jim crow" shows, bowling alleys, circuses, or billiard rooms. An illustration of some of the possible reasons for the Democrats' successful appeal to the majority of Lynn's shoemakers may be found in the controversy surrounding the proposed city charter in 1849 to 1850 and the first mayoralty contest.

Despite arguments to the contrary, Whigs generally disliked the town meeting, seeing it as a pyre of kindling, which demagogues too easily ignited with their inflammatory appeals to popular hatreds. They wished to conduct the town's business in an atmosphere of greater order, decorum, and propriety, free of interruptions, yelling, hisses, and boos; that is, away from the mob. They argued further that Lynn's population had grown so rapidly that the town meeting was outmoded and cumbersome: the prerogatives of government should be delegated to representatives rather than exercised directly. Lynn's population contained too many elements from which demagogues could fashion mobs to intimidate their opponents. One troubled observer, for example, said that Lynn had "a very large proportion of irresponsible and floating population who, under our present government, are not sufficiently under restraint."[131]

The Democrats rejected these arguments and, in their rebuttal, revealed the main tenets of their political philosophy. The town meeting was the "most perfect" system of two government because it "is based upon the true republican principle, that the people are the safest repository of power." Under the existing system, law and custom required that the constables inform each citizen of the time of the town meeting and of the business to be transacted. Notice of the meeting appeared in all meeting places at least two days in advance. The people in turn voiced their sentiments and voted their wishes directly and not through the medium of elected officials. And who were the people? They were not a large foreign and floating population but "natives of the town and permanent residents, attached to their institutions, and always ready to cherish and defend them." They were distinguished for their "good conduct, morality, virtue and intelligence" and should not be regarded as "an infuriated populace." The Democrats also detected in the proposed charter the ubiquitous hand of the aristocracy.

The Democrats saw in the movement for a city charter the classic example of an aristocracy seeking to undermine a republic. They believed that "the history of all former republics is full of instruction on this point." "The people," they warned, "were prevailed upon to surrender their rights—to delegate their power by degrees." And as the people became "engrossed in their pursuits, they became careless of their duties as citizens, and permitted the crafty and ambitious few to rule and manage so as to accustom them to arbitrary power—to make laws and regulations to hedge them in and deprive them of their rights." In short, they concluded that in Lynn as under "all former republics" power had been "constantly stealing from the many to the few."

Specifically, they noted that the meetings of the new government would be in the evening, "as they do in other cities," and would make attendance difficult for citizens in distant wards but easy for people from "the central wards" or business district of Lynn. In addition, the new government took power from the people and vested it in a handful of men largely because "a small body is much easier managed than a large one." Furthermore, "the mayor would have the power of an autocrat," with exclusive power of nomination of all officers to be chosen by the Board of Aldermen. He would appoint all the constables and assistants, city marshall and assistants and remove them at will. He would take from the fire companies the right to nominate the chief engineer and fire wards. Although the Democrats strongly condemned the charter of 1849, they conceded that if Lynn were to have a new city form of government they "ought at least to have a liberal one," a system that protected rather than hedged the rights of the people.[132]

A majority of people apparently agreed with this position. They defeated the first proposed charter and accepted the second by a vote of 1047 to 987. The modified plan reduced the salary and powers of the mayor, provided for the popular election of overseers and assessors, and provided remuneration for school committeemen. And in 1850,

George Hood, a prominent leader in the Lynn Democratic party and a leading critic of the first charter, won election to the office of mayor.

The returns from the various wards suggest the sources of Democratic strength. The Swampscott fishermen had not changed their party loyalty in more than a decade; they gave Hood 105 votes to his opponent's 11. But Hood's supporters were most numerous in Woodend where the largest portion of Lynn shoemakers lived. Hood received 328 votes to Thomas Bowler's 74, a margin of better than 4 to 1. The tallies were reversed in the business districts of downtown Lynn, the area of the town in which the largest shoe manufacturers lived and kept shop. According to tax rolls, the gap between rich and poor was greatest in the wards where the Whig candidate ran strongest. Ward 4, consisting of the Quaker Pudding Hill and the area around the bank and railroad station, gave Hood 174 votes and his opponent 317. The margin was about the same in Ward 5 around Market Street, Bowler defeating Hood 313 to 163. Thus, the shoemakers of Woodend and the fishermen of Swampscott formed the backbone of the Democratic vote, while the businessmen of Wards 4 and 5 composed the bulk of the Whig tally.[133]

The Democrats also appeared in the garb of the people's tribune in the several cases of child beating in the schools. An earlier section detailed the efforts of the moral reformers to inculcate stringent standards of discipline and obedience in the public schools. Resistance from refractory pupils sometimes provoked corporal punishment and, in turn, produced strong reactions from irate parents. In 1848, the school committee felt compelled to request parents to refrain from accosting teachers who had beaten their children. Yet the child beating continued. In 1852, an Irish boy in Ward 6 suffered a caning at the hands of Reverend Mr. Richards, a member of the school committee.[134] A year later, a teacher beat Josiah Hand. The Whigs tended to support the upholders of strong discipline in the schools, while the Democrats voiced opposition. One defender of corporal punishment argued that his opponents were "total strangers to all discipline, whether mental or moral," whether "in schools or families."[135] There was an implied connection here between disorder in the schools and disorder in the streets, taking the form of smoking and profanity, tumultuous assemblies and other forms of moral laxity that the schools were supposed to curb. A supporter warned against the dangerous opinion "that the teacher has not a right to punish, or that he has such a right only at the dictation of the parents."[136] The most celebrated case that brought divergent views of school discipline to the surface involved Samuel

King, a teacher in Ward 4, and the sons of several citizens. In 1851, the school committee, with the exception of George Hood, acquitted King of wrongdoing in punishing a boy. But the complaints against the stern, and some witnesses said lecherous, King mounted, and in 1857 the school committee fired him. The upper-class revered King, seeing him as the embodiment of the values they wished implemented in education and child rearing.[137] Despite King's departure from Lynn, the bourgeoisie enshrined King's memory in "Master King's Schoolboys Association," an organization made up mainly of manufacturers who had studied under King.[138]

The response of workingmen to the controversies surrounding the issues of corporal punishment in the schools, coercive moral reform, public relief, and antislavery suggest the formation of a common outlook that derived from a common social experience. And in the process of institution-building during the period 1830 to 1860, there were further indications that Lynn's voluntary institutions were increasingly reflecting class rather than neighborhood, age, or religion. Certain institutions such as the Academy, social clubs, reform societies, and Pine Grove cemetery were the vehicles for the fulfillment of needs felt by the middle class. In other areas of society—education, politics, and public policy—they exerted a profound influence, largely because they successfully merged the public interest with their own in a manner that evoked both compliance and support from a deferential society. Yet at the same time, workingmen felt and reacted against the class bias inherent in the society that was emerging under the aegis of the middle class. Both in their absence from middle-class institutions and in the institutions they created, they provided evidence for the formation of a working class in embryo. Their newspapers, trade societies, volunteer fire companies; and neighborhood social life all indicated a way of life separate, different, and sometimes opposed to the middle-class way. The cleavage that appeared first in their productive relationship and then reappeared in a multitude of forms throughout society, culminated finally in the great shoemakers strike of 1860.

# 11. The Great Shoemakers' Strike

The Great Shoemakers' Strike was not like a thunderclap from a clear sky nor like a summer squall that raged briefly and then blew out to sea. Instead, the strike of 1860 marks a turning point in Lynn's history: it was an end and a beginning. It marked an end to an appearance of harmony in the community; an end to the passive acceptance of the immutable laws of supply and demand by many deferential working people; an end to patient waiting, an end to the belief that the system would soon right itself, that manufacturers would regulate the shoe industry, set production quotas, prices, fair wages, and the ground rules of fair competition. Though unbeknownst to shoemaker and manufacturer alike, the strike of 1860 also marked the end to the putting-out system. Within a decade the method of production that had existed for half a century would give way to the factory system, and the shoemakers would begin abandoning the ten-footers and moving into the immense edifices that housed machines like the Blake stitcher and a host of other devices that soon followed, converting the shoemaker into a machine operative.

But the strike of 1860 was also a beginning. Industrial conflict between labor and capital would become almost commonplace in Lynn during the next half century. The strike of 1860 was merely the first of many open conflicts, unfolding in the same pattern, the same opponents, the same grievances, and many of the same methods. And the distinctive features of the new system, which journeymen dimly perceived in the 1830s and 1840s, would become clearer, sharper, inescapable: the gulf between worker and employer, the great disparity in the distribution of wealth, sharp differences in housing patterns, life style, education, and social habits; in brief, the labor question, that conflict of labor and capital, which seemed before to lurk only at one's elbow but now came to the fore. Trends present in the generation before 1860 became accelerated. Transiency in the work force, for example, became more marked. If in 1857, 180 jobless, homeless men took lodging in the jail, in the 1870s the figure reached into the thousands. The composition of neighborhoods more closely reflected class, and certain social institutions were more clearly the domain of a single class.

The immediate cause of the 1860 uprising was an expansion in the productive capacity of the shoe industry and its worsening impact on workingmen. In the absence of machinery and a further division of labor, increased production came in two ways. First, more workers became engaged in production. In the state of Massachusetts the number of males employed in making shoes grew from 29,252 in 1850 to 45,001 in 1855 and then dropped slightly to 43,068 in 1860. The number of female binders or stitchers increased from 22,310 in 1850 to 32,826 in 1855 and then dropped sharply to 19,215 in 1860, largely because of the introduction of the sewing machine. In 1850, Lynn manufacturers employed nearly 4,000 shoemakers; a decade later they employed 5,000. Probably more important than a larger work force in Lynn was the larger number of people outside the town who worked for Lynn bosses.

In the 1830s, Lynn manufacturers were drawing upon labor in the surrounding towns of Essex County. During the next decade they extended the labor market into New Hampshire and Maine. Lynn began to resemble an immense central shop, with dozens of express wagons carrying materials from Lynn to the countryside and returning with finished shoes. The expressmen either worked for the Lynn manufacturers or were self-employed labor contractors. The putting-out system blended nicely with traditional employment. In a declining agricultural region it allowed the outworker and his family to remain on the land and supplement their income from farming with wages from shoemaking. But the great spurt in production during the 1850s also suggests that the outworkers were giving more of their time to shoemaking than to farming. In fact, many outworkers did not live on the land at all. Instead, they moved to towns like Northwood, Farmington, and Dover, New Hampshire, which became manufacturing satellites to Lynn and Haverhill. By 1855, outworkers were making approximately three-fifths of the shoes Lynn bosses sold. From 1845 to 1855 the number of workers employed by Lynn manufacturers increased 57 percent, but shoe production increased 286 percent. In 1860, five express teams were delivering about 9000 cases of shoe work to workers in several New Hampshire towns. Thus, not only were more people engaged in production, but they were also producing more.

Increased output was partly due to a growing concentration on cheap shoes that required less training and skill. A trade journal of the shoe industry reported in 1860 that there were relatively few shoemakers who could make welted walking shoes or spring heel pumps. Most were making the cheaper, simpler set heel pumps, a shoe anyone could learn to make "in twelve easy lessons."[1]

The location of the central shops within Lynn is an indication of the manufacturers' dependence on outworkers. In 1850, there were only five central shops located in the vicinity of the railroad depot. A decade later there were 58.[2] The avenues that connected employer to worker ran along the railway lines and roads that radiated out from Lynn. The Lynn bosses were, therefore, practicing a form of colonialism. To survive in a highly competitive industry, they incessantly sought to reduce costs, and the largest item of cost was labor. They sent parcels of materials prepared in the central shop to outworkers who would assemble the parts at cheaper rates than workers in Lynn. This was the principal source of the widespread anger among the Lynn townspeople. It appeared that manufacturers were giving preference to outsiders, selfishly pursuing their own interests at the expense of the Lynn shoemakers and the town itself.

But this colonial system, with Lynn as the mother country and the farming villages as dependent satellites, began to show signs of strain. Independent shoe bosses began to appear in towns throughout the hinterland, bypassing the Lynn bosses and directly employing local people in their limited vicinity. The competition among Lynn bosses that had been intensive became more so with the appearance of new entrepreneurs eager to exploit a cheap labor supply at their doorstep.

By the mid-fifties the Lynn manufacturers did possess one important advantage, the sewing machine. This invention of Elias Howe and Isaac Singer was the single most important technological innovation in the shoe industry prior to 1860: the Lynn manufacturers bought them as fast as they could be made. An observer reported in 1856 that the demand for the machine was "immense and without a parallel."[3] Machine sewn work was superior to the hand sewn, and a machine operator could produce many times the number of uppers than could a binder. In 1860, one girl could stitch enough uppers to supply twenty shoemakers. The Lynn manufacturers either established their own battery of machines in the central shop and hired the operators directly or subcontracted the work to machine sewers who had their own sewing businesses. It was the advent of the sewing machine that largely explains the struggle of the female binders, who also struck in 1860. In that year, their wages had dropped to less than $.40 a day. Although rapid adoption of the sewing machine gave the Lynn bosses an advantage over their emerging rivals in the countryside, there is evidence that outworkers, probably with support from their employers, were acquiring the machines. The Massachusetts Legislature in 1858 ruled that the sewing machine of an owner-operator could not be attached for a bad debt.

Another indication of the intensified competition among manufacturers was the dedication in 1859 of a new shoe exchange in Boston.[4] Commission merchants established and operated the exchange, drawing their commissions by buying from the manufacturers and selling to wholesale purchasers. The shoe exchange would operate as an auction center at which shoe buyers from various parts of the country would place bids with commission merchants who, in turn, would allow the manufacturers to compete with one another for the orders the merchants held. The auction system in one way signified a step backward in the evolution of the shoe industry because the manufacturer would no longer deal directly with the buyer but rather indirectly through the commission merchant. It was as if the industry was returning to an earlier era when small bag bosses from Lynn carried in their shoes to the commission merchants. The reappearance of this system was further evidence of the cutthroat competition among hundreds of bosses.[5]

The demand for shoes throughout the United States did not keep pace with production. Despite expansion westward and rapid growth in population, it appears that infant shoe industries were arising in areas that had in the past purchased shoes made in New England. The South and the West remained large purchasers, but areas like upper New York, Ohio, Illinois, Michigan, Indiana, and Wisconsin were beginning to develop their own shoemaking centers. Lynn records occasionally mentioned natives who migrated westward and resumed their old lines of work.

A larger workforce, increased output, further decentralization, and an insufficient growth in demand brought crisis to capitalism in the shoe industry. Depressions became sharper and more frequent, each depression more severe than the one before. Unlike an earlier period in which depression seemed to affect the entire economy, as in 1837, for example, the economic slumps seemed to hit the shoe business alone. In the 1850s, for example, there were sharp declines in 1852, 1855, 1857 and again in late 1859, bringing wage cuts and massive unemployment. Yet as inventories disappeared and new orders resumed, wages failed to return to their pre-depression level, providing further evidence that the shoe industry was a sick industry.

The depression of 1857 was the catalyst that precipitated action among the Lynn cordwainers. The depression in Lynn was "extraordinarily severe," with whole families out of work and wages down to $.50 a day. Citizen groups held emergency meetings to provide relief to the destitute, but at the same time insisted they could only help in alleviating the effects of unemployment and could do nothing for the causes. Some also counseled patience and more stringent measures of frugality and self-discipline.[6] The Democratic organ in Lynn recognized the intensive competition among workers in a cheap labor market, but could only request manufacturers to hire just Lynn jours and for the jours themselves to go into farming or "go a fishing."[7] The journeymen seemed to emerge from the depression with a determination to deal with their problems in their own way.

Preparations for collective action began in the summer of 1858, a few months after the shoe business showed signs of recovery. Approximately 600 shoemakers gathered during July to hear a lecture on the rights of labor and to lay plans for a permanent organization—the Journeymen Cordwainers' Mutual Benefit Society—a name Lynn shoemakers traditionally chose for their organizations.[8] From the outset they resolved to build a strike fund from membership dues and a daily assessment of one penny. The featured speaker was Thomas G. Haynes, an itinerant organizer from Philadelphia, who explained the structure of the shoe industry, the growing power of capital, and the necessity for journeymen cordwainers throughout New England to combine in self defense. He assured them also that organizing efforts were proceeding in virtually every shoe manufacturing town in eastern Massachusetts.[9] During the next year and a half the Journeymen Cordwainers Society began to take shape under the leadership of committees that met with virtually every shoemaker in Lynn. Membership grew by the hundreds, each man pledging himself to contribute to the strike fund. In June of 1859, the Protective Leagues and Associations met in Boston and voted to strike at a date to be set by the leadership.[10] Although the Protective Leagues and Associations sought a simultaneous strike by all its branches, some leagues struck in the fall of 1859. The Lynn Society waited. It issued its bill of wages in early February and reported a week later that 1126 shoemakers pledged themselves to the wage schedule, while only 10 refused.[11] The action came none too soon; a new slump in the shoe business began in the early winter of 1860. The journeymen thus pledged themselves to withhold their labor until their employers had signed the bill of wages. The strike officially began on Wednesday, February 22, George Washington's Birthday, a day they intentionally chose to link their own militant spirit with that of a national hero. On Wednesday morning, thousands of shoemakers marched to the central shops and turned in their "wood" (lasts).

The strike that began on February 22, 1860, therefore, was not a spontaneous uprising of disorganized workingmen but the culmination of nearly two years of almost continuous preparation and careful planning. Despite the absence of machinery and factories in which large numbers of workers regularly assembled, the shoemakers were capable of a discipline and organization of a high order. Their administrative structure was based upon the ward or neighborhood, with executive and standing committees composed of representatives from the various sections of Lynn. They also created a special police force of 100 men, later enlarged to 200, to maintain discipline within the ranks and adherence to the policies of the organization. In other words, the administrative structure followed the neighborhood in the same way as earlier organizations—the volunteer fire companies, cooperative stores, political parties, and the earlier journeymen's societies. The journeymen also sent organizers into the surrounding towns of Essex County to persuade shoemakers to lay down their tools and strike for the same bill of wages the Lynn jours had drafted.[12]

The strike of 1860, in the portion of the total population participating, was probably the largest in Massachusetts history.[13] At the peak of the strike in early March, there were 40,000 or more people who took part in the meetings and parades that the workingmen sponsored. The female shoe binders greatly augmented the strikers' ranks in Lynn when they voted in early March to strike for their own price list. Elsewhere in New England the strike reached the manufacturing centers of New Hampshire—Dover, Northwood, Farmington, Middleton, Milton—and for a time forced expressmen to return unfinished work to Lynn and Haverhill manufacturers. The strike also reached deep into central Massachusetts, breaking out in the Worcester County towns of Milford and Grafton. Yet the largest turnouts were in the surrounding towns of Essex County.

It has been said that the early strikes in the United States resembled popular demonstrations more than they do the modern strike, which typically involves only the employees. The nature of the strike in Lynn, and elsewhere for that matter, illustrates the accuracy of that observation.

When thousands of Lynn journeymen and binders slogged through the snow on March 7, they did not march alone. Joining them were fire companies, militia units, cornet bands, neighbors, and friends whose support demonstrat the interlocking network of social relationships that existed in the mid-nineteenth-century New England town. One of the outstanding features of the strike was the breadth of support the journeymen and binders were able to evoke. This suggests that they were not viewed as malcontents, troublemakers, outsiders, foreigners or radicals whose grievances were thought ill-founded and whose actions threatened to destroy society. In other words, one finds none of the hysteria, fear, and dark foreboding that often characterize the response of the middle class to the actions of working people. The vehement denunciations, the cry of anarchy and mob rule, and the demand for the forcible suppression of lawlessness in the streets that came from the *Daily Advertizer*, the organ of conservative business interests in Boston, did not echo throughout Massachusetts, nor did these warnings deter citizens from tendering their support. They knew from personal experience that such dire warnings were groundless. The sheer size of the workforce in eastern Massachusetts engaged in shoe production, and the presence of the journeymen and binders in citizens organizations was partly the reason. In other words, many of the volunteer firemen, the militiamen, and band members were themselves journeymen and binders. In addition, those who were not, eagerly expressed their own support for neighbors and friends in an organized manner, working through organizations which admittedly had not been founded for that purpose. Their favorable response to the journeymen's and binders' cause also suggests that the shoe manufacturers were unable either to neutralize or win the support of these social institutions. It means also that the bulk of the people in many towns felt more in common with the shoemakers than with the bosses. If one examines the course of the strike in Lynn, one can discern the nature of the town's response.

Formal government in Lynn dissolved during the strike. There were no meetings of the city government, yet important decisions were made. Although the actual source of decision making is difficult to locate, power tended to gravitate toward a small group of anonymous persons and a few aldermen who met in secret session with the mayor. Executive and police powers lay with the mayor, Edward S. Davis, a former shoe manufacturer, secretary of the antislavery society, and Republican of Whig background. Davis was a pathetic figure: weak, indecisive, almost cowardly. He was elected as a friend of the people, one who would not oppress them with unpopular policies. But Davis's own behavior during the strike showed that he was merely a figurehead; stronger and more determined persons were in command. At a mass meeting on the first night of the strike he mumbled through a speech in a manne that was as confused as it was inaudible. He broke down the next day and retired to his bed, incapacitated some said because of nervous exhaustion, but more likely because he feared to see and hear the displeasure of the vast majority of his constituency. After his embarrassing appearance at the mass meeting, Davis did not reappear in public while the strike lasted, nor did he ever stand again for election. Yet he did continue to put his signature to the directives that emerged from his private meetings.

Outside intervention was almost immediate, unpopular with most Lynn people but necessary for the defense of the manufacturers' property rights. The success of the strike hinged on the journeymen's and binders' ability to prevent the making of shoes. Because the strike was almost unanimous within Lynn, the manufacturers depended entirely on makers outside the town and a few scabs whom they lodged in their attics and cellars. The journeymen could halt the making of shoes outside Lynn in two ways. One was to enlist the support of outworkers who would voluntarily join the strike and refuse to work for Lynn bosses at the old prices. This was the option which the leadership and a majority of strikers chose, largely because they feared violence. The second way was to halt the movement of raw materials from Lynn to the outworkers, a course of action which a large, aggressive minority favored. The scattered incidents of disorder and occasional fighting that occurred in the streets on the first day were triggered by the efforts of manufacturers to ship cases of materials out of Lynn on express wagons or railway cars. These incidents precipitated the decision of some city authorities to seek outside aid.

The intervention took several forms. On Thursday, February 23, the second day of the strike, the Attorney General of the Commonwealth, Stephen Phillips, arrived in Lynn. Phillips, a Whig from Salem with close ties to party colleagues in Lynn, came at the request of the mayor and a handful of aldermen. He in turn summoned General Sutton, commander of the Fourteenth Regiment, and instructed him to activate the Lynn Light Infantry, one of two militia companies of the Fourteenth based in Lynn. At the same time, Mayor Davis and his advisors took additional measures to protect the free movement of raw stock out of Lynn. They requested city officials in Salem, South Danvers, and Boston to send details of police officers. They also issued a call for one hundred special deputies to bolster Lynn's own police force. When the strikers assembled in the streets of Lynn on Friday, February 24, they faced a force of more than a hundred men and police from Boston and South Danvers. They were also aware that the Lynn Light Infantry, armed with muskets and live ammunition, remained in the armory, ready to move at a moment's notice.

The use of massive police power was a shattering blow. Some citizens undoubtedly commended the mayor's action as the only effective means for curbing anarchy and lawlessness in the streets and upholding the right of the manufacturer to send his shoe stock where he chose without interference. A larger number were shaken by an action, which, more clearly than any other, revealed the cleavages that split Lynn into two warring camps. Lynn as a unified community was dead. It could no longer settle its own internal differences without outside intervention. Workers were angry and disillusioned. They also felt betrayed that their elected officials would instruct their own neighbors to shoot them down if they dared interfere with the movement of shoe stock. They were especially angry because the mayor had not granted them the chance to police their own ranks with the force of 200 journeymen whom they had chosen to insure compliance with the decisions of the Journeymen's Society. The introduction of armed force was the single most important event during the strike that demonstrated to workers their own lack of power, the manner in which their own officials viewed them, and the power of the manufacturers in the councils of government. It was for this reason that six months later they organized politically as a class and won control of nearly every position in the city government. Their strike leaders, Alonzo Draper and James Dillon, took control of the police force, immediately fired the police chief and his deputy and hired new police offers from the ranks of the journeymen.[14]

Although the Lynn shoemakers lacked support from the city authorities they won the backing of large segments of the nonshoemaker citizenry. The volunteer fire companies were colorful additions to their massive parades through the streets of Lynn. The Lynn Cornet Band invariably provided the martial music, while the Lynn City Guards acted as military escort to the thousands who jammed the streets in a procession stretching for a half mile or more. Journeymen painters hand-lettered and embellished the banners and placards which the jours and binders carried. Farmers in the countryside furnished several wagons loaded with potatoes, onions, and other vegetables for the strikers and their families, while a lumber dealer donated a stand of trees and a partial shipment of wood for fuel. The Swampscott fisher-men, on one occasion, supplied 1000 pounds of fish and scores of bushels of clams for an immense collation in Rocks Pasture on the out-skirts of Lynn. And Alonzo Lewis, poet, historian, archivist, teacher and surveyor, provided the "Cordwainers' Song" which became a strike anthem:

> Shoemakers of Lynn, be brave!
>   Renew your resolves again;
> Sink not to the state of slave,
>   But stand for your rights like men!
>
> Resolve by your native soil,
>   Resolve by your fathers' graves,
> You will live by your honest toil,
>   But never consent to be slaves!
>
> The workman is worthy [of] his hire,
>   No tyrant shall hold us in thrall;
> They may order their soldiers to fire,
>   But we'll stick to the hammer and awl.
>
> Better days will restore us our right,
>   The future shall shine o'er the past;
> We shall triumph by justice and right,
>   For like men we'll hold onto the last!
>
> The peaceable people of Lynn
>   Need no rifles to keep them at peace;
> By the right of our cause we shall win;
>   But no rum, and no outside police.[15]

The petty bourgeoisie in Lynn were more cautious. As the strike dragged on into March and reached a stalemate, concerned citizens sought to mediate the conflict. Lewis Josselyn, editor of the Lynn *Bay State*, a former candidate for mayor and a leader of the Democratic party, chaired a meeting of grocers, provisions dealers, master mechanics, and other small merchants who assembled in mid-March to determine a policy. They acknowledged that the shoe industry was the foundation of Lynn's economy and that a cessation of business harmed everyone, including men like themselves who depended on retail trade and construction. They conceded to the journeymen the right to with-hold their labor and to the manufacturers to withhold their material, and in the face of these conflicting but legitimate rights urged conciliation.

They could do little more, they argued, because the problem lay outside Lynn and was inherent in the structure of a system and industry that encompassed an area far larger than Lynn alone. In other words, the private ownership of property was accepted as given—inviolate and unalterable. The concerned citizens, therefore, resolved to mitigate the suffering and hardship that accompanied the strike. They appointed a committee to work with the striking journeymen in soliciting money and supplies for families in need.

The strike in Lynn petered out in April, and it is difficult to say if the strikers won or lost. The journeymen and binders who signed the price list originally pledged themselves to withhold their labor until all the bosses had signed the bill of wages. But because the manufacturers could reach no agreement that would be binding on all, they responded differently to the strikers' demands. Some agreed to the bill of wages, while others held out to the end. The strikers, in turn, began to break ranks. There were some who agreed with Joseph Conner's call for "war to the knife, and the knife to the hilt," and by mid-April it appeared that many journeymen had returned to work, some of them depositing their wage increases into a fund for the relief of journeymen still on strike. There undoubtedly was intense bitterness among shoemakers who felt betrayed by their fellows who broke the original agreement and returned to work before all had gained employment at the new wages. Partly to assuage these feelings and provide jobs, a group of citizens, including some journeymen, formed the Lynn Boot and Shoe Company, a joint-stock manufactory with each share at ten dollars, to give employment at the new wage rates.

The strike revealed much of Lynn's past, making visible what the slow passage of time had obscured. For a brief time, Lynn's history was compressed into a single moment. The old patterns of deference retained much of their strength in binding many working people to middle-class citizens. Some trusted in their employers' good judgment on all matters, relied upon their leadership, and sought to emulate them in every particular. Others were profoundly aware of their own distinctiveness and the many ways in which they differed from their employers, but were usually immobilized and made passive by a deeply rooted fatalism. They suffered patiently and did their best to survive the conditions of hardship and insecurity that had been the lot of their kind throughout history. So too did there remain political, religious, sectional, and moral differences that cut across class lines and presented the appearance of a multitude of interest groups with diverse membership. But the single most important change that made the

Lynn of 1860 different from the Lynn of 1800 was the tendency toward the formation of class and class consciousness. Lynn was a town but no longer a community: a people growing apart, two parts with two bodies of shared experiences, each part creating traditions, values, and institutions that answered to their distinctive needs. Two people, then, divisible not by age, nor by neighborhood, nor by nationality, but by the ownership of the means by which they lived, one possessing and able to buy others, the other dispossessed and selling themselves to live, one owning power and the other seeking it.

# Notes

## Notes to Chapter 1

1. Most of this interpretation is based on early chapters in Alonzo Lewis and James R. Newhall, *History of Lynn, Essex County, Massachusetts* (Boston: John Shorey, 1865).

2. In 1772, Lynn ranked tenth in tax levies and dropped to eleventh in 1782. *Lynn Scrapbooks* 25: 39. The *Lynn Scrapbooks* are collections of articles that originally appeared in local newspapers. Sometimes the original source and author are identified; many times they are not.

3. There were 281 Newhalls, 259 Breeds, 195 Alleys, and 162 Johnsons, see *Lynn Directory*, 1832, p. 32.

4. Warren Mudge Breed, "Some Abandoned Industries of Lynn," *The Register of the Lynn Historical Society*, 14: 184–89.

5. Ibid.

6. One old Lynn resident recalled that in 1790 Salem supplied Lynn "almost entirely" with West India goods. And up to 1825, "we had our Sunday clothes there made by merchant tailors." *Lynn Scrapbooks* 47: 25.

7. *Lynn Scrapbooks* 23: 6. There were no grocery stores in Lynn in 1810.

8. Lewis and Newhall, *History of Lynn*, pp. 297–500, for biographical sketch of Gray.

9. Best account of these efforts to establish new forms of employment is Warren M. Breed, "Some Abandoned Industries of Lynn," pp. 178–207.

## Notes to Chapter 2

1. Warren Mudge Breed, "Banks and Bankers of Old Lynn," *The Register of the Lynn Historical Society* 20 (1916): 37. Breed reported there were 18 banks of issue in Massachusetts, three of them in Boston and two in Salem. Lynn manufacturers usually went either to Boston or Salem for discounts.

2. Blanche E. Hazard, *The Organization of the Boot and Shoe Industry in Massachusetts before 1875* (Cambridge, Mass.: Harvard University Press, 1921), pp. 23ff.

3. Figure is from the *Boston Palladium* of 1827, quoted in Lewis and Newhall, *History of Lynn*, p. 335.

4. *Lynn Directory*, 1832, contains an historical sketch of the shoe inudstry by Alonzo Lewis.

5. Lewis and Newhall, *History of Lynn*, p. 328.

6. Howard Kendall Sanderson, *Lynn in the Revolution* (Boston: W. B. Clarke, 1909), vol. I, p. 9.

7. James R. Newhall, *Centennial Memorial of Lynn, Essex County, Massachusetts* (Lynn: Thomas Breare, 1876), pp. 50–65 for historical sketch of the early shoe industry.

8. For an account of Breed's career, see James R. Newhall, *Centennial Memorial of Lynn*, pp. 60–61.

9. Another merchant-capitalist from Lynn, Benjamin Ireson, pushed markets for Lynn shoes into the Caribbean and Mediterranean areas. See *Lynn Scrapbooks* 2: 54.

10. Quoted in James R. Newhall, *Centennial Memorial of Lynn*, pp. 71–72.

11. For a brief description of the extent of shoemaking in Lynn in 1783, see *Lynn Scrapbooks* 2: 15. The author estimated there were fifty small shops in 1783.

12. For text of petition and signers, see *Lynn Scrapbooks* 2: 15.

13. Letter from Jacob Ingalls, reprinted in *Lynn Scrapbooks* 2:52.

14. Lynn's trade with the South was double-edged in its impact. One writer believed that heavy dependence on Southern buyers, who often did not pay their bills, made the business unstable and risky. He wrote, "It was not until the West was opened that the manufacturers began to thrive, and only those who were very careful and prudent before that day, were able to accumulate much property." See *Lynn Scrapbooks* 2: 51. Nathan D. Chase was another manufacturer who blamed the South for the frequency of failure among Lynn shoe bosses. See *Lynn Scrapbooks* 23: 2.

15. Firm of Daniel Silsbee and Micajah Burrill, Jr. See *Lynn Scrapbooks* 2: 50. Their major market for shoes was Balitmore.

16. *Lynn Scrapbooks* 2: 52, 53. John D. Atwill was in business in Petersburg, Va., before 1805.

17. *Lynn Scrapbooks* 13: 61, obituary of David Taylor, includes discussion of his operations in New Orleans.

18. Secretary of the Commonwealth. *Statistics of the Condition and Products of Certain Branches of Industry in Massachusetts*, 1837, 1845, 1855. Comparative employment figures for textile and shoes:

|                 | 1837   | 1845   | 1855   |
|-----------------|--------|--------|--------|
| Cotton Goods    | 19,754 | 20,710 | 34,787 |
| Boots and Shoes | 39,068 | 45,877 | 74,326 |

19. Text of letter, Ebenezer Breed to Amos Rhodes, Philadelphia, May 16, 1793, reprinted in Lewis and Newhall, *History of Lynn*, p. 524.

20. A thorough account of the changes in the organization of production can be found in John Philip Hall, "The Gentle Craft: A Narrative of Yankee Shoemakers" (unpublished Ph.D. Dissertation, Columbia University, 1953).

21. *Lynn Scrapbooks* 24: 8, for a description of an early central shop.

22. *True Workingman*, December 27, 1845.

23. Malcolm Keir, *Manufacturing Industries in America: Fundamental Economic Factors* (New York: Ronald Press, 1920), pp. 220–21.

24. *First Census of the United States.*

25. *First Census of the United States; Second Census of the United States; Third Census of the United States.*

26. *Lynn Scrapbooks* 11: 23, for a description of early bag bosses. For modest size of many Lynn shoe firms, see Louis McLane, Secretary of the Treasury, *Report on Manufactures* 1832 (House Doc. 308). The term "jours" was often used in place of journeymen.

27. *Lynn Scrapbooks* 23: 1, for a description of these joint undertakings.

236

## Notes to Chapter 3

1. On the formation of the Lynn Mechanics' Rifle Corps, *Lynn Scrapbooks*, 17: 25; on launching of the *Industry*, Lewis and Newhall, *History of Lynn*, p. 373, and *Lynn Scrapbooks*, 6: 1; on founding of the Lynn Mechanics' Institute, *Lynn Scrapbooks*, 46: 2; on formation of Lynn Mechanics Bank, Ellen Mudge Burrill, *Essex Trust Company, Lynn, Massachusetts, 1814–1914* (n.p., n.d.), p. xxi; and on the creation of Lynn Mechanics Mutual Fire and Marine Insurance Company, Lewis and Newhall, *History of Lynn*, p. 398.

2. James R. Newhall, *Proceedings in Lynn, Massachusetts, June 17, 1879: Being the two hundred and fiftieth anniversary of the settlement* (Lynn, 1879), p. 113.

3. Lewis and Newhall, *History of Lynn*, pp. 351–52.

4. James R. Newhall, *Centennial Memorial of Lynn*, p. 28.

5. *Lynn Record*, August 14, 1833.

6. Benjamin F. Newhall, "Sketches of Saugus," no. 33. He further describes the encounter with the merchants as "a furnace of affliction to the seller, of indescribable agony."

7. *Awl*, November 9, 1844.

8. The town meeting recognized a connection between the oppression of the Mother Country and the privileged elite in America. One resolution, passed on December 16, 1773, attacked "A vile and corrupt ministry, supported by enemies and traitors to their Countrey, [who] have manifested the Stupidity to Sacrifice Liberty to avarise, and the wickedness when occasion Shall Serve to Riot on the Spoils of their Brathren."

9. *Lynn Mirror*, November 1, 1828.

10. *Awl*, September 11, 1844.

11. David Montgomery, "The Working Class of the Pre-industrial American City, 1780–1830," *Labor History*, 9, no. 1 (Winter, 1968): 3–22, shows evidence of group consciousness in Boston, New York, Philadelphia and Baltimore. The article is somewhat misleading because Montgomery often uses "mechanic" and "journeymen" interchangeably, leaving the impression of separation between master and journeymen mechanics where in fact it did not exist.

12. Sanderson, *Lynn in the Revolution*, I: 27.

13. Ibid., I: 27.

14. Lynn and Newhall, *History of Lynn*, p. 350.

15. For account of the founding of the Academy and the class nature of its support, see George H. Martin, "The Lynn Academy," paper read to Lynn Historical Society meeting, April 16, 1908. MS, Lynn Historical Society.

16. West Lynn was the major business center of the town, largely because of the opening of the Salem-Boston turnpike in 1803. See sketch of Life of Isaiah Breed, Lynn *Daily Evening Item*, July 14, 1892.

17. Margaret E. Porter, "Old Woodend and Its Neighboring Territory," *Lynn Historical Society Register*, 15 (1912): 106–32.

18. See mention of the event in *Lynn Scrapbooks*, 6: 3.

19. Alfred Mudge, *Memorials: Being a Genealogical, Biographical and Historical Account of the Name MUDGE in America, from 1638 to 1868* (Boston: Alfred Mudge, 1868), pp. 119–209; Lewis and Newhall, *History of Lynn*, pp. 366, 370, 373, 377; *Lynn Scrapbooks*, 26: 25.

20. Account of conflict, *Lynn Scrapbooks* 6: 19. Also reminiscences of old Lynn Hotel, *Lynn Scrapbooks*, 6: 43. For biographical sketch of Paul and Ellis Newhall and their role in founding of republican movement, see *Lynn Scrapbooks*, 20: 74.

21. Lewis and Newhall, *History of Lynn*, pp. 366, 368; James R. Newhall, *Centennial Memorial of Lynn*, p. 73. Party spirit was equally intense in 1806. See *Lynn Scrapbooks*, 32: 26.

22. For movement to establish a bank, see *Lynn Scrapbooks*, 23: 3.

23. Ellen Mudge Burrill, *Essex Trust Company*, p. 2.

24. For account of efforts to charter a bank and for list of first incorporators, see Warren M. Breed, "Banks and Bankers of Old Lynn," paper read to meeting of Lynn Historical Society, January 10, 1917, MS, Lynn Historical Society. First meeting was held in Paul and Ellis Newhall's building, political headquarters of the Republicans.

25. Nathan M. Hawkes, "John Fuller of Lynn," *The Register of the Lynn Historical Society* 18: 72–108, gives good account of Joseph Fuller's political activities and his role in establishing a bank.

26. Lewis and Newhall, *History of Lynn*, p. 368.

27. Ibid., p. 367.

28. *Lynn Scrapbooks*, 26: 24, 25, 27, 40. Most militia units of the 8th Regiment, Essex County, were organized in the period from 1800–1814.

29. Ellen Mudge Burrill, "Lynn in Our Grandfather's Time," *The Register of the Lynn Historical Society* 21 (1917): 65.

30. *Lynn Scrapbooks*, 17: 19.

31. Ibid., 11: 15.

32. For a description of hard times in Lynn during the embargo and the depression that followed the war of 1812, see *Lynn Scrapbooks* 23: 9. Shoe firm of Daniel Silsbee and Micajah Burrill, Jr., lost $30,000 during the war of 1812. See item in *Lynn Scrapbooks*, 2: 50.

33. *Lynn Mirror*, September 6, 1828.

34. For a brief introduction to the career of Lee, see James M. Buckley, *A History of Methodism in the United States* (New York: Harper and Brothers, 1898), I: 257–60; and for an account of the conditions confronting Methodism in New England, M. L. Scudder, *American Methodism* (Hartford: SS Scranton, 1870), pp. 241–42.

35. For an account of the origins of Methodism in Lynn and its early growth, see George Henry Martin, "The Unfolding of Religious Faith in Lynn," *The Register of the Lynn Historical Society* 16 (1912): 60–65; and for a hostile view of the Methodist "heresy," Parsons Cooke, *A Century of Puritanism and a Century of Its Opposites* (Boston: S. K. Whipple, 1855), pp. 227–69.

36. For names of incorporators of First Methodist Church, see *Lynn Scrapbooks*, 2: 12.

37. Martin, "Religious Faith in Lynn," p. 63.

38. Cooke, *Century of Puritanism*, p. 258.

39. Martin, "Religious Faith in Lynn," p. 63.

40. Benjamin F. Newhall, "Sketches of Lynn," Sketch number 37, in scrapbook in Lynn Historical Society.

41. Martin, "Religious Faith in Lynn," p. 63.

42. Connection between Methodism and manufacturing also had a sectional twist. Heavier concentration of shoemaking in Woodend (East Lynn), made that section more republican. See *Lynn Scrapbooks*, 11: 9.

43. The tie between Methodism and Republicanism produced different results elsewhere. An example is the case of James O'Kelley. An ardent republican, Methodist preacher and presiding elder of the Southern District of Virginia, O'Kelley attempted to apply republican principles to the structure of the Methodist Church. At a General Conference in Baltimore, November 1792, he introduced a measure that would allow any

Methodist preacher who was dissatisfied with a parish assignment by the bishop to appeal to the General Conference. His motion defeated, O'Kelley and his followers withdrew from the Methodist Church and formed the Republican Methodist Church "in which all the preachers were to stand, as nearly as possible, on an equal footing." See account of the secession in William H. Daniels, *The Illustrated History of Methodism in Great Britain and America* (New York: Methodist Book Concern, 1879), pp. 527–29.

44. Hawkes, "John Fuller of Lynn," p. 101, for discussion of Joseph Fuller's political career.

45. Description of outfit in *Lynn Scrapbooks*, 32: 39.

46. For connection between Quakers and Lynn Academy, private school for upper class, see *Lynn Scrapbooks*, 10: 50.

47. Lye's journal is in the Lynn Historical Society. It covers the years from 1817–1832. Also see Henry F. Tapley, "An Old New England Town as Seen by Joseph Lye, Cordwainer," *The Register of the Lynn Historical Society*, 19 (1915): 36–40, for comments on Lye's journal entries.

48. Account of early Quaker community, *Lynn Scrapbooks*, 23: 35.

49. *Lynn Directory*, 1832, gives figures for citizens with most common surnames. Also see *Lynn Vital Records* for births, deaths and marriages under same names for continuity of families over two centuries.

50. *Lynn Scrapbooks*, 23: 38.

51. Also see description of Swampscott fishermen on election day in *Lynn Scrapbooks*, 13: 7.

52. Account of Quaker community and publicly supported school, *Lynn Scrapbooks*, 23: 35. The school was governed by a board appointed by the Quaker meeting.

53. Even temperance societies were organized along neighborhood lines. See *Lynn Scrapbooks*, 23: 12, for account of the Gravesend Temperance Society.

54. *Lynn Scrapbooks*, 17: 19, for description of neighborhood fire companies and their sponsors.

55. *Lynn Scrapbooks*, 28: 19. Volunteer unit #8, for example, was equipped with a suction engine purchased by West Lynn businessmen. David Taylor put up $200.

56. *Lynn Scrapbooks*, 24: 46–47, gives account of "Early Firefighters" and process toward securing town support.

57. Records of fire companies can be found in manuscript collection of Lynn Historical Society. See, for example, records of "Silver Grey Fire Association"; and "Names of the Members of the Lynn Fire Club, With Their Residences and Places of Business."

58. *Lynn Scrapbooks*, 17: 25. Lynn Mechanics' Rifle Corps composed mainly of Woodenders, residents of East Lynn.

59. *Lynn Scrapbooks*, 32: 12, gives description of military units in the town in 1835.

60. Same was true of gang rivalries between Black Marsh and Westenders. See *Lynn Scrapbooks*, 47: 13.

61. *Lynn Scrapbooks*, 17: 16–17.

## Notes to Chapter 4

1. For a statement of this notion, see Lewis and Newhall, *History of Lynn*, p. 91.

2. The figures for the late 1850s and 1860 are deceptive; they overstate the number of firms. The Lynn directories in the 1850s listed as shoe manufacturers men who took no active part in running a business. They were merely investors or, at most, advisers to

those who actually conducted the business. In 1860, there were probably about 150 shoe firms.

3. *Lynn Record,* September 13, 1837. The *Record* also reported that the term "bos" was being applied to the manufacturer.

4. United States Secretary of the Treasury [Louis McLane], *Report on Manufactures,* 1832 (House Document 308).

5. United States, "Seventh Census of the United States, 1850—Schedule of Manufactures," MS, Massachusetts State House.

6. The statistical information on the manufacturers is compiled chiefly from two sources: the Lynn directories for 1832, 1841, 1851, 1854, 1856, 1858, and 1860; and the *Vital Records of Lynn, Massachusetts to the End of the Year* 1849 (Salem: Essex Institute, 1905, 1906), two vols. The vital records list births, deaths, and marriages in Lynn.

7. The portion of new manufacturers who married in Lynn was undoubtedly larger than the figure indicates. The *Vital Records* terminate in 1849; those who married in the 1850s would be unlisted.

8. For the extent of Quaker domination of Lynn business, see *Lynn Scrapbooks,* 23: 37. Also items on Quaker community in Lynn, *Lynn Scrapbooks,* 23: 35.

9. Sally H. Hacker, "The Friends: Laws and Social Customs of the Quakers," unpublished paper read to meeting of the Lynn Historical Society, March 29, 1899. MS, LHS.

10. For the extent of this business practice in the seventeenth century, see Bernard Bailyn, *The New England Merchants in the Seventeenth Century* (Harper Torchbook edition, 1964), pp. 87–91.

11. Biographical sketch of Pratt in article on "Lynn, 1629–1892," in *Shoe and Leather Reporter,* August 4, 1892.

12. Warren M. Breed, "Banks and Bankers of Old Lynn," paper read to meeting of the Lynn Historical Society, January 10, 1917. MS, LHS.

13. Lynn *Daily Evening Item,* "Life and Times of Nathan Breed," April 10, 1908.

14. Nathan Breed, Micajah Pratt, and a shoe merchant in Boston provided the capital for shoe outlets in the West. Their agent was the young George Hood, who became the first mayor of Lynn in 1850, and leader of the Democratic Party. See *Lynn Scrapbooks,* 34: 29.

15. On the founding of the Lynn Mill Dam and Eastern Railroad, see Ellen Mudge Burrill, "Lynn in Our Grandfather's Time," paper read to the meeting of the Lynn Historical Society, March 20, 1918. MS, LHS.

16. For an account of the struggle between business factions for control of the Mechanics' Bank, see *Lynn Scrapbooks* 47: 26. The bank building itself was transferred from West Lynn to Front and Broad Streets, in the heart of the Quaker business community, and symbolized the importance of the Quaker group in the town's business affairs. Also see Warren M. Breed, "Banks and Bankers of Old Lynn," p. 16.

17. See *Lynn Scrapbooks,* 47: 28, for an account of the controversy over location of the railway line through Lynn.

18. "Life and Times of Nathan Breed," Lynn *Daily Evening Item,* April 10, 1908; biographical sketch of Isaiah Breed, Lynn *Daily Evening Item,* July 14, 1892. Also see appropriate sections in "Lynn, 1629–1892," in *Shoe and Leather Reporter,* August 4, 1892.

19. Biographical sketch of Robinson in "Lynn, 1629–1892," *Shoe and Leather Reporter,* August 4, 1892.

20. An account of Thompson's career in *Lynn Scrapbooks,* 18: 97. Also see *The Register of the Lynn Historical Society* 15 (1912): 63.

21. Benjamin F. Newhall, "Sketches of Saugus," numbers 33 and 34. Newhall's "Sketches" were originally written sometime during the 1860s. They can be found in a scrapbook in the Lynn Historial Society. For a biographical sketch of Newhall, see Lewis and Newhall, *History of Lynn*, pp. 570–71.

22. Benjamin F. Newhall, "Sketches of Saugus."

## Notes to Chapter 5

1. Lewis and Newhall, *History of Lynn*, p. 371. Of the figure for 1810, Newhall states that it was reached "by careful estimation," yet cites no source. Figures on production, then, are estimates only.

2. *Lynn Mirror*, January 19, 1828. The editor also estimated shipping costs. The study was made in response to the Massachusetts General Court's inquiry into transportation needs of Massachusetts towns.

3. *Lynn Mirror*, December 17, 1836; *Lynn Record*, December 31, 1835; *Lynn Record*, December 14, 1836 also gives figures on employment.

4. *Lynn Directory*, 1832; *Lynn Record*, December 14, 1836.

5. *Lynn Mirror*, April 25, 1837, for first account of depression in the shoe trade.

6. *Lynn Mirror*, June 1, 1837, for impact of depression on population growth; *Lynn Record*, August 28, 1839.

7. *Lynn News*, September 14Æ 1855.

8. Great Britain. House of Commons, 1854–55, British Sessional Papers, *Report of the Committee on the Machinery of the United States of America*, p. 21.

9. *Lynn News*, July 20, 1855. It also estimated that first operators earned wages as high as $14 per week; average at $6.

10. *Lynn News*, January 25, 1856.

11. The *Lynn Daily Evening Item*, October 29, 1895, contains the reminiscence of Elizabeth A. Keene who worked as a machine stitcher in the late 1850s. Her wages were $3 per week.

12. *Lynn Directories*, 1841, 1851, 1858.

13. Louis McLane. *Report on Manufactures*, 1832, pp. 224–25; *Eighth Census of the United States*, "Schedule of Manufactures." MS, Mass. State House.

14. Stanley Lebergott, *Manpower in Economic Growth: The American Record Since 1800* (New York: McGraw, 1964), p. 139.

15. Lye's journals cover the years from 1817 to 1832. MSS, LHS.

16. Stanley Lebergott, *Manpower*, p. 117.

17. *Lynn Record*, September 13, 1837.

18. David N. Johnson, *Sketches of Lynn or The Changes of Fifty Years* (Lynn: Thomas P. Nichols, 1880), pp. 2, 7.

19. This information was obtained from Lynn tax records. The records are in two parts: first are "Inventories of Estates," which gave itemized inventories of taxable property; the second, "Assessments and Taxes," record of the taxes levied on the items in the estates. The "Inventories" did not mention poultry. MSS, Lynn City Hall.

20. "Lynn Tax Records," volumes for 1832, 1837, 1842, 1849, 1855, and 1860.

21. Johnson, *Sketches of Lynn*, p. 30.

22. John R. Commons, "American Shoemakers, 1648–1895," *Quarterly Journal of Economics*, 24: 55ff. A shilling was worth about $.17.

23. Israel Buffum's Account Book is in the Lynn Historical Society.

24. See *Vital Records of Lynn*, vol. 2; and small piece on Israel and Ruth Buffum in *Lynn Bay State*, October 28, 1858.

25. Joseph Lye, MSS, LHS.

26. *Lynn Mirror*, January 27, 1827.

27. Ibid., August 9, 1828. The paper carried an ad for 200 shoemakers.

28. *Lynn Mirror*, June 3, 1837 for population in 1830, 1836, 1837.

29. Johnson, *Sketches of Lynn*, p. 151.

30. Ibid.

31. *The Lynn Star*, September 5, 1836, gives prices for five basic commodities.

32. *The Star*, September 5, 1836; *Lynn Mirror*, November 5, 1836 compares prices for 1829 and 1836.

33. *Lynn Mirror*, November 5, 1836.

34. Johnson, *Sketches of Lynn*, p. 155. Also see account in *Lynn Scrapbooks*, 11: 47.

35. *Lynn Record*, August 28, 1839; *Lynn Focus and Essex County Journal*, May 16, 1837.

36. Johnson, *Sketches of Lynn*, p. 164.

37. *Democratic Sentinel and Republican*, February 20, 1841, for an attack on the order system.

38. Nathan D. Chase in *Lynn Scrapbooks*, 24: 19.

39. *Essex County Washingtonian*, June 22, 1843, indicates that commodity prices remained fairly high.

40. *The Awl*, July 24, 1844.

41. Ibid., September 25, 1844.

42. Ibid., September 25, 1841.

43. Ibid., January 4, 1845.

44. Ibid., July 5, 1845; August 23, 1845.

45. Ibid., September 20, 1845.

46. Ibid., April 26, 1845.

47. *True Workingmen*, December 27, 1845.

48. *Lynn News*, July 13, 1849.

49. Ibid., November 29, 1855.

50. *Lynn News*, July 13, 1849, gives statistics for employment and production.

51. Ibid., November 29, 1855.

52. Lynn *Bay State*, September 15, 1851, for biographical sketch of Newhall and a description of his business.

53. *Lynn News*, November 16, 1855.

54. *Lynn News*, July 13, 1849, estimated that part of the influx was transient, with six to seven hundred workers coming to Lynn for summer employment.

55. See estimates of wages for binders and makers and cost of living in *Annual Report of Board of Heatlh of Lynn*, 1850. (City Document #7), p. 14.

56. George Teel to his wife in Lowell, October 2, 1846; in scrapbook in Lynn Historical Society, originally printed in a newspaper of July 29, 1899. Text of letter: "I work 16 hours for 83 cents per day here, on my present work, which only leaves me $3.25 clear my board."

57. *Lynn News*, July 13, 1849.

58. Reprinted in *Lynn News*, April 8, 1852.

59. *Lynn News*, October 7, 1853.

60. Quoted in *Lynn News*, January 5, 1855.

61. *Lynn News*, August 17, 1855.

62. Ibid., November 29, 1855.

63. Description of panic of 1857 in *Lynn News*, May 12, 1857. Also see *Lynn News*, October 6, 1857, October 27, 1857.

64. *Lynn News*, December 15, 1857. This corroborated by Nathan D. Chase, a former Lynn manufacturer. See *Lynn Scrapbooks*, 11: 49.

65. *Lynn News*, May 18, 1858. Also see *Lynn News*, December 14, 1858, for account of the wages of outorkers in New Hampshire employed by Lynn bosses.

66. Lynn *Bay State*, February 1, 1860.

67. *Lynn Scrapbooks*, 24: 7.

68. *Lynn Record*, October 8, 1835; for Isaiah Breed's role in establishing the school, see sketch of his life in Lynn *Daily Evening Item*, July 14, 1892.

69. *Shoe and Leather Reports*, "Lynn, 1629–1892," August 4, 1892, p. 14.

70. Nathan D. Chase in *Lynn Scrapbooks*, 14: 17.

## Notes to Chapter 6

1. Donald G. Mathews, "The Second Great Awakening as an Organizing Process, 1780–1830: An Hypothesis," *American Quarterly*, 21, no. 1 (Spring, 1969): 25–43.

2. Joseph Gusfield, *Symbolic Crusade* (Urbana: University of Illinois Press, 1963), pp. 5–6. "Abstinence was becoming a symbol of middle class membership and a necessity for ambitious and aspiring young men. It was one of the ways society would distinguish the industrious from the ne'er-do-well; the steady worker from the unreliable drifter."

3. See Clifford S. Griffin, "Religious Benevolence as Social Control, 1815, 1860," *Mississippi Valley Historical Review*, 44 December 1957): 423–44, for an account of the efforts of middle class evangelicals to use religion and morality to prevent "political and social upheavals."

4. *The Star*, October 1, 1836, reported that plaintiffs were treated with "much roughness and contempt."

5. In addition to the Cheever case, there is a report from David Johnson, *Sketches of Lynn*, pp. 412–13, which further confirms Lynn's leading role in the early moral reform movement. At the ordination of John Pierpont Jr. in October of 1843, one man present was a Dr. Pierce of Brookline. Pierce recalled that he had attended 94 ordinations and that Pierpont's ordination in Lynn was "the first one where intoxicating drinks were not used; and the first ordination at which ladies were present."

6. For an account of the Cheever case, see George Faber Clark, *History of the Temperance Reform in Massachusetts, 1813–1883* (Boston: Clarke and Carruth, 1888), p. 33.

7. *Lynn Record*, April 17, 1833.

8. Edward Warren (ed.), *The Life of John Collins Warren: Compiled Chiefly from his Autobiography and Journals*, 1 (Boston: Ticknor and Fields, 1860): 14–19.

## Notes to Chapter 7

1. *Lynn Mirror*, December 30, 1826. *Lynn Scrapbooks* 24: 11, gives a brief sketch of several of the Society's founders. Also see 23: 27. For a list of officers and ward representatives, *Weekly Messenger*, December 15, 1832.

2. A clear statement of this view can be found in the *Lynn Record*, May 28, 1835. Also see *Lynn Mirror*, December 23, 1826 for statement of purpose and constitution of the Society for the Promotion of Industry, Frugality and Temperance.

3. *Lynn Record*, July 25, 1835; *Lynn Mirror*, November 4, 1826.

4. *Lynn Mirror*, January 20, 1827, for list of Officers of the Lynn Institution for Savings.

5. This is borne out by resistance the temperance movement continually encountered in West Lynn. Caleb Wiley, grocer and rum dealer in West Lynn, was a frequent defendant before the Justice of the Peace for liquor violations. See *The Star*, August 20, 1836, for an account of one such court action; others in *The Star*, October 1, 1836; and in the *Lynn Bay State*, November 22, 1849.

6. *Lynn Mirror*, March 15, 1828, for citizens' complaints against cost of poor relief. On the founding of the poor house, see *Lynn Scrapbooks* 12: 12.

7. *Lynn Mirror*, January 13, 1827.

8. Ibid.

9. This is supported by the recollection of Nathan Chase: "All kinds [of persons] were put in there for want of a better place." *Lynn Scrapbooks* 23: 10.

10. *Lynn Mirror*, September 23, 1826.

11. Ibid., May 5, 1827, May 19, 1827, February 9, 1828.

12. Ibid., March 15, 1828.

13. Ibid.

14. *Lynn Mirror*, March 8, 1828.

15. *Weekly Messenger*, March 9, 1833. From March 2, 1832 to March 1, 1833, the poor house received $475.71 in goods for the shoes the inmates made.

16. *Lynn Mirror*, March 14, 1829, March 5, 1831.

17. Ibid., March 31, 1829. Report of the auditor for 1829 attributed the decline in outdoor relief to new practices in dispensing provisions at the Poor House rather than granting orders drawn on local grocery stores. *Lynn Mirror*, March 5, 1831.

18. *Lynn Record, March* 7, 1832; *Weekly Messenger*, March 9, 1833.

19. Ibid., July 24, 1833.

20. Ibid.

21. Ibid., March 5, 1835.

22. *Essex Democrat*, March 18, 1831.

23. *Lynn Freeman and Essex County Whig*, February 12, 1842; *Essex County Washingtonian*, February 1, 1844; *Lynn News*, January 23, 1832.

24. *Lynn News*, January 5, 1855, January 11, 1856.

25. A partial exception, which will be explored in Chapter Ten, was the offer of the town's wealthy to set up a soup house in 1842. Many shoemakers spurned the offer and argued that higher wages would do more to alleviate poverty than a soup house. *Lynn Freeman and Essex County Whig*, December 17, 1842, explains the original proposal for a soup house.

26. *Lynn News*, May 19, 1854.

27. *Lynn Pioneer*, March 15, 1848.

28. *Lynn Scrapbooks* 17: 45.

29. *Lynn Directory*, 1832, pp. 29–31, for the bylaws adopted in 1828.

30. *Lynn Mirror*, June 10, 1826.

31. Michael B. Katz, *The Irony of Early School Reform: Educational Innovation in Mid-Nineteenth-Century Massachusetts* (Cambridge, Mass.: Harvard University Press, 1968), gives an excellent account of the motives and policies of the "reformers."

32. This impulse to "educate" children extended to the founding of Sunday Schools as well as to changes in the public school. Robert Rantoul recalled that "Hannah Hill, somewhere between 1809 and 1810, became impressed with the danger resulting to the children and society from the running at large on Sunday of a tribe of vagrant boys and

girls, residing about the wharves of Beverly." The purpose of Hannah Hill's new Sunday School was "to teach morals and faith [to] that very dangerous class of neglected children." See Robert Rantoul, "Mr. Rantoul's Connexion with Town and Parochial Affairs—His Views of Religion," Essex Institute *Historical Collections* 6, no. 2 (April, 1864): 89.

33. "Report from Lynn," in Massachusetts State Board of Education, *Eighteenth Annual Report of the Board of Education*, 1855, p. 128. Also see Katz, *Irony of School Reform*, p. 131, for summary of the reformers' intent.

34. Lynn School Committee, *Annual Report for* 1847−48, p. 7.

35. Massachusetts, *First Annual Report of the Board of Education*, 1837, p. 29; *Lynn Scrapbooks* 1: 15, for description of the prudential system of governance.

36. Massachusetts, *Tenth Annual Report of the Board of Education*, 1847, p. 151.

37. Massachusetts, *First Annual Report of the Board of Education*, 1837, p. 37.

38. Lynn, "Lynn Town Records, 1822−1835," p. 373, MS in Lynn City Hall.

39. Massachusetts, *Fifth Annual Report of the Board of Education*, 1842, pp. 66−67.

40. Massachusetts, *First Annual Report of the Board of Education*, 1837, p. 28.

41. Lynn, "Lynn Town Records, 1833−1835," p. 370, MS in Lynn City Hall.

42. "Report from the School Committee of Lynn," in Massachusetts, *Twenty-Second Annual Report of the Board of Education*, 1859, p. 62.

43. Lynn School Committee, *Annual Report for* 1847−48, p. 8.

44. *Lynn News*, July 26 1850, February 20, 1852, December 20, 1853, February 3, 1857, May 5, 1857.

45. Lynn School Committee, *Annual Report for* 1847−48, p. 7.

46. Ibid., p. 5.

47. Stephen Willner Nissenbaum, "Careful Love: Sylvester Graham and the Emergence of Victorian Sexual Theory in America, 1830−40 (unpublished Ph.D. Dissertation, University of Wisconsin, 1968), pp. 23, 29, 31, 98, 221, 255.

48. Quoted in Wisconsin State Superintendent of Public Instruction, *Twelfth Annual Report* (Madison, 1860), pp. 58−59 in section entitled "Privies in the Schools."

49. Massachusetts, *Fifth Annual Report of the Board of Education*, 1842, p. 126; *Tenth Annual Report of the Board of Education*, 1847, p. 253.

50. For study of the bundling custom, see Dana Doten, *The Art of Bundling* (Countryman and Farrah and Rinehart, 1938).

51. For a description of paw-paw or props and kindred vices, see William J. Snelling, *Expose of the Vice of Gaming, As it Lately Exists in Massachusetts* (Boston, 1833). On the origins of paw paw, see Mitford Mathews (ed.), *A Dictionary of Americanisms: On Historical Principles*, vol. II (Chicago: University of Chicago Press, 1951), pp. 1195, 1319.

52. "Mr. Rantoul's Connexion with Town and Parochial Affairs—His Views of Religion," Essex Institute *Historical Collections*, vol. 6, no. 2 (April, 1864), pp. 79−90. Rantoul also gives an excellent description of the festivities that accompanied 'Lection Day in the area around Salem.

53. *Lynn Mirror*, May 28, 1831. Also see "Old 'Lection Day," in *Lynn Scrapbooks*, 1: 7.

54. *Lynn Mirror*, October 6, 1827.

55. [Worcester] *Massachusetts Spy*, quoted in *Lynn Mirror*, October 27, 1827.

56. *Lynn Mirror*, July 1, 1826.

57. For a good account of the movement in Massachusetts, see George Faber Clark, *History of the Temperance Reform in Massachusetts, 1813−1883* (Boston: Clarke and Carruth, 1888).

58. Edward Warren (ed.), *Life of John Collins Warren*, p. 15. This study gives a good

account of the changing attitudes towards drinking during the lifetime of a man whose career spanned the crucial period of the moral reform movement.

59. Alice Felt Tyler, *Freedom's Ferment* (Harper Torchbook edition, 1962), p. 312.

60. John A. Krout, *The Origins of Prohibition* (New York: Alfred Knopf, 1925), p. 37. Also see Lebbeus Armstrong, *The Temperance Reformation*, p. 22 for an account of a New York farmer and lumber dealer who could not obtain the services of a single laborer without first offering a ration of liquor.

61. *Lynn Scrapbooks* 23: 6.

62. *Lynn Mirror*, August 12, 1837. Editor Charles F. Lummus gives a vivid account of the extent of drinking in Lynn.

63. "Reminiscences" in *Lynn News*, September 3, 1847.

64. *Lynn Scrapbooks* 23: 6.

65. *Lynn Mirror*, August 12, 1837.

66. *Lynn Scrapbooks* 24: 6, 11.

67. Ibid., 23: 7.

68. "Mr. Rantoul's Establishment in Business—Intemperance and Pauperism," Essex Institute *Historical Collections* 5, no. 6 (December 1863): 241–47.

69. *Lynn Record*, July 24, 1839, for an account of the pervasiveness of heavy drinking in Lynn.

70. A similar opinion of the connection between the quickening of economic activity and the beginnings of the temperance movement is found in Edward Warren (ed.), *Life of John Collins Warren*, pp. 15–16.

71. The basic strategy for fostering temperance was to humiliate the drinker, treat him as a social pariah. As one advocate put it: "Let the inebriate see and feel the desolation that his course brings upon himself and his family." See *Lynn Mirror*, February 11, 1837.

72. *Lynn Mirror*, November 24, 1827.

73. Ibid.

74. *Lynn Mirror*, October 14, 1837.

75. *Lynn Record*, May 28, 1835. The statement was part of a resolution the town meeting passed in Lynn on May 4, 1835.

76. Ibid., July 24, 1833.

77. This is the main theme of the moralistic short stories found in Lynn newspapers. See *Lynn Mirror*, July 28, 1837, for the story of "Harry the Apprentice"; and *Lynn Mirror*, November 10, 1827, June 21, 1828, July 26, 1828.

78. *Weekly Messenger*, December 15, 1832, April 6, 1833.

79. *Lynn Mirror*, July 28, 1828.

80. "Life and Times of Nathan Breed," Lynn *Daily Evening Item*, April 10, 1908.

81. *Lynn Mirror*, May 17, 1838; *The Locomotive*, June 8, 1842, July 27, 1842.

82. *Lynn Bay State*, September 1, 1851. Some fire companies were known as temperance outfits, others as tipplers. For a description of a "drinking" fire company's celebration see *Lynn Tattler*, February 19, 1848.

83. *Lynn Forum*, July 21, 1846, for an account of a meeting of the cold water army in Lynn Lyceum.

84. A vigorous debate between the forces of coercion and those of moral suasion can be found in the *Essex County Washingtonian*, November 23, 1843.

85. As early as March 1833 the town meeting voted to request that county officers grant no licenses for retailing spiritous liquors. See *Lynn Record*, March 27, 1833.

86. Henry Fenno (ed.), *Our Police: The Official History of the Police Department of the City of Lynn* (Lynn: Nichols, 1895). For police report on illegal drinking and gambling, see

*Lynn Pioneer,* April 15, 1847. The statistics on arrests for drunkenness and illegal sale of liquor can be found in the annual reports of the city marshal in the city of Lynn's annual reports.

87. See *Lynn News,* December 16, 1853, March 3, 1857 for accounts of petitions initiated by Nathan and Isaiah Breed calling on city authorities to prosecute violators of liquor laws.

## Notes to Chapter 8

1. Douglas C. Miller, *Jacksonian Aristocracy: Class and Democracy in New York, 1830–1860* (New York: Oxford University Press, 1967), especially pp. 128–54.

2. See, for example, Samuel Lane Loomis, "The Tramps Problem," *Chautauquan* 19 (June, 1894): 308–13; Shirley Plumer Austin, "Coxey's Commonweal Army," *Chautauquan,* 19 (June, 1894): 332–36; *Forum,* 15 (August, 1893): 753–66.

3. Robert V. Bruce, *1877: Year of Violence* (Indianapolis: Bobbs-Merrill, 1959).

4. Stephan Thernstrom, *Poverty and Progress: Social Mobility in a Nineteenth Century City* (Cambridge: Harvard University Press, 1964), p. 97.

5. Howard M. Gitelman, "The Waltham System and the Coming of the Irish," *Labor History,* 8, no. 3 (Fall, 1967): 250–51.

6. Evelyn Knowlton, *Pepperell's Progress* (Cambridge, 1948), quoted in Gitelman, "Waltham System," p. 250.

7. Stephan Thernstrom, "Working Class Social Mobility in Industrial America," unpublished paper read at Anglo-American Colloquium of the Society for Labour History, London, June 23, 1968. In possession of author.

8. An example of the efforts of mill owners and their supports to blame outsiders can be found in Liston Pope, *Millhands and Preachers* (New Haven: Yale University Press, 1942).

9. The data on geographical and occupational mobility is drawn from two sources: the Lynn town directories which appeared in 1832, 1841, 1851, 1854, 1856, 1858 and 1860; and the *Vital Records of Lynn,* two volumes, which record the vital statistics of births, deaths and marriages in Lynn up to 1850. The census manuscripts are a preferable source, but not until 1850 does the census enumerate each person by name. For the sake of consistency I relied on the directories throughout the period 1832–60.

10. See "Reports of the City Marshal" in *Lynn City Documents* for the years 1855, 1859, 1860 and 1861. In the 1870s the number of tramps who were given food and lodging in Lynn increased greatly, rising to 3,294 in 1874, 2,958 in 1875, and to 2,825 in 1876. See James R. Newhall, *History of Lynn,* 2: 66.

11. Donald B. Cole, *Immigrant City: Lawrence, Massachusetts, 1845–1921* (Chapel Hill: University of North Carolina Press, 1963), p. 184, and chapter on strike of 1912.

12. The term "leader" is used loosely to include any shoemaker whose name appeared in newspaper accounts of the journeymen's activities. This would include men who were officers of the organization, committee members, contributors to the newspaper, speakers at meetings, delegates to conventions, and so on.

13. Edward P. Thompson, *The Making of the English Working Class* (Vintage Paperback edition, 1966), p. 10; Eric Hobsbawm, *Primitive Rebels: Studies in Archaic Forms of Social Movement in the 19th and 20th Centuries* (New York: W. W. Norton, 1959).

14. Oscar Handlin, *Boston's Immigrants: A Study in Acculturation* (Cambridge: Belknap Press, 1959), p. 74.

15. Rowland Berthoff, *British Immigrants in Industrial America* (Cambridge: Harvard University Press, 1959), p. 21.

16. Oscar Handlin, *The Uprooted* (Grosset and Dunlop, 1951), p. 218; Berthroff, *British Immigrants,* p. 125.

17. David Brody, *Steelworkers in America: The Nonunion Era* (Cambridge, Mass.: Harvard University Press, 1960), pp. 96–111. It should be noted that Brody stresses the employers' drive for lower production costs rather than the ethnic background of the workforce to explain the deplorable working conditions in the steel industry.

18. Barbara M. Solomon, "The Growth of the Population in Essex County, 1850–1860," Essex Institute *Historical Collections* 95 (1959): 82–103. This study is based on the census manuscripts for 1850 and 1860.

19. *Annual Report of the Board of Health of Lynn,* 1850; *Lynn News,* January 21, 1853.

20. *Shoe and Leather Reporter,* August 4, 1892, sketch of "Lynn, 1639–1892," included a brief account of Micajah Pratt's career as a manufacturer. The author noted that in 1830 Pratt began sending shoes to Maine to be made, "and families worked for him for a quarter of a century and sent their children up to Lynn to work for him there."

21. For an introduction to the debate over the existence of a wage earning class, the outlook of workingmen and their political loyalties, see the excellent survey in Edward Pessen, *Jacksonian America: Society, Personality, and Politics* (Homewood, Ill.: The Dorsey Press, 1969), pp. 384–93.

22. Two sections of Lynn became independent towns between 1850 and 1855, Swampscott (pop. 901) in 1851 and Nahant (pop. 237) in 1852.

23. The figures are based primarily on state reports. Secretary of the Commonwealth, *Statistics of the Condition and Products of Certain Branches of Industry in Massachusetts,* 1837, 1845, 1855.

24. This table was compiled from the occupational listings of adult males in the directories.

25. These figures are somewhat deceptive. After 1850, there were more jointly owned firms than a decade or two before. In addition, some men who merely invested capital in operating firms were listed as "shoe manufacturer" in the directories, even though they took no active part in the business.

26. The tables on property holding and the distribution of real wealth were compiled from tax records for the years 1832, 1837, 1842, 1853, and 1860. The records listed ratable polls—adult males over twenty-one years of age—and the kinds and amounts of property they held, if any. The categories of wealth I arbitrarily constructed. They do not appear in the original records. I did begin a study of personal property but soon discovered that some people did not declare the wealth they had deposited in the bank. The state of Massachusetts apparently exempted personal savings accounts up to $500. After 1850, the year Lynn became a city, the tax records are organized by ward.

27. Alan L. Olmstead, "The Bank for Savings in the City of New York in the Ante-Bellum Years: 1819–1861" (unpublished M.A. thesis, University of Wisconsin, 1966).

28. This information is drawn from savings deposit records, 1826–1860, MSS, Lynn Institute for Savings.

*Notes to Chapter 9*

1. *Lynn News,* April 18, 1860.
2. Edward P. Thompson, *Making of the English Working Class,* pp. 9–10.

3. Blanche E. Hazard, *Organization of the Shoe Industry in Massachusetts before* 1875, for stages of development. There is revealing information on the operations of small bosses in John P. Hall, "The Gentle Craft: A Narrative of Yankee Shoemakers" (unpublished Ph.D. Thesis, Columbia University, 1953), pp. 134–44.

4. For a biographical sketch of Thompson, see David Johnson, *Sketches of Lynn,* p. 454.

5. *Lynn Bay State*, January 24, 1850. Robinson employed 375 men and women, plus nine cutters. The author of the article noted that three-fourths of Robinson's employees lived in Lynn.

6. For an extensive account of the shoemaker's work routine and the social life within the shop, see David Johnson, *Sketches of Lynn,* pp. 30–50.

7. *The Awl*, February 1, 1845, August 29, 1845. The term "grinder" was first used in the pages of *The Awl*, but in such a way as to suggest it was in common usage among shoemakers sometime earlier.

8. For a description of the order system, See Johnson, *Sketches of Lynn,* pp. 86–105; *Shoe and Leather Reporter*, August 4, 1892.

9. *The Awl*, August 14, 1844.

10. *Lynn News*, July 3, 1849. Also see *Lynn Record*, January 15, 1834; *Democratic Sentinel and Republican*, February 20, 1841.

11. *The Awl*, July 24, 1844, August 14, 1844. Also see *Lynn Record*, April 22, 1840; *Essex Tribune*, January 4, 1834.

12. *The Awl*, August 14, 1844.

13. Ibid., July 31, 1844.

14. *The Awl*, July 24, 1844; *Lynn Chronicle*, November 21, 1835; *Lynn Focus and Essex County Journal*, May 16, 1837; *Lynn Record*, March 18, 1840. Payment in depreciated paper was apparently common throughout the United States. See Lebergott, *Manpower,* p. 146.

15. *The Awl*, July 24, 1844.

16. *Lynn Forum*, March 25, 1848; *Lynn Record*, April 22, 1840.

17. *The Awl*, July 24, 1844.

18. Ibid., August 7, 1844.

19. *Annual Report of the Board of Health of Lynn*, 1850(City Document #7) p. 14. Average age at death for farmers was 64.89, for shoemakers it was 43.41.

20. *The Awl*, August 14, 1844.

21. *Lynn Mirror*, December 31, 1831.

22. *The Awl*, August 21, 1844.

23. Ibid., July 24, 1844.

24. Ibid., July 24, 1844.

25. *Lynn Mirror*, March 3, 1832.

26. *The Awl*, July 24, 1844. "Jours" was often used in place of journeymen.

27. *The Awl*, September 4, 1844, July 17, 1844.

28.*Lynn Chronicle*, November 28, 1835. Also see *Essex County Washingtonian*, June 20 1844. At a meeting of the journeymen on June 14, 1844, there was a resolution approved calling for creation of a committee to examine the quality of shoes produced.

29. Edward Pessen, *Most Uncommon Jacksonians: The Radical Leaders of the Early Labor Movement* (Albany: State University of New York Press, 1967), p. 174.

30. George Lichteim, *The Origins of Socialism* (New York: Prager, 1969).

31. See Chapter Three.

32. *Lynn Record,* November 9, 1839; *The Awl*, October 2, 1844.

33. *The Awl*, July 17, 1844. The Journeymen's Society denied that it intended to "injure our employers."

34. *Lynn Mirror*, January 10, 1829.

35. *Lynn Chronicle*, November 21, 1835; *The Awl*, August 14, 1844.

36. *The Awl*, July 17, 1844.

37. For the names of some "good" bosses, see *The Awl*, July 24, 1844.

38. *Lynn Record*, November 4, 1840.

39. *The Awl*, August 21, 1844.

40. Ibid., June 14, 1845.

41. Ibid., November 28, 1844.

42. Ibid., November 28, 1844.

43. Ibid., December 28, 1844.

44. *Lynn Mirror*, April 15, 1828.

45. *Lynn Tattler*, June 24, 1848.

46. *The Awl*, March 22, 1845, April 1, 1845. Also see *Lynn Mirror*, June 5, 1828, for allegation of favoritism in loan policies.

47. *The Awl*, July 17, 1844; *Essex County Washingtonian*, June 20, 1844.

48. *The Awl*, July 24, 1844.

49. *The Awl*, July 24, 1844. Similar sentiment expressed in letter from "Fourier," *Lynn Freeman and Essex County Whig*, June 5, 1842.

50. *The Awl*, March 22, 1845.

51. Maurice F. Neufeld, "Realms of Thought and Organized Labor in the Age of Jackson," *Labor History* 10, no. 1 (Winter, 1969): 5–43.

52. *The Awl*, August 21, 1844.

53. *The Awl*, November 9, 1844; *The True Workingman*, November 22, 1945.

54. *The Awl*, August 7, 1844.

55. Ibid., September 11, 1844.

56. Ibid., August 28, 1844.

57. Ibid., October 2, 1844.

58. Ibid., October 2, 1844.

59. Ibid., August 21, 1844, November 9, 1844, April 26, 1845.

60. Herbert Gutman, "Protestantism and the American Labor Movement. The Christian Spirit in the Gilded Age." *American Historical Review* 72 (October, 1966): 74–101.

61. *The Awl*, August 14, 1844. One does find scattered evidence of Biblical metaphor and language, but the dominant framework of thought was secular rather than religious.

62. *The Awl*, August 21, 1844.

63. Ibid., January 25, 1845.

64. Ibid., November 9, 1844.

65. Ibid., April 26, 1845. Also see letter from a Fourier disciple, *Lynn Freeman and Essex County Whig*, June 5, 1842.

66. *The Awl*, July 24, 1844, July 31, 1844.

67. Ibid., November 9, 1844.

68. Ibid., August 21, 1844.

69. Ibid., July 24, 1844.

70. Ibid., July 24, 1844.

71. Ibid., April 19, 1845.

## Notes to Chapter 10

1. John Breed Newhall, "Early Lewis, Broad and Nahant Streets," a paper read to meeting of the Lynn Historical Society, April 13, 1905. MS in Lynn Historical Society.;

2. There is a good account of Nahant's development as a resort for the wealthy in Lewis and Newhall, *History of Lynn,* pp. 62–63.

3. *Essex County Washingtonian,* September 12, 1844.

4. *Lynn News,* December 17, 1847.

5. *Lynn Pioneer,* May 24, 1848.

6. *Lynn Mirror,* July 24, 1830.

7. Ibid., July 24, 1830.

8. Ibid., June 26, 1830.

9. *The Awl,* June 14, 1845.

10. *Lynn Mirror,* February 5, 1831, letter from a "Poor Man."

11. *The Awl,* July 26, 1845. For discrimination between rich and poor in churches, see *Essex County Washingtonian,* May 9, 1844. The poor sat on plain boards, the rich on cushions.

12. George H. Martin, "The Lynn Academy," paper read to meeting of the Lynn Historical Society, April 16, 1908. MS in Lynn Historical Society. There were 70 pupils enrolled in the Academy in 1832. Also see Ellen Mudge Burrill, "Lynn in Our Grandfathers' Time," paper read to meeting of the Lynn Historical Society, March 20, 1918. MS in Lynn Historical Society.

13. *Catalogue of the Officers, Teachers, and Pupils of the Lynn High School, December 21, 1854* (Lynn: W. W. Kellogg, 1854). The roster also lists the parent or guardian of the pupil.

14. *The Awl,* July 24, 1844.

15. "Records of the Social Library in the Town of Lynn, 1818-October 9, 1847," MS, Lynn Public Library.

16. Johnson, *Sketches of Lynn,* p. 196ff.

17. Ibid., pp. 234–42.

18. "First Annual Report of the Trustees of Pine Grove Cemetery Corporation, made to the Proprietors, January 7, 1850," *Lynn City Documents,* 1850 (Document #4), pp. 3–9.

19. "List of Subscribers, February 15, 1850, to stock in Pine Grove Cemetery Corporation," *Lynn City Documents,* 1850 (Document #4), pp. 14–16.

20. *Lynn Bay State,* July 25, 1850.

21. *Lynn News,* February 13, 1852.

22. Ibid., August 26, 1853.

23. Ibid., April 22, 1853, May 5, 1853.

24. "Minutes of Meetings and By-Laws of Lynn Lyceum, from 1831 to 1834," MS Lynn Historical Society. This includes names of officers and members.

25. Broadside on program at Lynn Lyceum for April 15, 1845. Lynn Historical Society.

26. *Weekly Messenger,* October 20, 1832.

27. *Lynn Mirror and Independent Whig,* January 9, 1836.

28. *Constitution and By-Laws of the Young Men's Christian Association* (Lynn: W. W. Kellogg, 1857).

29. *Lynn Mirror,* April 10, 1830; *Lynn Mirror and Essex Democrat,* August 3, 1830.

30. *Lynn Mirror,* September 4, 1830. Article also lists officers of the Society.

31. *Lynn Mirror and Essex Democrat,* August 3, 32. *Lynn Record,* January 1, 1834, January 8, 1834, January 15, 1834, January 29, 1834. The issue of January 8, 1834 gives a list of ward and committee officers for both societies. Also see *Essex Tribune,* January 4, 1834.

33. *Lynn Record,* June 18, 1834; *Lynn Chronicle,* August 29, 1835, for officers of the United Trade Society of Journeymen Cordwainers of Lynn.

34. *Lynn Chronicle,* November 21, 1835.

35. *The Awl,* July 17, 1844.

36. For the notice of its founding, see *Lynn News,* February 8, 1859. Also, March 15, 1859, March 27, 1859. For reprints of articles from *New England Mechanic,* see *Lynn News,* April 27, 1859, May 18, 1859. I have been unable to find copies of the *New England Mechanic.*

37. *Lynn Record,* January 15, 1834. Editor Henshaw also admitted that he received a flood of letters protesting the combination stores. He printed only a few. See *Lynn Record,* December 24, 1834.

38. *Lynn Record,* August 9, 1837. Shoemakers probably saw the hand of the manufacturers determining editorial policy. The *Record's* publisher was Jonathan Buffum, a manufacturer, who was the brother-in-law of Nathan Breed, bank director, manufacturer and owner of a combination store.

39. *The Awl,* December 14, 1844. The editor of *The Awl* also charged that the *Lynn News* was supported in this position by the *Essex County Whig,* the [Worcester] *Massachusetts Spy,* and the *Boston Atlas.*

40. *The Awl,* September 27, 1845. The Workingmen's Reading Room was located at Buffum's Hall on Union Street.

41. *Lynn Scrapbooks* 32: 5.

42. For a listing of N.E.P. stores in Lynn and the amount of their capital stocks, see "Valuations and Taxes" for 1849 and 1853, MSS in Lynn City Hall. Also see items on N.E.P. stores in *Lynn Pioneer,* July 1, 1847, September 30, 1847, October 7, 1847, April 5, 1848.

43. *The Awl,* August 21, 1844, November 9, 1844, April 26, 1845.

44. *The Awl,* August 7, 1844.

45. *The Awl,* August 14, 1844. For a wage list of Philadelphia Cordwainers, see *Lynn Forum,* July 24, 1847.

46. *The Awl,* July 31, 1844.

47. Membership lists are often included with the constitutions and by-laws of the units. See, for example, *Constitution of Silver Grey Engine Company No.* 10 (Lynn: Bay State Press, 1856), and Silver Grey's "Record Book," MS, Lynn Historical Society. *Constitution of Niagara Engine Company No.* 9; *Constitution of Engine and Hose Company No.* 5; *established March* 15, 1837 (Lynn: James R. Newhall, 1837). Also see *Regulations at Fires, As Adopted by the Engineers of Lynn, for* 1837 [broadside]. All in Lynn Historical Society. For social composition of fire companies, see *Lynn Tattler,* February 19, 1848.

48. *Lynn Tattler,* April 22, 1848; *Lynn Pioneer,* March 2, 1848, April 12, 1848.

49. *Lynn Forum,* September 15, 1846; *Lynn Pioneer,* April 12, 1848.

50. A similar pattern in the transformation of institutions from private to public took place in other towns. Of the origins of fire and police forces, the authors of one study observed: "Here again, private interest and the community's general welfare overlapped. This curious mixture between public and private enterprise came to be a recurrent characteristic of American municipal development." Charles N. Glaab and A. Theodore Brown, *A History of Urban America* (New York: Macmillan, 1967), pp. 16–17.

51. *The Awl,* July 31, 1844.

52. See *Constitution of the Lynn Fire Club* (Lynn: James R. Newhall, 1834) and *Names of the Members of the Lynn Fire Club, With Their Residences and Places of Business* [broadside], Lynn

Historical Society.

53. Four shoemakers who were among the leaders of the 1850 strike came from one engine company, Empire No. 5. They were A. C. Wyman, Abel Bates, George P. Sanderson, and D. L. Estes. See *Lynn City Documents: Annual Reports for the Year* 1862 (Lynn, 1863), p. 51.

54. *The Awl*, January 25, 1845. Emphasis in original.

55. *Young Hickory*, October 14, 1844.

56. *The Awl*, November 23, 1844.

57. Ibid., February 8, 1845.

58. Ibid., April 26, 1845.

59. Ibid., January 25, 1845.

60. Ibid., February 1, 1845.

61. Ibid., February 8, 1845.

62. Ibid., January 25, 1845.

63. Ibid., February 8, 1845.

64. Ibid., September 11, 1844.

65. Ibid., January 25, 1845.

66. Ibid., February 8, 1845, March 8, 1845.

67. *Lynn Record*, November 16, 1836.

68. *Lynn News*, November 12, 1847.

69. For election returns in the 1860 contest, see *Lynn Weekly Reporter*, December 15, 1860. The editor observed that "of the officers elected to constitute the city government for the ensuing year we can say but little, because we know but few of them personally or by reputation."

70. *Weekly Messenger*, April 6, 1833; *Lynn Record*, May 28, 1835.

71. *Lynn Mirror*, December 30, 1826, January 24, 1827, August 15, 1829, January 2, 1830, January 16, 1830; *Lynn Record*, December 12, 1832. In 1832 the words "Industry and Frugality" were deleted.

72. George Faber Clark, *History of the Temperance Reform in Massachusetts*, 1813–1883 (Boston: Clarke and Carruth, 1888), p. 8.

73. Clark, *Temperance Reform*, p. 10.

74. Arthur M. Schlesinger, Jr., *The Age of Jackson* (Boston: Little, Brown, 1953), p. 256: "The Democrats were further encouraged by the enactment under Whig auspices of a law forbidding the sale of liquor in quantities of less than fifteen gallons, an obvious piece of class legislation."

75. *Lynn Scrapbooks* 23: 7. Nathan Chase stated that temperance did not gain massive support until the appearance of the Washingtonian movement.

76. Lebbeus Armstrong, *The Temperance Reformation* (New York: Fowler and Wells, 1852), pp. 148–49, for an account of a speech by a reformed drunkard.

77. Clark, *Temperance Reform*, p. 53.

78. *The Awl*, August 28, 1844; *Essex County Washingtonian*, May 16, 1844, June 20, 1844. The *Washingtonian* frequently carried notices of upcoming meetings of the Journeymen Cordwainers' Society and the names of partic pants in the meetings.

79. *The Awl*, June 28, 1845.

80. *Essex County Washingtonian*, April 6, 1846; *The Awl*, December 21, 1844.

81. Armstrong, *Temperance Reformation*, pp. 36–37, for a critique of moral suasion and the argument for legal coercion.

82. *Lynn News*, December 21, 1858.

83. *Essex County Washingtonian*, November 23, 1843.

84. *Essex County Washingtonian,* March 30, 1843.

85. *Essex County Washingtonian,* November 23, 1843.

86. *The Old Rat,* October, 1847.

87. *Lynn News,* March 3, 1857.

88. "Life and Times of Nathan Breed," Lynn *Daily Evening Item,* April 10, 1908.

89. *True Friend,* November 11, 1845.

90. *Lynn News,* December 15, 1857.

91. Ibid., December 21, 1858.

92. *Lynn Mirror,* May 20, 1837.

93. Ibid., May 20, 1837.

94. *Lynn News,* November 24, 1857.

95. *The Awl,* March 1, 1845.

96. *Lynn News,* November 24, 1857.

97. For an introduction to the subject, see Benjamin Percival, "Essex and Lynn Abolitionism," a paper read to meeting of the Lynn Historial Society, November 12, 1908. MS in Lynn Historical Society. Leaders of the Comeouters were Stephen S. Foster and Thomas Parnell Beach, neither of whom were from Lynn. For an attack on Comeouters, see *The Locomotive,* July 6, 1842, August 3, 1842; and *Lynn Freeman and Essex County Whig,* July 2, 1842.

98. Percival, "Lynn Abolitionism."

99. *Proceedings of the Society of Friends in the Case of William Bassett* (Worcester: Joseph Wall, 1840), offers a critique of older Friends for the moral complacency that so offended younger members like Bassett. For an exposition of Bassett's views, see his editorial in *Essex County Washingtonian,* November 16, 1843.

100. *The Awl,* July 17, 1844.

101. *Lynn Mirror,* July 29, 1837.

102. *The Awl,* September 6, 1845.

103. Ibid., April 26, 1845.

104. *Lynn Chronicle,* August 8, 1835

105. *Lynn Chronicle,* August 22, 1835; *Lynn Record,* August 30, 1835, September 7, 1835.

106. *Lynn Chronicle,* September 5, 1835. *The Chronicle* was a Democratic organ. For the presence of racism in Lynn, see letter on "Prejudice Against Color," *Essex County Washingtonian,* November 16, 1843.

107. *Lynn Chronicle,* August 29, 1835.

108. *The Awl,* July 24, 1844.

109. Ibid., August 14, 1844.

110. Ibid., March 1, 1845, August 14, 1844.

111. Ibid., October 9, 1844.

112. *Lynn News,* November 17, 1848.

113. *The True Workingman,* November 22, 1845.

114. *The Awl,* September 11, 1844, November 9, 1844, November 23, 1844, January 18, 1845, January 25, 1845.

115. *The Awl,* February 8, 1845.

116. Ibid., January 18, 1845.

117. Ibid.

118. *The True Workingman,* November 22, 1845.

119. Ibid.

120. *The Awl,* February 8, 1845.

121. For references to condition of workingmen in foreign lands, see *The Awl*, July 24, 1844, July 31, 1844, August 7, 1844.

122. *The Awl*, February 22, 1845, an article entitled "Patronize the Producer." The author noted that it cost $1 to ship a barrel of flour from Ohio to Massachusetts, yet a barrel of flour cost $5 more in Massachusetts than in Ohio.

123. *The Awl*, February 22, 1845.

124. "Hitchinson Family Memorabilia," MSS, Lynn Historical Society.

125. Shoemakers served on vigilance committees for both parties. These committees were organized by ward. The members apparently distributed ballots, watched the polls and rounded up supporters. See lists of vigilance members for both parties in the *Lynn Daily Journal*, November 11, 1837.

126. The prominence of manufacturers and professionals among town officials is evident from a cursory examination of election outcomes. Lists of town officers regularly appeared in newspapers and in the town directories.

127. *Lynn Mirror*, November 8, 1828; *Lynn Record*, November 14, 1832, November 16, 1836. The vote in 1828 was Adams 346, Jackson 25; in 1832, Antimason 478, National Republican 218, Jackson, 193.

128. *Lynn News*, March 17, 1848.

129. *Lynn Daily Journal*, November 11, 1837; *Lynn Chronicle*, November 21, 1835, November 28, 1835; *Lynn Focus* and *Essex County Journal*, May 16, 1837; *Democratic Sentinel and Republican*, February 20, 1841; *Young Hickory*, October 12, 1844; *Lynn Forum*, February 5, 1848. *The Forum* charged that one-third of the Mechanics Bank's loans went to the directors and another third to their relatives and the Eastern Railroad.

130. *Lynn Record*, May 13, 1840. The Lynn delegation to the Whig convention in Baltimore included Isaiah Breed, F. S. Newhall, John Lovejoy, Josiah Newhall, Thomas N. Saunderson, Micajah Pratt, Daniel Farrington, Edward S. Davis, Andrews Breed and David Taylor, nearly all of them manufacturers. One Democrat charged that the only shoemakers who were Whigs were "toad eaters and broken bosses." Another shoemaker alleged that Lynn employers handed out Whig ballots on election eve and promised their employees no reduction in wages. See *Lynn Record*, April 22, 1840.

131. *Lynn News*, March 22, 1850, March 29, 1850.

132. *Report of the Committee Against the Adoption of the City Charter* (Lynn: J. B. Tolman, 1849); *Address of the Committee Against the City Charter* (Lynn: Bay State Press, 1850).

133. *Lynn Bay State*, May 9, 1850.

134. In the case of Reverend Mr. Richards, George Hood, leader of the Democratic Party in Lynn, was the only member of the school committee who refused to back Richards. See *The Grindstone*, February 28, 1852.

135. See Chapter Seven.

136. *Lynn News*, January 27, 1857.

137. For a defense of King, see *An Exposition of the Course Pursued by the School Committee of the City of Lynn in Relation to Samuel W. King* (Lynn: W. W. Kellogg, 1857).

138. For a sketch of the association, see *The Register of the Lynn Historical Society* 12 (1908): 27.

## Notes to Chapter 11

1. Reprinted in *Lynn News*, December 14, 1859. Also see *Lynn Bay State*, February 1, 1850, August 28, 1851. *The Awl*, July 17, 1844, contains a protest against "that injurious

practice of taking apprentices for a few weeks or months, and learning them to make one kind of a shoe, or what is called a shoe."

2. *Lynn News*, October 31, 1860.

3. Ibid., January 25, 1856.

4. Ibid., March 1, 1859.

5. A former shoe manufacturer, Benjamin F. Newhall, was extremely bitter toward the merchants. He stated that they had "control of a large amount of ready money, and an almost unlimited credit" and could therefore "take the greatest advantage of every fluctuation in the market, as well as of every financial depression." "There are no merchants in the country that grind the manufacturers down to so small, or next to nothing profit as the wholesale merchants of Boston." In his "Sketches of Saugus," Scrapbook, Lynn Historical Society.

6. *Lynn News*, May 12, 1857, November 25, 1857, December 15, 1857, August 3, 1858.

7. *Lynn Bay State*, April 1, 1858.

8. Ibid., July 29, 1858.

9. *Lynn News*, May 18, 1858, July 27, 1858; *Lynn Bay State*, July 29, 1858, August 5, 1858.

10. *Lynn News*, June 15, 1859.

11. *Lynn News*, February 15, 1860, February 22, 1860; *Lynn Bay State*, February 9, 1860.

12. *Lynn News*, February 22, 1860 lists committee members. See lists of ward representatives in *Lynn News*, February 29, 1860.

13. The details of the strike can be found in the *Lynn News*, and *Lynn Bay State*, the *Lynn Weekly Reporter*, the Boston *Daily Evening Transcript*, and the Boston *Atlas and Daily Bee*. Of the Lynn papers, the *Bay State*, a Democratic organ, was sympathetic to the strikers and gave the most complete coverage of the events.

. *Lynn Bay State*, December 13, 1860, for election returns. *List of City Officers for the Year 1861* (Lynn: Bay State Press, 1861). Nineteen new men were added to the police force after the election of 1860. Nearly all were shoemakers prominent in the strike. A number of strike leaders enlisted as a unit when the Civil War broke out. They formed the Lynn Mechanics Phalanx, Company C of the Fourteenth Massachusetts Regiment.

15. "Cordwainers Song," from scrapbook in Lynn Historical Society.

# Bibliography

## I. PRIMARY WORKS

### A. Manuscripts

Lynn Historical Society. Israel Buffum. Account Book, 1806–1837. Records of Buffum's earnings, price per pair of shoes, names of employers, schedule of wage payment, types and value of commodities received.

———. "Engine Company Returns," 1837. Names, location and members of fire companies.

———. "Records of Silver Grey Fire Association." Meeting Proceedings, names of officers and members.

———. "Hutchinson Family Memorabilia."

———. "Minutes of Meetings and By-Laws of Lynn Lyceum from 1831 to 1834." Includes names of officers, members, amount of dues.

———. Journal, 1817–1832 [by Joseph Lye]. Daily record of earnings, types of shoes made, price per pair, names of employers, wages received. Also includes occasional comments on social, political and religious issues.

Lynn City Hall. "Assessments and Taxes," for the years 1832, 1837, 1842, 1849, 1853 and 1860. Names of ratable polls, amount and value of personal and real property, taxes levied.

———. "Inventories of Estates," for the years 1832, 1837, 1842, 1849, 1853 and 1860. Names of ratable polls and itemized inventory of real and personal property and assessed value.

City Clerk's Office, Lynn City Hall. "Lynn Town Records, 1822–1835." Proceedings of town meetings.

Lynn Institution for Savings. Saving Deposit Records, 1826–1860. Names of depositors, dates of deposits and withdrawals.

Lynn Public Library. "Records of the Social Library in the Town of Lynn, 1818—October 9, 1847." Meeting proceedings, number of volumes, names of officers and members.

United States. Schedule of Manufactures, Seventh Census of the United States, 1850. Massachusetts State House. Names of shoe manufacturers, capital investment, number of male and female employees.

———. Schedule of Manufactures, Eighth Census of the United States, 1860. Massachusetts State House.

## B. Published Public Documents

Lynn. *Annual Report of the Board of Health of Lynn,* 1850 (City Document #7).

———. *Catalogue of the Officers, Teachers and Pupils of the Lynn High School, December* 21, 1854 (Lynn, 1854).

———. "First Annual Report of the Trustees of Pine GroveCemetery Corporation, Made to the Proprietors, January 7, 1850," *Lynn City Documents,* 1850 (City Document #4).

———. "List of Subscribers, February 15, 1850, to Stock in Pine Grove Cemetery Corporation," *Lynn City Documents,* 1850 (City Document #4).

———. *Regulations at Fires, As Adopted by the Engineers of Lynn, for* 1837 (Lynn, n.d.).

———. *Vital Records of Lynn, Massachusetts to the End of the Year* 1849, 2 vols. (Salem: Essex Institute, 1905, 1906).

Lynn City Marshal. *Annual Reports,* 1855, 1859, 1860, 1861.

Lynn School Committee. *Annual Report for* 1847−48 (Lynn, 1848).

Massachusetts. Secretary of the Commonwealth. *Statistics of the Condition and Products of Certain Branches of Industry in Massachusetts,* 1837, 1845, 1855, 1865.

———. State Board of Education. *Annual Reports,* 1838−1855. United States. *Census of the United States,* 1790−1860.

———. Secretary of the Treasury [Louis McLane]. *Report on Manufactures,* 1832 (House Executive Document 308).

Wisconsin. State Superintendent of Public Instruction, *Twelfth Annual Report* (Madison, 1860).

Great Britain. House of Commons, 1854−55, British Sessional Papers, *Report of the Committee on the Machinery of the United States of America.*


## C. Newspapers (all published in Lynn unless otherwise noted)

*The Awl,* 1844−45.
*Democratic Sentinel and Republican,* 1841.
*The Engine,* 1838.
*Essex County Washingtonian,* 1843−44.
*Essex Democrat,* 1831.
*Essex Tribune,* 1834.
*Free Democrat,* 1848.
*The Grindstone,* 1852.
*Josselyn's Lynn Daily,* 1855.
*The Locomotive,* 1842.
*Lynn Bay State,* 1852−60.
*Lynn Chronicle,* 1835.
*Lynn Daily Journal,* 1837.
*Lynn Focus and Essex County Journal,* 1837.
*Lynn Forum,* 1846−48.
*Lynn Freeman and Essex County Whig,* 1841−42.
*Lynn Mirror,* 1826−37.
*Lynn News,* 1846−61.
*Lynn Pioneer,* 1846−48.
*Lynn Record,* 1830−40.
*Lynn Tattler,* 1848.

*The Old Rat,* 1847.
*The Organ,* 1854.
*The Protectionist,* 1842.
*The Sizzler,* 1848.
*The Star,* 1836.
*Temperance League,* 1852.
*True Friend,* 1845.
*True Workingman,* 1845.
*Weekly Messenger,* 1832–33.
*Weekly Reporter,* 1856–60.
*Young Hickory,* 1844.
(Boston) *Atlas and Daily Bee,* 1860.
(Boston) *Daily Evening Transcript,* 1860.

## D. Books, Articles, Pamphlets

Armstrong, Lebbeus. *The Temperance Reformation.* New York: Fowler and Wells, 1853.
Committee Against the City Charter. *Address of the Committee Against the City Charter.* Lynn, 1850.
———. *Report of the Committee Against the Adoption of the City Charter.* Lynn, 1849.
*Constitution of Engine and Hose Company No. 5, Established March* 15, 1837. Lynn, 1837.
*Constitution of Niagara Engine and Hose Company No.* 9, Lynn, 1836.
*Constitution of Silver Grey Engine Company No.* 10. Lynn, 1856.
*Constitution of the Lynn Fire Club.* Lynn, 1834.
*An Exposition of the Course Pursued by the School Committee of the City of Lynn in Relation to Samuel W. King.* Lynn, 1857.
*Lynn Directories,* 1832, 1841, 1851, 1854, 1856, 1858, 1860.
Lynn Fire Club. *Names of the Members of the Lynn Fire Club, With Their Residences and Places of Business.*
*Lynn Scrapbooks,* vols. 1–48. Reminiscences and historical recollections, chiefly by contemporaries of antebellum Lynn. Authors and original sources of publications frequently unidentified. Lynn Public Library.
Newhall, Benjamin F. "Sketches of Saugus." Series of thirty or more articles, originally published around 1860; collected in scrapbook, Lynn Historical Society.
*Proceedings of the Society of Friends in the Case of William Bassett.* Worcester, 1840.
Young Men's Christian Association. *Constitution and By-Laws of the Young Men's Christian Association.* Lynn, 1857.

## II. SECONDARY WORKS

Austin, Shirley Plumer. "Coxey's Commonweal Army." *Chautaquan* 19 (June 1894): 332–36.
Bailyn, Bernard. *The New England Merchants in the Seventeenth Century.* New York: Harper Torchbook, 1964.
Berthroff, Rowland. *British Immigrants in Industrial America.* Cambridge, Mass.: Harvard University Press, 1959.
Breed, Warren Mudge. "Banks and Bankers of Old Lynn." *The Register of the Lynn Historical Society* 20 (1916): 35–64.

_____ . "Some Abandoned Industries of Lynn." *The Register of the Lynn Historical Society* 14 (1910): 178−207Æ

Brody, David. *Steelworkers in America: The Nonunion Era*. Cambridge: Mass.: Harvard University Press, 1960.

Bruce, Robert V. *1877: Year of Violence*. Indianapolis: Bobbs-Merrill, 1959.

Buckley, James M. *A History of Methodism in the United States*. Vol. 1. New York: Harper, 1898.

Burrill, Ellen Mudge. *Essex Trust Company, Lynn, Massachusetts, 1814−1914*.

_____ . "Lynn in Our Grandfathers' Time." Paper read to meeting of Lynn Historical Society, March 20, 1918. MS, Lynn Historical Society.

_____ . "Lynn in Our Grandfathers' Time." *The Register of the Lynn Historical Society* 21 (1917): 36−108.

Clark, George Faber. *History of the Temperance Reform in Massachusetts, 1813−1883*. Boston: Clarke and Carruth, 1888.

Cole, Donald B. *Immigrant City: Lawrence, Massachusetts 1845−1821*. Chapel Hill: University of North Carolina Press, 1963.

Cooke, Parsons. *A Century of Puritanism and a Century of Its Opposites*. Boston: S. K. Whipple, 1855.

Daniels, William H. *The Illustrated History of Methodism in Great Britain and America*. New York: Methodist Book Concern, 1879.

Fenno, Henry. *Our Police: The Official History of the Police Department of the City of Lynn*. Lynn, 1895.

Gitelman, Howard M. "The Waltham System and the Coming of the Irish." *Labor History* 8, no. 3 (Fall, 1967): 227−53.

Glaab, Charles N. and Theodore Brown. *A History of Urban America*. New York: Macmillan, 1967.

Griffin, Clifford S. "Religious Benevolence as Social Control, 1815−1860." *Mississippi Valley Historical Review* 44 (December 1957): 423−44.

Gusfield, Joseph. *Symbolic Crusade.* Urbana: University of Illinois Press, 1963.

Gutman, Herbert George. "Protestantism and the American Labor Movement: The Christian Spirit in the Gilded Age." *American Historical Review* 72 (Octob er 1966): 74−101.

Hacker, Sally H. "The Friends: Laws and Social Customs of the Quakers." Paper read to meeting of the Lynn Historical Society, March 29, 1899. MS, Lynn Historical Society.

Hall, John Philip. "The Gentle Craft: A Narrative of Yankee Shoemakers." Unpublished Ph.D. Dissertation, Columbia University, 1953.

Handlin, Oscar. *Boston's Immigrants: A Study in Acculturation*. Cambridge, Mass.: Belknap Press, 1959.

_____ . *The Uprooted*. Grosset and Dunlop paper edition, 1951.

Hawks, Nathan M. "John Fuller of Lynn." *The Register of the Lynn Historical Society* 18 (1912): 72−100.

Hazard, Blanche E. *Organization of the Boot and Shoe Industry in Massachusetts Before 1875*. Cambridge, Mass.: Harvard University Press, 1921.

Hobsbawm, Eric. *Primitive Rebels: Studies in Archaic Forms of Social Movements in the 19th and 20th Centuries*. New York: Norton, 1959.

Johnson, David N. *Sketches of Lynn: The Changes of Fifty Years*. Lynn: Thomas Nichols, 1880.

Katz, Michael B. *The Irony of Early School Reform: Educational Innovation in Mid-Nineteenth Century Massachusetts*. Cambridge, Mass.: Harvard University Press, 1968.

260

Keir, Malcolm. *Manufacturing Industries in America: Fundamental Economic Factors.* New York: Ronald Press, 1920.

Krout, John A. *The Origins of Prohibition.* New York: Alfred Knopf, 1925.

Lebergott, Stanley. *Manpower in Economic Growth: The American Record Since 1800.* New York: McGraw, 1964.

Lewis, Alonzo and James R. Newhall. *History of Lynn, Essex County, Massachusetts.* Boston: John Shorey, 1865.

Lichteim, George. *The Origins of Socialism.* New York: Praeger, 1969.

"Life and Times of Nathan Breed." Lynn *Daily Evening Item.* April 10, 1908.

"Life of Isaiah Breed." Lynn *Daily Evening Item,* July 14, 1892.

Loomis, Samuel Lane. "The Tramp Problem." *Chautauquan* 19(June 1894): 308–13.

Martin, George Henry. "The Lynn Academy." Paper read to meeting of the Lynn Historical Society, April 16, 1908. MS, Lynn Historical Society.

———. "The Unfolding of Religious Faith in Lynn." *The Register of the Lynn Historical Society* 16 (1912): 47–72.

Mathews, Donald G. "The Second Great Awakening as an Organizing Process, 1780–1830: An Hypothesis." *American Quarterly* 21 no. 1 (Spring 1969): 23–43.

Mathews, Mitford, ed. *A Dictionary of Americanisms: On Historical Principles.* Vol. II. Chicago: University of Chicago Press, 1951.

Miller, Douglas C. *Jacksonian Aristocracy: Class and Democracy in New York, 1830–1860.* New York: Oxford University Press, 1967.

Montgomery, David. "The Working Classes of the Pre-industrial American City, 1780–1830." *Labor History* 9, no. 1 (Winter 1968): 3–22.

Mudge, Alfred. *Memorials: Being a Genealogical, Biographical and Historical Account of the Name MUDGE in America, from 1638 to 1868.* Boston: Alfred Mudge, 1868.

Neufeld, Maurice F. "Realms of Thought and Organized Labor in the Age of Jackson." *Labor History* 10, no. 1 (Winter 1969): 5–43.

Newhall, James R. *Centennial Memorial of Lynn, Essex County, Massachusetts.* Lynn: Thomas Breare, 1876.

———. *Proceedings in Lynn, Massachusetts, June 17, 1879: Being the two hundred and fiftieth anniversary of the settlement.* Lynn, 1879.

Newhall, John Breed. "Early Lewis, Broad and Nahant Streets." Paper read to a meeting of the Lynn Historical Society, April 13, 1905. MS, Lynn Historical Society.

Nissenbaum, Stephan Willner. "Careful Love: Sylvester Graham and the Emergence of Victorian Sexual Theory in America, 1830–40." Unpublished Ph.D. Dissertation, University of Wisconsin, 1968.

Olmstead, Alan L. "The Bank for Savings in the City of New York in the Ante-Bellum Years: 1819–1861." Unpublished M.A. Thesis, University of Wisconsin, 1966.

Percival, Benjamin. "Essex and Lynn Abolitionism." Paper read to meeting of the Lynn Historical Society, November 12, 1908. MS, Lynn Historical Society.

Pessen, Edward. *Jacksonian America: Society, Personality and Politics.* Homewood, Ill.: Dorsey Press, 1969.

———. *Most Uncommon Jacksonian: The Radical Leaders of the Early Labor Movement.* Albany: State University of New York, 1967.

Pope, Liston. *Millhands and Preachers.* New Haven: Yale University Press, 1942.

Porter, Margaret E. "Old Woodend and Its Neighboring Territory." *The Register of the Lynn Historical Society* 15 (1912): 106–32.

Rantoul, Robert. "Mr. Rantoul's Connexion with Town and Parochial Affairs—His Views of Religion." Essex Institute *Historical Collections* 6, no. 2 (April 1864): 79–90.

————. "Mr. Rantoul's Establishment in Business-Intemperance and Pauperism." Essex Institute *Historical Collections* 5, no. 6 (December 1863): 241–47.

Sanderson, Howard Kendall. *Lynn in the Revolution,* 2 vols. Boston: Clarke, 1909.

Schlesinger, Arthur M., Jr. *The Age of Jackson.* Boston: Little, Brown, 1953.

Scudder, M. L. *American Methodism.* Hartford: S. S. Scranton, 1870.

Solomon, Barbara M. "The Growth of the Population in Essex County, 1850–1860." Essex Institute *Historical Collections* 95 (1959): 82–103.

Tapley, Henry F. "An Old New England Town as Seen by Joseph Lye, Cordwainer." *The Register of the Lynn Historical Society* 19 (1915): 36–40.

Thernstrom, Stephan. *Poverty and Progress: Social Mobility in a Nineteenth Century City.* Cambridge, Mass.: Harvard University Press, 1964.

————. "Working Class Social Mobility in Industrial America." Unpublished paper read at Anglo-American Colloquium of the Society for Labour History, London, June 23, 1968.

Thompson, Edward Palmer. *The Making of the English Working Class.* Vintage paperback edition, 1966.

Ware, Norman. *The Industrial Worker, 1840–1860.* Quadrangle paperback edition, 1964.

Warren, Edward, ed. *The Life of John Collins Warren: Compiled Chiefly from his Autobiography and Journals.* Vol. 1. Boston: Ticknor and Fields, 1860.

# Index

263